JOURNEY

DAVID JEREMIAH

Faith
Words

Published in association with Yates & Yates, LLP, www.yates2.com

Special thanks to William Kruidenier and Robert J. Morgan
Managing Editor: Myrna Davis

Editorial and Design Services:
Mark Gilroy Creative, LLC with Thinkpen Design, Inc.

www.markgilroy.com
www.thinkpendesign.com

FaithWords
Hachette Book Group
237 Park Avenue
New York, NY 10017

www.faithwords.com

Printed in U.S.A.

First Edition: January 2012

10 9 8 7 6 5 4 3 2

FaithWords is a division of Hachette Book Group, Inc.
The FaithWords name and logo are trademarks of Hachette Book Group, Inc.

ISBN: 9781455506194

RRD-C

INTRODUCTION

Most of us get excited about taking a trip, whether it is a weekend excursion, a family reunion, or a long-planned vacation to a place of our dreams. Part of the excitement is the planning, the anticipation, and the hopeful expectation of what our journey will bring. Some could say that we "long for" those times of retreat and refreshment.

Our lives are often like a journey, with unexpected mishaps, missteps, and mistakes. But as believers our lives are also filled with surprising moments of joy, faith for each trial and triumph, and a deep-seated peace with the knowledge that the God of the universe is traveling that same road with us. Just as we look forward to a holiday or a special trip, as Christians we live in anticipation of the crossing we will take with Him someday, knowing that it will be unlike anything we can expect or imagine.

As you begin your journey into the next year, take time each day to remember your Creator, to read His Word, to consider all that He has done for you. Our hope is that the *Journey* 365-day devotional provides refreshment, encouragement, and blessing to you throughout the coming year as you live in anticipation of His return.

Blessed are those whose strength is in you,
whose heart is set on pilgrimage.

—PSALM 84:5

JANUARY

OUR HOPE FOR YEARS TO COME

The Lord is my strength and my shield; my heart trusted in Him, and I am helped; therefore my heart greatly rejoices, and with my song I will praise Him.

PSALM 28:7

This verse provides a happy formula for the New Year. Notice the progression.

First, we realize that *the Lord* is our strength and shield. No matter what unfolds from day to day or from month to month, He will give us sufficient strength, and His presence will surround us as a shield.

Second, our hearts can fully *trust Him*. We can relax, rest, and lean on Him, knowing He is fully able to do all He has promised.

Third, as we recognize who He is and trust Him, we *are helped*. There's no sense of panic as it relates to the uncertain future. He helps us in everything at every time. The past, the present, and the future are His.

Fourth, our heart can therefore *rejoice*. Today is a day for a joyful and glad attitude. And that leads to a song of *praise*. We can have a hymn in our hearts today—like this one: "O God our Help in ages past, our hope for years to come; be Thou our Guide while life shall last, and our eternal home."

Under the shadow of Thy throne Thy saints have dwelt secure;
sufficient is Thine arm alone, and our defense is sure.

ISAAC WATTS

THE LAST LECTURE

For we know that if our earthly house, this tent,
is destroyed, we have a building from God, a house
not made with hands, eternal in the heavens.

2 CORINTHIANS 5:1

When Professor Randy Pausch learned he was dying of pancreatic cancer, he gave a talk to his students at Carnegie Mellon University. His presentation circulated widely on the Internet, and then it appeared in book form titled *The Last Lecture*. In an interview with *Reader's Digest*, Pausch said that his life was measured now in months, not years, and that he simply wanted to do what good he could do "on my way out of the building."

That's reminiscent of Paul's teaching in 2 Corinthians 5. We're laboring now in an earthly tent that is passing away, but we have an eternal house in the heavens. Therefore we make it our aim to be well pleasing to Him, "whether present or absent." We don't know if our remaining days on earth are measured in years, months, weeks, or minutes. Our times are in His hands, and our goal is to do all the good we can on our way out of the tent. "Therefore we make it our aim, whether present or absent, to be well pleasing to Him" (verse 9).

O Lord, help me to do all the good I can, by all the means I can,
in all the ways I can, in all the places I can, in all the times I can,
to all the people I can as long as ever I can.

JOHN WESLEY

THE BLIND MAN OF BETHSAIDA

And he looked up and said, "I see men like trees, walking."

MARK 8:24

Jesus never does anything half-way, but sometimes He *does* work in stages. In Mark 8, the disciples only partially understood His teachings and they didn't fully grasp what He was saying. "How is it you do not understand?" He asked (verse 21).

In verse 22, Jesus taught them a lesson. Meeting a blind man in Bethsaida, Jesus healed him in stages. At first, the man saw people as trees walking. Then Jesus put His hands on his eyes again, and his sight was restored 20/20.

This two-stage miracle is very encouraging. When we're confused about some aspect of Bible study, when life seems blurry, or when we're bothered by events we can't explain, we're seeing trees walking. But how wonderful to grow in the grace and knowledge of our Lord and Savior! As we walk with the Lord day by day, we find that our focus improves, our knowledge grows, our wisdom increases. And even if things are still a little blurry just now, we can be assured that with the Great Physician we'll understand it better by and by.

*The simplicity of the Gospel gives what the complexity
of human wisdom promises but never delivers.*

JOHN MACARTHUR

DAVID JEREMIAH

JANUARY 4

BE GROUNDED

*There is hope for a tree, if it is cut down, that it will sprout again,
and that its tender shoots will not cease. Though its root may grow
old in the earth, and its stump may die in the ground, yet at the
scent of water it will bud and bring forth branches....*

JOB 14:7-9

In 2004 in Sweden, researchers found the oldest known living
plant on earth, a 13-foot-tall Norway spruce. The visible part
of the tree—the part above ground—is about 600 years old; but
the tree's roots predate Abraham. Whenever a stem or trunk dies,
a new one emerges from the root stock, and that's what gives the
tree its incredible longevity.

The Bible says we're like trees planted by the waters that
spread our roots by the river (Jeremiah 17:8). We are told to be
rooted and grounded in love (Ephesians 3:17) and rooted and
built up in Him, established in the faith (Colossians 2:7). Jesus
warned of the danger of springing up quickly, but, having no
roots, withering away (Matthew 13:6).

Personal Bible study is the best way to sink your roots deeply into
the faith. At the beginning of this New Year, make up your mind to
read and meditate on God's Word daily. You'll be like a tree planted
by rivers of water that brings forth its fruit in season (Psalm 1:3).

*As a tree by the waters grows, in spite of drought all around it,
so I, by drawing upon the life of Christ, grow into His strength.*

W. PHILLIP KELLER

The Source of Everything

*But who am I, and who are my people, that we should
be able to offer so willingly as this? For all things come
from You, and of Your own we have given You.*

1 Chronicles 29:14

When it came time to build the first temple in Jerusalem,
King David set the example by being the first to give.
He gave 3,000 talents of gold and 7,000 talents of silver out of
his pocket—about $3.14 billion and $106 million respectively
in today's dollars. But then he surprised everyone by saying, in
essence, "I'm giving away someone else's money."

When David prayed a prayer of thanksgiving for the resources
given by all the people, he made it plain that whatever they had
given came first from God. It's so easy for us to forget the origin of
everything we own. Wherever you are right now, look around—
everything you see is a gift from God. Those gifts include the eyes
with which you see and the breath that keeps you alive. Every
human heartbeat should be a silent refrain of thanksgiving to the
God who created the heart and gives it life. Be careful today not to
take credit for something that heaven first gave as a gift.

When we give to God, it is not a credit to our own creativity
and resourcefulness, but to His.

> *Evangelical repentance is not at the beck
> and call of the creature. It is the gift of God.*
>
> A. W. Pink

LEARNING TO THINK ETERNALLY

Commit your works to the Lord, and your thoughts will be established.

PROVERBS 16:3

In his book *Maximum Achievement*, corporate trainer Brian Tracy writes, "Virtually everything you do is the result of habit. The way you talk, the way you work, drive, think, interact with others, spend money and deal with the important people in your life are all largely habitual." But then he says, "The good news is that all habits are learned, and they can therefore be unlearned."[1]

It's easy to see the habits in our lives. We brush our teeth, dress ourselves, and drive to work the same way. Those habits may or may not need changing. But here's one habit we should definitely unlearn: our tendency to consider the temporal implications of life's choices and events before we consider the eternal. The apostle Paul learned to emphasize the eternal after meeting Christ. He said that his only goal was to know "Christ Jesus [his] Lord" (Philippians 3:8).

What do you think of first when deciding or reacting in life—the here and now or the life to come? Start a new habit based on today's events: Think first of the eternal difference your choices will make.

> *Every action of our lives touches on some*
> *chord that will vibrate in eternity.*
>
> E. H. CHAPIN

[1] BRIAN TRACY, *Maximum Achievement* (NEW YORK: SIMON & SCHUSTER, 1993), 90-91.

SPIRITUAL TO-DO'S

*Look to yourselves, that we do not lose those things
we worked for, but that we may receive a full reward.*

2 JOHN 8

There are two words that, at first glance, might not seem to go with one another: procrastination and priorities. We think of procrastinators as people who put off doing what should be done—that is, life's priorities. But that doesn't mean procrastinators put off everything. They do what is important to them—even procrastinators have priorities!

And that applies to everyone. All of us have things we choose to do each day based on our personal set of values. And if the disciplines of the spiritual life are continually excluded from our day—week after week, month after month—then it means they don't have the value in our lives that would move them higher on our list of priorities. We need to be honest with ourselves and with God. Calling ourselves Christians, but failing to manifest Christlike characteristics in our life—prayer, service, acts of compassion, study of God's Word, worship—sets up a disconnect for which we will one day give account.

Take stock today. Are you procrastinating about the real priorities in your spiritual life? This would be a good day to move them higher on your "To-Do" list.

We have left undone those things which we ought to have done.

Book of Common Prayer, "GENERAL CONFESSION"

DAVID JEREMIAH

GRACE TO GIVE

*But as you abound in everything—in faith, in speech,
in knowledge, in all diligence, and in your love for us—
see that you abound in this grace [of giving] also.*

2 CORINTHIANS 8:7

How often do you use, or hear others use, the word "grace" in conversation? It is one of the most often-used words in Christianity, but one of the hardest to define. For instance, "grace" is the word at the root of spiritual gifts in the New Testament, and as such represents special favor or ability from God. Grace, directly or indirectly, almost always refers to power or ability from God to live supernaturally.

For that reason, when it came time for Paul to ask the church at Corinth to participate in his financial rescue plan for the suffering church in Jerusalem, he knew it would only happen by the grace of God. Why? Because he was asking people with few and limited means to give generously. So in 2 Corinthians 8:1-9 the word "grace" appears four times, and twice more in chapter nine on the same subject. It takes God's grace to give, and even more grace to give sacrificially—the same kind of grace Jesus Christ displayed when He intentionally became poor that we might be made rich (2 Corinthians 8:9).

If you struggle to give, ask God to give you grace.

A giving Saviour should have giving disciples.

J. C. RYLE

These Old Skinflints

Freely you have received, freely give.

Matthew 10:8

According to Clive Anderson's book, *Travel with C. H. Spurgeon*, one day the great London pastor spoke to a group about his various ministries for the impoverished and destitute of the city. Afterward he passed his hat around for the collection. No one put anything into it, and some in the crowd wondered what Spurgeon would do next. The famous preacher simply bowed in prayer and said, "I thank you, O Lord, that at least these old skinflints have given me my hat back!"

There's no shortage of "skinflints," but how different to be in the presence of those who radiate grace! How wonderful to be a Grace-Giver. We may not always have much to give, but there's something wonderful about being generous with our time, treasure, and talents—ready to give an extra dollar, spend an extra moment, tackle an extra task, or go an extra mile.

It's not enough just to return the hat. We should put something into it. God's grace is freely given that we might freely give.

As thou, Lord, hast lived for others, so may we for others live; freely have Thy gifts been granted, freely may Thy servants give.

Somerset Lowry

David Jeremiah

OUR BILLFOLDS GO ALONG FOR THE RIDE

I had it in my heart to build a house of
rest for the ark of the covenant of the LORD....

1 CHRONICLES 28:2

According to economists, some industries seem virtually recession proof. During the current downturn, spending on pets has increased, as has spending on candy. Fast food hasn't taken much of a hit, nor has doling out money for entertainment and recreation. Despite some belt-tightening and lifestyle adjustments, we usually find ways of spending on the things that are important to us.

How we manage what God has given us is a leading indicator of our priorities.

In 1 Chronicles 28, King David had a leadership conference for his government officials. He rose to his feet and addressed the group, giving them a vision of the temple he longed to build for the Lord in Jerusalem. It was in his heart. As a result, he dedicated his own fortune to the project, and he challenged his leaders to do the same, saying, "Who then is willing to consecrate himself this day to the LORD?" (1 Chronicles 29:5)

When we consecrate ourselves to the Lord, our billfolds go along for the ride.

Money requires discipline, as do the
decisions that money makes possible.

FRED SMITH, SR.

SAUL OF TARSUS

*Then Saul arose from the ground, and when his
eyes were opened he saw no one. But they led him
by the hand and brought him into Damascus.*

ACTS 9:8

How strange that Saul of Tarsus was blinded by the very light that would soon light up his life! Journeying toward Damascus to imprison Christians, he fell to the ground when a sudden light burst on him. It was the glorified Jesus, which tells us something wonderful about our Lord's current appearance in the heavens.

Psalm 104 (NIV) says that the Lord wraps Himself in light as a garment. In 1 Timothy 6:16, we read that He dwells in unapproachable light. When John saw Him in Revelation 1, "His countenance was like the sun shining in its strength." In the Eternal City, there will be no need for sun or moon, for the Lamb is its light. And on the Mount of Transfiguration, the disciples saw Jesus resplendent in a portion of the glory that is eternally His.

By faith, we can walk in the light of His presence now. We can visualize our glorified Jesus, seated on the throne of heaven and be reflectors of His light today. "They looked to Him and were radiant" (Psalm 34:5).

I know that the light of His presence with me doth continually dwell.

FANNY CROSBY

DAVID JEREMIAH

GOD'S HARVEST LAW

Do not be deceived, God is not mocked;
for whatever a man sows, that he will also reap.

GALATIANS 6:7

Why are Isaac Newton's three Laws of Motion (inertia, resultant force, reciprocal action) and his Law of Universal Gravitation (Law of Gravity) called laws? Why is Michael Faraday's Law of Induction (law of electromagnetism) called a law? Because they are universal physical certainties that have never been proved not to govern the situations to which they apply.

Just as there are laws in the physical realm, so there are laws in the spiritual realm. One found in Galatians 6:7 is the universal Law of the Harvest: ". . . for whatever a man sows, that he will also reap." That spiritual law is based on observations from the first-century world of agriculture: plant a seed and, absent unnatural forces, it will germinate and lead to a harvest. Paul applied that universal law to spiritually-based actions. If we sow a godly action, we will reap a godly blessing. If we sow an ungodly action, we reap godly discipline or judgment. Strangely, people who know the Law of Gravity applies to them feel they are exempt from the effects of God's Harvest Law.

Before you act this week, decide what kind of harvest you want to reap—and sow accordingly.

Holiness in the seed shall have happiness in the harvest.

THOMAS ADAMS

PICKED LAST

He said to another, "Follow Me."
But he said, "Lord, let me first go and...."

LUKE 9:59

In the book, *Teaching Children Physical Education,* George Graham warns against letting school teams "choose up sides." He rightly says the custom is "excruciatingly painful to children and creates lasting, haunting impressions as adults." It "should be banned from schools—against the law. It simply hurts too much to stand and wait, only to be picked last or next to last."[1]

If this brings back bad memories of gym class, you know what he's talking about.

But what happens when we pick God last?

Lord, I will follow You, but first let me earn a living, raise a family, take a trip, pay the bills, get an education, enjoy myself, go out with my buddies, have a little fun, save up some money.

Jesus Christ isn't *something* we include in the mix of events that makes up our lives. He is *someone* whom we call Master, Lord, and King. He's the First who orders all other events according to His will. We can never say, "Lord, let me first...," but "Lord, You are First!"

"Christ... is first in everything" (Colossians 1:18, NLT).

Oh! Yes, I do love Jesus, because He first loved me.

CHARLES H. SPURGEON

1 GEORGE GRAHAM, *Teaching Children Physical Education* (CHAMPAIGN, IL: HUMAN KINETICS, 2008), 183.

TO BE FOUND FAITHFUL

Moreover it is required in stewards that one be found faithful.

1 CORINTHIANS 4:2

"Steward" used to be a common concept, most notably in the form of a "stewardess"—when airline flight attendants were all females. Now, stewards are mostly found in labor unions (shop steward), fancy restaurants (wine steward), and cruise ships (ship's steward).

The earliest, and still the best, biblical example of a steward is Joseph—the favorite son of Jacob who was sold as a slave into Egypt by his jealous brothers. So rich was the blessing of God on Joseph that his Egyptian master, the wealthy Potiphar, made Joseph the overseer and manager (steward) of his entire household. Joseph was responsible for everything: finances, the other servants and employees, and Potiphar's reputation as it related to all his affairs. A steward's chief occupation is to do what his master would want done. A steward's responsibilities can be summed up in two words—loyalty and faithfulness.

Look around and within at what God has given you: gifts, talents, money, property, opportunities, and possibilities. Every Christian is a steward of God—He has provided—we are to be faithful.

*Our need is not to prove God's faithfulness but
to demonstrate our own, by trusting Him both
to determine and to supply our needs according to His will.*

JOHN MACARTHUR

WORK AND WAGES

*Now he who plants and he who waters are one, and each one
will receive his own reward according to his own labor.*

1 CORINTHIANS 3:8

*H*ow to Succeed in Business Without Really Trying opened on
Broadway in 1961 and went on to win a Pulitzer Prize
for Drama (1962) and seven Tony Awards. After its 1,417
performances, it was later made into a movie of the same name
and reprised on Broadway in 1995. It told the story of the
seemingly miraculous rise of a young window washer to the
Vice-Presidency of the World Wide Wicket Company.

Such miraculous transformations in the business of life
are mostly the stuff of fiction. For most people, success is
achieved slowly and steadily, the result of hard work, diligence,
resourcefulness, and focusing on the long view. And not
surprisingly, the same is true in the spiritual life. It's not surprising
that the term "labor" occurs 19 times from Acts through Revelation,
almost always referring to the labor involved in making spiritual
progress. If you are averse to hard work generally, you'll probably
resist laboring to see Christ "formed in you" (Galatians 4:19).

God has promised rewards for those in Christ who labor
faithfully for Him and for His kingdom. The work is now—the
wages are soon to come.

Faith believes as if it did not work, and it works as if it did not believe.

THOMAS WATSON

DAVID JEREMIAH

JANUARY 16

TAKING ROOT: DRINK IN THE SON

The righteous shall...grow like a cedar in Lebanon.

PSALM 92:12

Phillip Keller once wrote a book entitled *As a Tree Grows* in which he explored the comparison the Bible makes between Christians and cedars. He pointed out that every tree in the forest competes with all its fellows for light. On the upper surface of each leaf or needle of a cedar or other pine there is an innumerable array of stomata with light-absorbing cells. "By means of the complex process of photosynthesis sunlight is used by the leaf to produce carbohydrates for its growth. This explains why, in order to flourish and grow, a leaf automatically responds to light falling on it and turns toward it."[2]

Jesus said, "I am the light of the world" (John 8:12). He is the "Sun of Righteousness" with healing in His rays (Malachi 4:2).

Whenever we read the Gospels and study the life of Christ, we are soaking up the Son. Whenever we search out biblical truth about Christ—and we can find it in Leviticus as well as in Luke—we are turning our leaves toward the light.

If light be pleasant to our eyes, how pleasant is that light
of life springing from the Sun of righteousness!

JOHN FLAVEL, SEVENTEENTH CENTURY PURITAN

2 W. PHILLIP KELLER, *As a Tree Grows* (CHARLOTTE: COMMISSION PRESS, 1966), 29-30.

The Blind Demoniac

Then one was brought to Him who was demon-possessed,
blind and mute; and He healed him....

MATTHEW 12:22

Satan is in the Eye-Blinding Business. The Bible warns that the "god of this age" has blinded the minds of unbelievers "lest the light of the gospel of the glory of Christ, who is the image of God, should shine on them" (2 Corinthians 4:4). This is why we have friends and loved ones who seem impervious to our testimony and resistant to our witness.

Jesus Christ is in the Sight-Restoring Business. The prophet Isaiah predicted that He would come "as a light to the Gentiles, to open blind eyes, to bring out prisoners from the prison, those who sit in darkness from the prison house" (Isaiah 42:6-7).

There's a great prayer we can echo about this in 2 Kings 6:17. Elisha asked the Lord regarding his servant: "Lord, I pray, open his eyes that he may see." Let's turn that into our own prayer for a brother, sister, son, daughter, friend, or spouse who needs the Lord Jesus. And as we pray, we can do so with confidence, "for the eyes of the Lord are on the righteous, and His ears are open to their prayers" (1 Peter 3:12).

I once was lost but now am found; was blind, but now I see.

JOHN NEWTON

THE QUAKER'S NEIGHBOR

You cannot serve both God and money.

MATTHEW 6:24 (NIV)

A Quaker watched as his new, wealthy neighbor unpacked truckloads of furniture, clothing, and decorative items. He then went to greet the man and said to him, "Neighbor, if thee hath need of anything, please come to see me and I will tell thee how to get along without it."

We are bombarded with TV commercials and Internet ads for beautiful furniture, nice cars, and the ultimate American dream of owning a home. What they don't advertise though, is how quickly those things, as legitimate as they are, will begin to own us if we aren't careful. To be sure, God does not expect us to live without the necessities of life, but He does encourage us to strike a balance between earthly needs and heavenly purposes, valuing the treasures we lay up for ourselves in heaven rather than becoming attached to the material things that will fade away on that glorious day when Christ returns.

After all, "It is He who gives [us] power to get wealth," but we must use those riches to invest in our heavenly future (Deuteronomy 8:18).

It is not to make money that I believe a Christian should live. The noblest thing a man can do is, just humbly to receive, and then go amongst others and give.

DAVID LIVINGSTONE

JANUARY 19

HEART-CHECK

*For the Lord does not see as man sees; for man looks
at the outward appearance, but the Lord looks at the heart.*

1 SAMUEL 16:7

As a man and his son came out of church one Sunday
morning, the man complained that the service went too
long. His little boy said, "Daddy, I thought it was pretty good
since you only had to pay a dime."

Though this story is humorous, it makes an important
point. Some people might look at the man's offering and laugh,
believing it to be small and insignificant. But it is not the amount
that is shameful; it is the state of the man's heart. The Bible says,
*"So let each one give as he purposes in his heart, not grudgingly or of
necessity; for God loves a cheerful giver"* (2 Corinthians 9:7).

Because God gives to us out of love, He would much rather
receive a small gift given wholeheartedly than a large offering
from a grumbling heart. With that in mind, every time we give to
the Lord, we should do a quick heart-check to make sure we are
giving willingly and cheerfully because no matter the amount, it is
our heart that God sees and values above all else.

*The world asks, "How much does he give?"
Christ asks, "Why does he give?"*

JOHN RALEIGH MOTT

DAVID JEREMIAH

DARK NIGHTS

You have tested my heart; You have visited me in the night;
You have tried me and have found nothing; I have purposed
that my mouth shall not transgress.

PSALM 17:3

La noche oscura del alma—The Dark Night of the Soul. That's the name of the poem written by St. John of the Cross, a sixteenth century Spanish poet. Written while St. John was in prison for trying to reform his monastic order, "the dark night" represents the difficulties and trials we experience on the road to heaven.

"Dark night" also pictures the isolation we feel during times of spiritual tests. We sometimes lie in bed at night, surrounded by darkness, longing for sleep, but consumed with our thoughts and questions. The psalmists, especially David, were candidly honest about their literal and spiritual dark nights. David made good use of his sleepless nights, crying out to God for relief and answers (Psalm 22:2; 42:8). And he relied on the natural order of things to remind him that "weeping may endure for a night, but joy comes in the morning" (Psalm 30:5b).

If you are in the midst of your own dark night, use the time wisely. If there are tears, let them water the words you pour out to God, remembering that joy comes in the morning.

Faith is a plant that can grow in the shade,
a grace that can find the way to heaven in a dark night.

WILLIAM GURNALL

FAITHFUL AND TRUE

He who calls you is faithful, who also will do it.

1 THESSALONIANS 5:24

Modern consumers have developed a cynical streak when it comes to shopping. On the one hand, they fear that "planned obsolescence" on the part of the manufacturer will cause their product to have a short life. On the other hand, they fear that if they buy the "extended warranty" (and don't read the fine print), there will be a loophole that keeps the warranty from applying "in your particular situation."

The "Yeah, right" syndrome is pervasive in our culture. We have been disappointed so often that we find it difficult to know who to trust and what to believe. And, by cultural osmosis, that attitude creeps into the spiritual life and impacts our willingness to trust God. Can He be trusted implicitly in what He says? A good example of a promise from God with an extended warranty is in Jeremiah 31:35-37 where God promises that the universe—sun, moon, stars—will remain stable as a sign of His faithfulness in His promises to the Jews. God's promises are "exceedingly great and precious" (2 Peter 1:4), and you are invited to test them (Psalm 34:8).

God is faithful and thus is His Word. Millions have proven His promises to be true; none have proven them otherwise.

God promises to keep His people, and He will keep His promises.

C. H. SPURGEON

DAVID JEREMIAH

BRANCH OUT

His Lord said to him, "Well done, good and faithful servant;
you have been faithful over a few things, I will make you
ruler over many things. Enter into the joy of your lord."

MATTHEW 25:23

If we want to take root and to grow in our faith, it's necessary to branch out in service. Try serving God in little things. It's wonderful to accomplish great things for Christ, but sometimes our greatest works are in the little things.

Leslie Flynn relates the legend of an angel who, at the start of a church construction project, announced he would award a prize to the person who made the most significant contribution to the finished product. Everyone worked hard, wanting to win—the architect, the contractor, the craftsmen, the artists, the clergy, and the carpenters.

The winner turned out to be an elderly peasant woman who every day carried hay to the ox that pulled the stones for the stonecutters.[3]

Our faith grows as we serve, and we serve best when we're faithful in little things. Try branching out in a new area of Christian service, however small; and be faithful so that one day the Lord of the Harvest will say, "Well done!"

God expects us to take advantage of every opportunity to be a doer of
good.... Keep on keeping on. Who does God's work will get God's pay.

LESLIE B. FLYNN

---

3 Leslie Flynn, *Keep On Keeping On* (Carlsbad, CA: Mangus Press, 2005), 106.

IRREVOCABLE PROMISES

For the Lord your God will bless you just as He promised you.

DEUTERONOMY 15:6

Some days are harder than others, and perhaps this is one of them for you. Life is full of frustrations, and we can grow mighty weary with financial pressures, family problems, church misunderstandings, and workplace conflicts. It sometimes seems like we're losing our minds.

But God is not losing His! Remember that nothing revokes His faithfulness. His promises to us are irreversible, unalterable, firm, and fixed. There are conditions to be met, of course; but outer circumstances must bend, in His time, to the purposes and promises of God for our lives.

Dietrich Bonhoeffer once said, "God does not give us everything we want, but He does fulfill His promises... leading us along the best and straightest paths to Himself." The Lord your God will bless you just as He has promised in His Word.

His promises are sure, His blessings are great, His grace is sufficient, His presence is near, His mercy is everlasting, and His truth endures to all generations. Cheer up! It's not as bad as it seems.

Let God's promises shine on your problems.

CORRIE TEN BOOM

EZEKIEL

Like the appearance of a rainbow in a cloud on a rainy day,
so was the appearance of the brightness all around it.
This was the appearance of the likeness of the glory of the Lord.

EZEKIEL 1:28

The first words of the Book of Ezekiel seem to give us the prophet's age: "Now it came to pass in the thirtieth year...." According to Numbers 4:23, Jewish priests began leading temple worship at age 30. But just when Ezekiel was ready to assume his life's work, he was seized in a raid and deported hundreds of miles to a Jewish refugee camp beside the Chebar River in Babylon. He was angry, disappointed, and bitter (Ezekiel 3:14).

God's answer was to open his eyes, giving him a glimpse of the heavenly throne itself and allowing him to see "the appearance of the likeness of the glory of the Lord." Seeing this, Ezekiel fell on his face and listened as the Lord commissioned him to a ministry he had never anticipated—one that still benefits us to this day.

There's an old hymn that says: "One look at His dear face, all sorrow will erase...." When our eyes are opened to the Lord, everything else falls into place, takes shape, and begins to make sense. *Sir, we wish to see Jesus* (John 12:21).

We would see Jesus, the great rock Foundation
whereon our feet were set with sovereign grace.

ANNA WARNER, AUTHOR OF "JESUS LOVES ME"

CAN AND WILL

The Lord will give strength to His people;
The Lord will bless His people with peace.

PSALM 29:11

Everybody has been corrected on the difference between "can I?" and "may I?" when asking a question—as in, "Teacher, can I get a drink a water?" "It's 'May I,' Johnny—and yes you may." "Can" refers to ability while "may" refers to permission or volition. Strangely, Christians get confused between ability and volition when it comes to trusting God.

We know that God "can" do anything. But we lose faith when it comes to God's willingness. We have no problem trusting Him for both His ability and His willingness to save us from the penalty of our sins. Somehow, we believe God can and will make our salvation a reality. But when it comes to trusting God for, say, our financial needs, we falter. We know God "can" meet our needs but we're not sure He will—in spite of what Jesus said: ". . . it *will* be given . . . you *will* find . . . it *will* be opened . . ." (Luke 11:9; italics added).

When you see "will" in Scripture associated with God's actions, take it as a promise from Him: He "can" and He "will" meet your need.

Whatever God did and was able to do and willing to do at any time,
God is able and willing to do again, within the framework of His will.

A. W. TOZER

A COSTLY OFFERING

I will offer to You the sacrifice of thanksgiving...

PSALM 116:17

During Old Testament times, approaching God was not a casual event, nor did it happen without some sort of sacrifice. Noah sacrificed the best of the animals he had carried through the flood, Abraham loved God so much that he was willing to offer his own son as a sacrifice, and Hannah promised God that if He would bless her with a son, she would *"give him to the Lord all the days of his life"* (1 Samuel 1:11). All of these sacrifices were costly to the giver and demonstrated immense love and respect for Almighty God.

The literal practice of burnt offerings may no longer be necessary because of Christ's sacrifice on the cross, but the idea of giving something of worth to the Lord before approaching Him is as important today as it was during the time of our ancestors. Some of the offerings we can give today are *prayer and praise* (Hebrews 13:15, Psalm 50:23), *our gifts* (Philippians 4:18), a *humble heart* (Psalm 51:17), and *our life* (Romans 12:1-2).

May we never come to the Lord empty-handed, but let us *"Enter into His gates with thanksgiving, and into His courts with praise"* (Psalm 100:4).

Like our fathers of old, we need to get into the practice of building altars everywhere we go and offering our precious things upon them.

JIM GERRISH

GROWTH SPURT

Live a life worthy of the Lord and... please Him in every way: bearing fruit in every good work, growing in the knowledge of God...

COLOSSIANS 1:10 (NIV)

God believes in growth! In the Garden of Eden, "the Lord God made every tree grow..." (Genesis 2:9). He designed grass to grow for cattle, and crops to grow for us (Psalm 104:14). He wanted the children of Israel to grow into a great nation (Genesis 48:16). We're to consider the lilies, how they grow (Luke 12:27). Even the Lord Jesus grew and became strong in spirit (Luke 2:40).

The Lord expects His saints to grow, too, like palm trees and cedars of Lebanon (Psalm 92:12). We're to grow up in all things into Him who is the head—Christ (Ephesians 4:15). Our faith is to grow more solid every day, and our love deeper (2 Thessalonians 1:3). Peter told us to desire the sincere milk of the Word, that we may grow thereby, and to grow in the grace and knowledge of our Lord Jesus Christ (1 Peter 2:2 KJV; 2 Peter 3:18).

Are there areas in our lives—whatever our ages—in which we need fresh growth? Focus on that area, memorize Scripture on that topic, pray for maturity, and ask God for a "growth spurt" in your life.

The mind grows by taking in, but the heart grows by giving out; and it is important to maintain a balanced life.

WARREN WIERSBE

GOING THE DISTANCE

But you must continue in the things which
you have learned and been assured of...

2 TIMOTHY 3:14

The 1976 Oscar-winning movie *Rocky* is the story of a small-time boxer who trained long and hard for the opportunity to fight heavyweight champion, Apollo Creed. When he lost the first fight against Creed, he resolved to train harder and fight him again. He said that all he wanted to do was "go the distance" with Creed. When he finally did go the distance, he was bloody, swollen, broken, and completely exhausted. But he had finished the fight!

The original Rocky Balboa was Paul in the New Testament. He was beaten; stoned; shipwrecked; in perils of waters, robbers, his own countrymen, in the city, in the wilderness, and at sea (2 Corinthians 11:22-31). Yet, his one desire was to go the distance for Christ, and he did. Paul was able to remain committed to Christ because he trusted Him with his future and his life.

We should all strive for complete commitment in our walk with Christ; and when the going gets rough, let us not quickly forget our promise. Resolve to go the distance for the glory of God!

The knowledge of Christ's love for us should cause us
to love Him in such a way that it is demonstrated
in our attitude, conduct, and commitment to serve God.

EDWARD BEDORE

A PERFECT FATHER

For whoever desires to save his life will lose it,
but whoever loses his life for My sake and the gospel's will save it.

MARK 8:35

When our children have a birthday, we forget about the tantrum they threw last week in the middle of the grocery store, put out of our mind the memory of the kitchen floor completely covered in apple juice, and resolve to think about something other than the countless times we've heard "No" and "Mine!" from our little ones. Somehow, all of that fades away and we celebrate our children with a cake, gifts, and a party because we love them.

We are the children of a perfect Father; and despite our many shortcomings, He loves us and gives us good things (Matthew 7:11). Why then do we often fail to give something back to Him? Why is it such a struggle to give ourselves to Him when He lovingly and sacrificially gave us the ultimate gift of His Son?

If we truly love our Heavenly Father, then let's begin demonstrating that love by offering our very lives as a living sacrifice, not withholding anything. After all, it was Christ Himself who set the example when He gave up His life that we might live.

He is no fool who gives what he cannot
keep to gain what he cannot lose.

JIM ELLIOT

JANUARY 30

PULL WEEDS

For as he thinks in his heart, so is he.

PROVERBS 23:7

About a hundred years ago, the British writer, James Allen, wrote a little book entitled *As a Man Thinketh*. He said the thoughts we cultivate in our minds will grow up and will show up in our attitudes, actions, and words. "A (person's) mind may be likened to a garden," he wrote, "which may be intelligently cultivated or allowed to run wild; but whether cultivated or neglected, it must, and will, bring forth. If no useful seeds are put into it, then an abundance of useless seeds will fall therein, and will continue to produce their kind."

In other words, every garden becomes a hopeless thicket of vines, grass, scrubs, briers, and nettles unless a dedicated gardener seeds, feeds, and weeds it. Our minds and our lives are the same. We've got to weed the bad thoughts out of our minds and the bad habits out of our conduct.

With God's help, we can cultivate our thoughts, pulling up weeds and planting the fertile seed of His Word. With Christ's help, we can rid our lives of bad habits, one by one.

Take care of your garden and keep out the weeds; fill it up with sunshine, kind words and kind deeds.

HENRY WADSWORTH LONGFELLOW

GOD'S ANVIL

"Is not My word like a fire?" says the Lord,
"and like a hammer that breaks the rock in pieces?"

JEREMIAH 23:29

When we hear attacks on the Bible, it's important to remember that they aren't new. The faith of every generation of Christians has been criticized and challenged; and opposition to God's Word is as old as Satan himself, who, in Genesis 3:1 asked, "Has God indeed said . . .?"

Consider this. The Bible was written in sixty-six installments over a period of 1600 years in three languages on three continents. It has more than forty authors from all walks of life, writing under diverse conditions, and writing on hundreds of controversial topics. Yet it all fits together, seamlessly and without error or contradiction. When we hold the Bible in our hands, we aren't holding an anthology or a bundle of scattered and miscellaneous thoughts. We're holding one comprehensive, cohesive volume with a logical beginning and ending, telling us one story centered around one Person—Jesus Christ.

It's as though a Master Author was behind it all, which there was. When we hear someone attack the Bible, we shouldn't be too alarmed. The Bible has a habit of outliving all its critics.

Hammer away ye hostile hands;
your hammers break, God's anvil stands.

CHARLES SPURGEON

FEBRUARY

RUTH AND BOAZ

*So [Ruth] fell on her face, bowed down to the ground,
and said to [Boaz], "Why have I found favor in your eyes,
that you should take notice of me, since I am a foreigner?"*

RUTH 2:10

Everyone knows what it feels like to visit a foreign culture or country—even to visit a neighborhood that is ethnically different from your own. Not only the language, but the foods, the currency, even the alphabet, seem foreign. How nice to meet someone who invites you in and makes you feel at home.

Ruth, a Moabite woman during the period of the judges in Israel, had that experience. As the Gentile daughter-in-law and widow of Israelites, she was shocked when a wealthy Israelite landowner named Boaz invited her to glean barley from his fields to provide food for Ruth and her mother-in-law, Naomi. In fact, Boaz married Ruth and brought her into the fold of God's people. Their marriage is a perfect example of what Christ has done for us. God invited us into His family through faith in Christ and provides for all our needs.

Have you accepted God's invitation to draw near and be nourished?

*From heaven he came and sought her to be his holy bride;
with his own blood he bought her, and for her life he died.*

SAMUEL JOHN STONE

DAVID JEREMIAH

PLANNING AHEAD

And he carried me away in the Spirit to a great
and high mountain, and showed me the great city,
the holy Jerusalem, descending out of heaven from God.

REVELATION 21:10

It happens, but rarely—a college freshman showing up in
September, suitcases in hand, seeing the campus for the first
time. Or a family moving to a new city without several prior visits
to check out schools, houses, shopping, and churches. In other
words, we have a built-in desire to know about the places in which
we are going to spend extended time. And logic suggests that the
longer we are going to be in a future place, the more effort we will
extend to learn about it.

But that logic often breaks down when it comes to the place
we are going to live for eternity. Think of it—Jesus Christ, at this
very moment, is preparing a place for us to dwell forever (John
14:1-3). Doesn't it behoove us to learn and know everything we
can about that place? We ought to be like Abraham who lived
his whole life in anticipation of "the city which has foundations,
whose builder and maker is God" (Hebrews 11:10).

If you're not sure where to start, use Revelation 21 as a guide to
your heavenly home, the New Jerusalem.

Those who have the new Jerusalem in their eye
must have the ways that lead to it in their heart.

MATTHEW HENRY

FEBRUARY 3

POWER FOR THE POWERLESS

*The fear of the LORD is the beginning
of knowledge, but fools despise wisdom and instruction.*

PROVERBS 1:7

The English historian, Lord Acton, wrote a letter to Bishop
Mandell Creighton in 1887 in which he penned these now
famous words: "Power tends to corrupt, and absolute power
corrupts absolutely." Drawing on Lord Acton's words, present-day
writer and actor Harry Shearer has wondered, "If absolute power
corrupts absolutely, does absolute powerlessness make you pure?"

Both those extremes—absolute power and absolute
powerlessness—were illustrated in the life of the king of ancient
Babylon, Nebuchadnezzar. He was a man in whose hands resided
absolute power. But his absolute power had corrupted him; he
did not fear God. Then the day came when Nebuchadnezzar
found himself powerless. A series of dreams left him confused
and disconcerted. He had no idea what they meant, nor did his
wisest advisors. He ultimately found himself humbled before the
God of Israel who gave the interpretation to His prophet, Daniel.

When we find ourselves powerless in the face of life's
circumstances, our best recourse is to confess our weakness to
God and rely on His power alone.

*O Love that wilt not let me go, I rest my weary soul in thee; I give thee back
the life I owe, that in Thine ocean depths its flow may richer, fuller be.*

GEORGE MATHESON

DAVID JEREMIAH

NOT "IF," BUT "WHERE"

And as it is appointed for men to die once, but after this the judgment.

HEBREWS 9:27

One of the most important things to remember about life as we know it is this: We are not living the life God created us to live. After Adam and Eve were expelled from the Garden of Eden due to their sin (Genesis 3), everything changed. And no change is bigger than death. Mankind was created to live eternally; but that eternal life is to be interrupted by death (the ultimate result of sin), followed by resurrection to eternal life. The question is, "Where will one's eternal life be spent?"

Again, the Garden of Eden is the model. God created mankind to fellowship with Him for eternity. Therefore, the Bible speaks of only two options for eternal life: with God (heaven) or not with God (hell). Jesus said in John 3:18 that failure to believe in God's plan for saving mankind from sin results in condemnation—spending eternity apart from God. But believing in God's plan results in being saved from condemnation and experiencing "everlasting life" (John 3:16). The question is not "if" we live eternally, but "where."

Make sure you have answered the question of "where" you will spend eternity by believing in Jesus Christ.

*The beginning of the way to heaven
is to feel that we are on the way to hell.*

J. C. RYLE

GOD KNOWS EVERYTHING

[God] reveals deep and secret things;
He knows what is in the darkness, and light dwells with Him.

DANIEL 2:22

As has been rightly observed, there is much that we do not know and even more that we do not know that we do not know. It seems there is no end to the discoveries man makes about the mysteries revealed in the heights of the universe and the depths of the oceans. While scientists address those realms of knowledge, the average person is consumed with his own list of "don't knows."

Should I take that job? Should I marry that person? Why has this illness or calamity come into my life? What does the future hold? These questions are the stuff of life for most of us and can be a reason for either fear or faith. But if we can take one lesson from the experience of King Nebuchadnezzar of Babylon, it is this: God knows the answer to every question and is perfectly capable of revealing it at just the right time. We may not have a dream that needs interpreting like Nebuchadnezzar, but the point is the same—God has the answers we need. When life presents questions that we cannot answer, we can turn to the One who has every answer.

Faith is a confession of trust, not a demand for an immediate answer. Let your confidence be in God, whatever His answer may be.

A man's heart is right when he wills what God wills.

THOMAS AQUINAS

DAVID JEREMIAH

PEACE

"'Blessed is the King who comes in the name of the LORD!'
Peace in heaven and glory in the highest!"

LUKE 19:38

When Isaiah the prophet foretold the birth of Israel's Messiah, "Prince of Peace" was one of the names given to Him. All of the names—"Wonderful, Counselor, Mighty God, Everlasting Father, Prince of Peace"—reflected the heaven from which He would come (Isaiah 9:6). And when Jesus came, and entered Jerusalem to prepare for His Passion, the crowds called out, "Peace in heaven and glory in the highest!" (Luke 19:38)

Heaven is indeed a kingdom of peace. And when Jesus taught His disciples how to live in a world characterized by a lack of peace, He taught them to pray that God's will would be done "on earth as it is in heaven" (Matthew 6:10). There is peace in heaven, and Jesus wants His disciples to have peace on earth until eternal peace is realized in the New Jerusalem. But how? Through prayer. The apostle Paul wrote that when we commit every care and concern to God through prayer, the heavenly peace of God will guard our hearts and minds (Philippians 4:6-7).

If you have lost your peace, get it back through prayer. Commit every troubling thought to God and receive heavenly peace in return.

When we lack the peace of God, we should turn to our peace with God.

ROBERT HORN

HERE TODAY, GONE TOMORROW

*And God will wipe away every tear from their eyes; there shall
be no more death, nor sorrow, nor crying. There shall
be no more pain, for the former things have passed away.*

REVELATION 21:4

How would you define pain? Since 1968, the most widely used definition of pain in clinical settings is the one set forth by pain researcher Margo McCaffery: Pain is "whatever the experiencing person says it is, existing whenever and wherever the person says it does." In other words, no one can tell another person that they are not in pain. Pain is as unique as the individuals who profess to experience it.

Think about any pain you may be experiencing now—relational pain, physical pain, emotional pain, spiritual pain. Regardless of the kind of pain you are experiencing now, it will "soon" be over. The Bible says that in the New Jerusalem "there shall be no more pain, for the former things have passed away." Whatever kind of pain you feel today, an eternal day is coming in which you will feel it no more if you live in the New Jerusalem. Every God-designed need and longing of the human spirit, soul, and body will be met completely in Christ.

Let today's pain lead you to tomorrow's pleasure in heaven.

God . . . shouts in our pains; it is His megaphone to rouse a deaf world.

C. S. LEWIS

WHO'S IN CHARGE?

The fear of the Lord is the beginning of wisdom,
and the knowledge of the Holy One is understanding.

PROVERBS 9:10

After the Colonies won the Revolutionary War, they were united by the Articles of Confederation, which, by 1787, had become inadequate. The colonies were on the verge of becoming thirteen small nations, and a Constitutional Convention convened to form a "more perfect union." From the beginning, however, the writing of this new constitution was so divisive that one delegate, Oliver Ellsworth, warned, "We grow more and more skeptical as we proceed. If we do not decide soon, we shall be unable to come to any decision."

It was the venerable Ben Franklin who struggled to his feet to ask: "In this situation of this assembly, groping as it were in the dark to find political truth, and scarce able to distinguish it when presented to us, how has it happened that we have not hitherto once thought of humbly applying to the Father of lights to illumine our understanding?"

Franklin was right. It isn't our government but our God who rules in the affairs of men. Let's pray for our leaders; for without God's illumination, none of them has answers to times like these.

It is impossible to rightly govern the world without God and the Bible.

GEORGE WASHINGTON

FEBRUARY 9

HEAVEN ON THE WAY TO HEAVEN

The kingdom of God is not eating and drinking,
but righteousness and peace and joy in the Holy Spirit.

ROMANS 14:17

Most people anticipate their vacations with relish. We plan them, study the tour guides, book our reservations, and look forward to our time away.

The reality of eternal life on a New Earth is more exciting than any trip or vacation; and with every passing day, our anticipation for heaven should grow brighter. How wonderful to visualize the great city of New Jerusalem with its gleaming walls and walkways, its translucent skyscrapers, its crystal river, and its centerpiece—the throne of God! No more pain, tears, suffering, or death!

But why wait?

Christians can experience heaven on the way to heaven. We have the King of heaven living in our hearts. We have the Word of God, more precious than gold, inscribed in our minds. We have the crystal river of the Holy Spirit flowing from our innermost being. The kingdom of God is not eating or drinking; it is righteousness, peace, and joy in the Holy Spirit.

With Jesus living in our hearts, we can experience heaven on the way to heaven.

The hill of Zion yields a thousand sacred sweets before
we reach the heavenly fields or walk the golden streets.

ISAAC WATTS

DAVID JEREMIAH

FEBRUARY 10

OCEAN LINER

A man's heart plans his way, but the Lord directs his steps.

PROVERBS 16:9

Someone once described the sovereignty of God as being like an ocean liner bound for port. While it is resolutely moving toward that destination, there are passengers aboard who are free to move about as they will. They are not in chains. In fact, they eat, sleep, play games, read, and talk as they please. All the while, the liner is still headed toward its predetermined port. It is a picture of both freedom and sovereignty harmoniously taking place at the same time.

As children of God, each of us has the Sovereign God as ruler in our hearts. This means that no matter what happens in life and whatever decisions we make, God resides in our hearts, steering us toward an ever-fixed mark. This is a comforting truth because as humans, we don't know what's best for our lives; and though we try to make good decisions, sometimes we just make the wrong ones. It's wonderful to know that while we're busy living and learning, God is at the helm of our life working all things together for good (Romans 8:28).

> *In the total expanse of human life, there is not a single square inch of which the Christ, who alone is sovereign, does not declare, "That is mine!"*
>
> ABRAHAM KUYPER

THE CROSS AND THE CROWN

*But God forbid that I should boast except
in the cross of our Lord Jesus Christ.*

GALATIANS 6:14

George Bennard was born into a miner's family in Ohio and came to Christ as a youth. He wanted to go to theological school, but family concerns kept him from the education he desired. In time, he became a traveling evangelist, diligently studying his Bible and reading all the books he could find. During one period of his ministry, he carefully studied the subject of the cross of Christ, praying for a deeper understanding of its meaning and power. As he preached from town to town, the words of a hymn began formulating in his mind. He sang portions of it at his meetings. Finally he finished his hymn and sang the completed version to friends, asking them, "Will it do?"

It has done very well. It's "The Old Rugged Cross."

One of the hymn's central ideas is that our trophies in this world are temporary and cannot compare to the power of the cross or to the crown to be awarded us when we stand before Jesus, "where His glory forever I'll share."

In an age of awards and trophies, let's keep our eyes on the cross and the crown.

So I'll cherish the old rugged cross, till my trophies at last I lay down; I will cling to the old rugged cross, and exchange it someday for a crown.

GEORGE BENNARD

DAVID JEREMIAH

LOVE

In this is love, not that we loved God, but that
He loved us and sent His Son to be the propitiation for our sins.

1 JOHN 4:10

There is something in the character of God and the culture of heaven that resulted in Jesus Christ coming to earth to die for the human race. Was it kindness? Compassion? Empathy? Sympathy? As God-like as those and other traits are, the Bible seems to focus on one trait as the defining characteristic of God: love. First John 4:8 and 16 say that "God is love," and the world's favorite Bible verse, John 3:16, says that it was because God "loved the world" that He sent Jesus to save us. Heaven is, and will be, brimming with love.

But the love of God is not for heaven alone; it is freely available for us to experience while on earth. Indeed, the "love of God has been poured out in our hearts by the Holy Spirit who was given to us" (Romans 5:5). Nothing can separate us from "the love of God" (Romans 8:39). And our hearts are continually being directed into "the love of God" (2 Thessalonians 3:5).

If you are feeling unloved, you do not have to wait for heaven to experience the reality of God's love. You can experience it now by believing in the gift of His love, Jesus Christ.

No less a person than God is needed to assure us of God's love.

RICHARD SIBBES

FEBRUARY 13

GOD OUR DELIVERER

He shall deliver you in six troubles, yes, in seven no evil shall touch you.

JOB 5:19

When Daniel's three friends—Shadrach, Meshach, and Abed-Nego—stood before the opening to a blazing furnace in Babylon, they had one of the most remarkable perspectives found in the pages of world history: "It doesn't matter if we are thrown into the furnace or not. If God chooses to deliver us, fine. If not, fine. Either way our trust is in Him."

How often do we face life's threatening moments with that kind of faithful resolve? It may not be life-or-death persecution for our faith that we face, but we may face a life-or-death situation of another kind: illness, divorce, unemployment, estrangement, or an unspeakable tragedy. But not everyone is delivered as Daniel's three friends were, so how do we interpret the scriptural promises of protection in light of actual outcomes? Here's how: we make up our minds about God at the door of the furnace, not once we're inside. As a result, we are prepared for any outcome. If we are delivered *on* earth, fine; if we are delivered *to* heaven, also fine. We let God be in charge of seeing us through our fiery furnaces.

God is our deliverer (Psalm 18:2), regardless of how, when, and where the deliverance occurs.

It is only the fear of God that can deliver us from the fear of man.

JOHN WITHERSPOON

DAVID JEREMIAH

LOVESICK

I charge you, O daughters of Jerusalem,
if you find my beloved, that you tell him I am lovesick.

SONG OF SOLOMON 5:8

Recently a lonely reader wrote to the advice columnist of an online magazine, asking: "I love someone who doesn't feel the same way. Everyone tells me to move on, but that's just not working. What do I do?"

Do you remember when your heart filled with joy because of a phone call from one you loved, or a note, a hug, or even the wave of a hand? Conversely, have you ever known the pain of loving but not being loved in return?

The woman in Song of Solomon could identify with that as she struggled with her feelings for Solomon. We can't control how another views us, nor can we command love from another person. But the Lord's love for us will never falter; we're secure in Him. Furthermore He promises to meet all our needs in life as we seek Him first (Matthew 6:33). If you feel lonely, rest in His love. Be proactive in meeting the needs of others, and trust Him to meet the deepest needs of your own heart in His own time and way.

Lord, I know not what I ought to ask of Thee; Thou only knowest what
I need; Thou lovest me better than I know how to love myself.

FRANCOIS FÉNELON

WHEN WE DON'T KNOW WHAT TO DO

Do not be afraid nor dismayed because of this great multitude, for the battle is not yours, but God's.... You will not need to fight in this battle.

2 CHRONICLES 20:15B, 17

In 2 Chronicles 20, King Jehoshaphat suddenly learned a great army was coming against him. In alarm, he gathered the people before the temple and led them in earnest prayer: "O our God..." he said, "we have no power against this great multitude that is coming against us; nor do we know what to do, but our eyes are upon You."

Just then a prophet declared a message from the Lord: "Do not be afraid nor dismayed... for the battle is not yours, but God's... Position yourselves, stand still and see the salvation of the Lord, who is with you."

The next day, King Jehoshaphat put the choir at the head of his army, and the nation went to war armed with hymns of praise. The enemy, falling into chaos, slaughtered itself, leaving the spoils and plunder to the people of Judah.

Sometimes our best strategy in facing a trial or temptation is to pray: "Lord, I don't know what to do, but my eyes are on You." Our Advocate has a way of fighting on our behalf as we position ourselves and sing songs of praise.

Anticipate your battles, fight them on your knees before temptation comes, and you will always have the victory.

R. A. TORREY

SITTING IN A PUDDLE

To be spiritually minded is life and peace.

ROMANS 8:6B

When we're disappointed or distraught—whether about health or money or prodigals or whatever—we need a biblical plan for recovering God's peace. Perhaps you're separated from someone you love, and the loneliness is intense. To love is to sometimes hurt. We need the peace that exceeds understanding.

Try underlining Bible verses. Sit down with a cup of tea and search the Scriptures, looking for verses to underline and memorize.

Try journaling. Write out your feelings, but also jot down the verses God gives you. You can also compose written prayers as the Psalm writers did long ago.

Try reading. Find an inspirational book. Whether an old classic like *Pilgrim's Progress* or something just off the press, read it with a highlighter in hand.

Try exercise. Even something as simple as walking around the block can clear your mind. Whatever you do, don't fall into self-pity. Sitting around in a puddle of worry isn't good for anyone. Whatever ailment we face, the Word of God is the medicine and the peace of God the cure.

If Christ's lordship does not disrupt our own lordship,
then the reality of our conversion must be questioned.

CHARLES COLSON

TRADING STRESS FOR A SONG

Let us go into His tabernacle; let us worship at His footstool.

PSALM 132:7

A Netherlands-based electronics firm is creating a bracelet that will change color and flicker from yellow to red when a person's emotions rise to unhealthy levels. It's being developed chiefly for stock traders on European exchanges. When trading becomes too intense and the trader's blood pressure rises, the device will issue a warning to "take a time-out, wind down, or reconsider their actions," said the manufacturer. The results, hopefully, will be beneficial to investors—to say nothing of the stock brokers themselves.

If everyone on earth were wearing such a bracelet right now, how many would be red. Would yours?

The greatest antidote to stress is worship. Worship is recognizing God's greatness and glory, and, in response, expressing our pleasure and praise. It's not about us, how we feel, or the kind of music we enjoy. It's about the One who is the same yesterday, today, and forever. It's about who He is and what He has done.

We don't need a bracelet on our wrists, but simply a heart of worship that adores and praises the greatness of God's glory.

God wants worshippers before workers; indeed the only acceptable workers are those who have learned the lost art of worship.

A. W. TOZER

TIME TOGETHER

Where has your beloved gone...? Where has your beloved turned aside...?

SONG OF SOLOMON 6:1

Marriage counselors are alarmed about the scant amount of time husbands and wives spend with each other and their children during the course of the week. We're a distracted generation. In olden times, families spent vast chunks of time together in the farmhouse and around the barn and in the fields. Today the average family hardly has time to eat a hurried sandwich together, and that's often done in the car after we've zipped past a drive-in where someone tosses food to us through the window.

A team of counselors recently suggested that any marriage can be improved by committing to a 30/30 plan—spending thirty minutes together for thirty days. We have to be intentional about scheduling time to protect priceless moments with those most precious to us. Block in date nights, family times, camping trips, regular meals, getaway weekends, and reading times with your youngsters at bedtime.

Even Solomon and Shulamith had trouble spending time with each other in Song of Solomon. The problem is as old as the Bible, but the answer is as modern as a good planning calendar.

> *The disciple of Christ is to be an expert*
> *merchant in the commodity of time.*[4]

J. H. JOWETT

4 J. H. JOWETT IN *Herald of Gospel Liberty*, JANUARY 12, 1922, 45

JOY

I thank my God upon every remembrance of you, always in every prayer of mine making request for you all with joy . . .

PHILIPPIANS 1:3-4

If you are delivering something to a friend, the best way to arrive with that delivery is to begin your trip with it. Therefore, when the angels from heaven arrived on earth with "good tidings of great joy"—the news of the birth of Jesus—it meant they left heaven with joy "in hand." And news of great joy could not have originated in heaven if heaven was not a place of great joy itself. Indeed, twice in the Book of Revelation heaven is exhorted to rejoice over the saving acts of God—not a hard thing for heaven to do (12:12; 18:20).

If Jesus wanted God's will to be done "on earth as it is in heaven" (Matthew 6:10), that means the joy of heaven should become the joy of God's people on earth. To prove that joy is dependent on the power of heaven and not the pleasures of earth, Paul wrote his epistle of joy (Philippians) while imprisoned by the Romans. Fifteen different times in that one letter Paul proves it is possible to know the joy of heaven in the midst of earth's hardest moments.

The secret to that joy, as Paul wrote, is to "rejoice in Christ Jesus" (Philippians 3:3).

It is the very joy of this earthly life to think that it will come to an end.

CHARLES SPURGEON

DAVID JEREMIAH

IT DOESN'T JUST HAPPEN

The fruit of the righteous is a tree of life, and he who wins souls is wise.

PROVERBS 11:30

On the hit TV show, *The Biggest Loser*, contestants work hard every week to drop pounds so they can remain on the show. They are held accountable by a gigantic scale that reveals their weight in front of millions of Americans. Going into the contest, they know weight loss doesn't just happen; they have to fight for it by breaking old habits and creating new, healthy ones. Desperate to lose weight and get healthy, they do whatever it takes to achieve their goal.

This should be our mentality as Christians. Becoming like Christ won't just happen; it takes discipline and the pursuit of righteousness. When we accepted Christ as our Savior, we made a commitment to Him; and it is our responsibility to put off the "old man" and "put on the new man...in true righteousness and holiness" (Ephesians 4:22, 24).

When we earnestly do this, we will be well on our way to achieving our goal of godly righteousness and pointing others toward Christ Jesus.

I know I can't do a thing to earn my salvation;
but now that I am His, I will do everything in my power
to show Him how much I love Him—and I live to please the
One I love who has transformed me with HIS love.

KATHERINE WALDEN

A Normal Day

The Lord is high above all nations, His glory above the heavens, who is like the Lord our God, who dwells on high, who humbles Himself to behold the things that are in the heavens and in the earth.

PSALM 113:4-6

What does your "normal" day look like? Perhaps you're at work, or keeping house and tending to the needs of children. Suddenly, by special delivery courier, you receive a message that you are in violation of a new law forbidding worship of God. And the penalty is death.

What would be your first response? When that happened to Daniel in Babylon, his day didn't change a bit. He prayed to God three times "as was his custom." He didn't even stop praying when the authorities showed up to say he wasn't allowed to pray! When we go into "crisis mode" as a response to bad or unexpected news, it reveals the depth of our "normal" life. If the life we live every day is deeply dependent on God through prayer, worship, and Bible study, then no news can shake that foundation. We keep on praying, worshipping, and studying just as we've always done. Yes, the content of our prayers may change, but the content of our character doesn't.

What is a normal day for you? Make sure it's the kind of day that prepares you to handle the abnormal when it comes.

We ought to behave ourselves every day as though we had no dependence on any other.

JONATHAN EDWARDS

THE UNFAILING HUSBAND

*For your Maker is your husband—the Lord Almighty
is his name—the Holy One of Israel is your Redeemer;
he is called the God of all the earth.*

ISAIAH 54:5 (NIV)

In the Old Testament, Jehovah presents Himself as the husband of the nation of Israel. In the New Testament, the church is pictured as the bride of Christ. How remarkable that the Bible consistently presents our Maker as our husband. Just as a caring man goes out of his way to enrich the life of his bride, God blesses us with loving provisions. He will never abandon, leave, forsake, neglect, nor forget us. He constantly demonstrates His love in expressions large and small. He gives us His name. He daily meets our needs. He lavishes His blessings. He has a mansion for us in heaven.

Sooner or later, we'll be disappointed by every friend on earth; none are perfect. But the Lord Jesus Christ will never let us down. When we are lonely, He comes calling. When we feel weak, He imparts strength. When we're hurt, His wounds provide strong medicine for inward healing. When we're aging, He reminds us of the eternal life bound up in His resurrection.

Your Maker is your husband—the Lord Almighty is His name.

*Let the love of husband be never so pure and fervent, it is but a faint
picture of the flame that burns in the heart of Jesus.*

CHARLES H. SPURGEON, IN HIS SERMON "BANDS OF LOVE"

FRIEND POWER

Though one may be overpowered by another, two can withstand him.
And a threefold cord is not quickly broken.

ECCLESIASTES 4:12

People with pets tend to exercise more, sleep better, and take fewer sick days than adults without pets. Pet owners also demonstrate higher levels of social interaction with other adults and often have lower cardiovascular risks as well. The most often cited reason for these benefits is "unconditional love."

Yes, humans and some animals enjoy a beneficial bond. But how much more would a human companion(s) be who displayed the same unconditional love—and so much more? God's statement in the Garden of Eden—that it is not good for man to be alone (Genesis 2:18)—has implications that go beyond marriage. Human beings were created by God as social beings, hardwired to relate to others as friends, spouses, extended family members, members of the Body of Christ, and partners in community life. Not only do we need what others can contribute to us, they need the strengths and gifts God has given us.

Are you walking through life with fellow pilgrims whose unconditional love manifests God's love to you? And are you being such a companion to others?

It is the best and truest friend who honestly tells us the truth about
ourselves even when he knows we shall not like it.

R. C. H. LENSKI

DAVID JEREMIAH

PERSPECTIVE

Your kingdom come. Your will be done on earth as it is in heaven.

MATTHEW 6:10

The English word "worldview" borrows its meaning from a German idea found in the word *Weltanschauung* (*Welt* = world; *Anschauung* = view or outlook). In both languages it means the same: the broad framework or set of values and principles by which one interprets life's experiences. Whether defined or not, everyone has a worldview—a way of understanding life, a perspective that governs one's mind, will, and emotions.

Heaven has a very clear perspective called the will of God. God intended for heaven's perspective to rule the earth as He made clear in the Garden of Eden (Genesis 2:16-17; 1:28-30). But mankind lost sight of God's perspective due to sin. Nonetheless, when Jesus inaugurated the kingdom of God in His ministry, He made it clear that it was time for God's perspective to again "be done on earth as it is in heaven." The only way to do that is to live in a close relationship with God Himself—trusting in His Son and being counseled and guided by His Spirit.

If you are a citizen of heaven already (Philippians 3:20), then living with a heavenly perspective on earth should come supernaturally to you.

Any worldview that cannot cope with death is fatally deficient.

ALISTER MCGRATH

CRAZY BUSY

Be still, and know that I am God.

PSALM 46:10A

In his book, *CrazyBusy: Overstretched, Overbooked and About to Snap,* Edward M. Hallowell wrote about the moment he knew he had crossed the dark side from busy to crazy busy. It was when he lost his temper at a rotary dial phone while on vacation. His cell phone wouldn't work, and he just about went nuts waiting for the dial to return to start with every number. Then, calming down, he timed the process. The entire dialing process took all of eleven seconds. "What a fool I had become," he wrote. "I had become a man in a hurry even when I had no need to hurry."[5]

Sometimes we're too busy to even notice we're busy. Our daily tasks weigh us down, and we unwillingly but unwittingly neglect what's most important—our inner nourishment and our family fellowship. Plan time for rest. Build some solitude into your routines. Establish plenty of time for spouse and family. Stop being crazy busy. Be still and remember Him who rules over all.

Be still, my soul: thy God doth undertake,
to guide the future as He has the past.

CATHARINA A. VON SCHLEGEL

---

5 ALINA GUGEND, "TOO BUSY TO NOTICE YOU'RE TOO BUSY," *The New York Times*, MARCH 31, 2007.

DAVID JEREMIAH

LIVING ABOVE THE WORLD

The hope of the righteous will be gladness,
but the expectation of the wicked will perish.

PROVERBS 10:28

William Tennent, a friend of George Whitefield, died one day—or so it seemed. People gathered for Tennent's funeral, but the doctor wasn't sure he was dead and sent the people home. The patient opened his eyes and explained that while unconscious he had envisioned himself in heaven. The glory was unutterable and there was indescribable joy.

For years afterward, Tennent testified that he felt such a "sense of divine things" that everything else seemed vain. "Such was the effect on my mind of what I had seen and heard, that if it be possible for a human being to live entirely above the world, and the things of it . . . I was that person."[6]

Anyone who has experienced the loss of a loved one knows sleepless nights and deep sorrow. But as a believer, we also know that during the dark hours we're not alone. God's comfort surpasses understanding. We anticipate heaven, and that enables us to live above the world.

> *I want to live above the world, though Satan's darts*
> *at me are hurled; for faith has caught the joyful sound,*
> *the song of saints on higher ground.*
>
> JOHNSON OATMAN

6 S. B. SHAW, *Touching Incidents* (MICHIGAN: J. W. HAZELTON, 1893), 154-156.

DRIVEN INTO SOVEREIGN ARMS

*. . .to console those who mourn in Zion, to give them beauty
for ashes, the oil of joy for mourning.*

ISAIAH 61:3

Kay Arthur was bitterly disappointed when she contracted a heart infection that forced her removal from the mission field. She and her family, serving in Mexico, were forced to return home. "I felt like a failure," she wrote. "It would be several years before I'd see how He'd use those formative years of study in Mexico to prepare me to write inductive Bible studies that would eventually reach 52 countries."

"My disappointments aren't over," Kay admits. "Pain and trials are almost constant companions, but never enemies. They drive me into His sovereign arms. There He takes my disappointments and works everything together for good."[7]

The Lord promises in Isaiah 61 to exchange our mourning with His oil of joy, and to give a garment of praise to those who are weighed down in spirit. Cast your burdens on the Lord and let Him become the strength of your heart. Let trouble drive you into His sovereign arms.

*The devil sometimes goes too far.
He drives us straight into the Lord's arms.*

RUTH BELL GRAHAM

7 KAY ARTHUR, "IN PERSON: MY DISAPPOINTMENTS, HIS APPOINTMENTS," *Moody Magazine*, JANUARY 1992, 30.

DAVID JEREMIAH

UTOPIA

For our citizenship is in heaven, from which
we also eagerly wait for the Savior, the Lord Jesus Christ.

PHILIPPIANS 3:20

Utopia is a fictional land conceived by Thomas More for his Latin novel, *On the Best State in a Republic.* This near-perfect society was discovered by a traveler on an island in the Atlantic, and it seemed to possess ideal social, political, and legal structures. It had few laws and no lawyers. Instead of fighting wars, it hired mercenaries. Instead of personal property, everything was held communally. Everyone was free to worship as they wished, and all appeared happy and whole.

But it exists only in fiction.

Ever since Adam and Eve lost their lease on Eden, humanity has been looking for Utopia. But we live in a world blighted by sin, selfishness, death, and destruction.

One day the times will reach fulfillment, Christ will return, the spiritual and physical realms will be merged, the New Earth will appear, the City of God will descend from heaven, and the dwelling place of God will be with men. He will be our God and we will be His people.

It won't be Utopia. It'll be heaven!

In the truest sense, Christian pilgrims have the best of both worlds.
We have joy whenever this world reminds us of the next,
and we take solace whenever it does not.

C. S. LEWIS

DO I HAVE FAITH?

Now faith is the substance of things hoped for,
the evidence of things not seen.

HEBREWS 11:1

The African impala is one of the most powerful and graceful animals in Africa. It can jump to a height of more than 10 feet and cover a distance of more than 30 feet in one jump. In spite of its great ability, an impala can be kept in an enclosure with a solid fence no more than three feet high. Impalas will not jump if they can't see where their feet will land.

Do impalas walk by faith or by sight? Don't laugh—there are many Christians who walk the same way. As a believer, if we are willing to take steps in life only when we can see exactly what's on the path, we don't have biblical faith. Abraham was a man who had true faith. God called him from his home in Mesopotamia and directed him to he-knew-not-where. He just obeyed God and left his home and walked one step at a time. Eventually, he arrived at his destination—not because he saw Canaan but because he saw the will of God for his life. The future can only be faced in two ways: with faith or with fear. How small is the enclosure that has you penned in?

For we walk by faith, not by sight. (2 Corinthians 5:7)

> *Knowing the Bible should lead to living the Bible*
> *which leads to honoring the Author of the Bible.*

DAVID JEREMIAH

MARCH

GRACE

Imitate me, just as I also imitate Christ.

1 CORINTHIANS 11:1

The term "understudy" is used in the theater for someone who learns the lines of the primary actor so that he or she can step into the role if necessary. Several famous stars began their careers as understudies. For example, Anthony Hopkins made a name for himself when he took over a role for Sir Laurence Olivier when the latter was stricken with cancer during a 1967 play at the National Theatre.

In a sense, all Christians are understudies. When Jesus ascended into heaven in Acts 1, He commissioned us to continue in His stead. We're to imitate Him, and to do so with such grace that others, too, can imitate Him by imitating us.

Just as Jesus was "full of grace" (John 1:14), we are to grow in the grace of our Lord (2 Peter 3:18). Our speech is to be with grace, seasoned with salt (Colossians 4:6). We are to sing with grace in our hearts (Colossians 3:16). And we are to be strong in the grace that is in our Lord Jesus Christ (2 Timothy 2:1).

We are understudies of His grace. What a role!

Grace is free, but when once you take it, you are bound forever to the Giver and bound to catch the spirit of the Giver.

E. STANLEY JONES, MISSIONARY

DAVID JEREMIAH

LION-HEARTED FAITH

But you, O Lord, be not far from me.... Save me from the lion's mouth.

PSALM 22:19A, 21A

We'd be surprised to read in the newspaper that a lion was loose in downtown Tel Aviv or Jerusalem. When we think of lions, we think of Africa. Yet in Bible times, the land of Israel was filled with lions; and the Bible contains several stories about them. There's Samson who killed a lion with his bare hands. And David, who as a shepherd boy, killed a lion that threatened his sheep. And, of course, the prophet Daniel was thrown to the lions.

Among the 150 references to lions in the Bible, two verses stand in stark contrast. In 1 Peter 5:8, Satan is compared to a lion prowling around for someone to devour. But he meets his match in Revelation 5:5, where Jesus is called the "Lion of the tribe of Judah."

When we feel the devil after us, we need to remember that we can't fight him off on our own any more than we could defend ourselves from an attacking lion. But we have a Lion on our side. Jesus is with us! That gives us a Lion's share of assurance.

> *"Don't you mind him," said Puddleglum.*
> *"There are no accidents. Our guide is Aslan."*

C. S. LEWIS, ABOUT THE CHRIST-FIGURE IN
The Lion, the Witch, and the Wardrobe

UNDERESTIMATING GOD

...and indeed the half of the greatness of your wisdom was not told me.

2 CHRONICLES 9:6

Because God is infinite, we always underestimate Him. Logically speaking, it's an unavoidable inevitability. The Lord has no boundaries or barriers, no limits or restrictions. He is endless in direction and duration, in space and time. His unfathomable attributes are bottomless seas without shores. Our minds can't grasp the depths of His presence, majesty, power, glory, and grace. There's no ceiling to His love, wrath, wealth, and intelligence. Our minds are astonished with God, and we can no more fit Him into our thoughts than we could fit the ocean into a thimble.

There is no way for us to comprehend the fullness of His infinity. So it would seem logical to say: Because God is inestimable, we always underestimate Him.

Nothing is a surprise to God, for He is the same yesterday, today, and forever. He sees the past, the present, and the future in one glance. Whatever our thoughts are about the return of Christ and our eternal home with Him, the reality will be even better. We'll say with the Queen of Sheba that the half was not told.

In the midst of the street is life's river, clear as crystal
and pure to behold; But not half of that city's bright glory
to mortals has ever been told.

JONATHAN B. ATCHINSON

WILL YOU BELIEVE HIM?

*"Men of Galilee, why do you stand gazing up into heaven?
This same Jesus, who was taken up from you into heaven,
will so come in like manner as you saw Him go into heaven."*

ACTS 1:11

When a jury listens as a witness gives testimony in a criminal or civil trial, the witness's character—his or her record of truth-telling—bears heavily on their decision. Does this witness have a history of honesty? Of telling the truth? Of living a life above reproach? Does the witness have anything to gain or lose by not telling the truth? If all indications point to honesty and integrity, the jury has no choice but to believe the witness's words.

The same thought process applies to what Jesus Christ said about His own return to earth. Throughout three years of public ministry, there is no record of His saying anything that was not true, not demonstrable, or not believable. Indeed, "the truth" was a central part of His teachings (John 8:32; 14:6). So, put yourself in the place of the jury concerning His testimony: "I will come again and receive you" (John 14:3). Since your future—indeed, your eternal destiny—depends on whether you believe His words or not, what should you do?

If you have not taken Jesus Christ at His word, now would be a good day to believe.

The truth of Scripture demolishes speculation.

R. C. SPROUL

THE REAL YOU

Search me, O God, and know my heart . . .
and see if there is any wicked way in me.

PSALM 139:23-24

On the three days preceding Ash Wednesday on the Christian church calendar, just prior to the beginning of Lent, raucous celebrations are held in many countries around the world. In America, the celebrations are called Mardi Gras, and in most other countries, Carnival. One of the main features of these festivals is masks that hide the true identity of the participants.

Given what takes place at Mardi Gras and Carnivals, hiding one's identity is understandable. It's also understandable when world rulers and others in authority try to hide their true identity—their true motives and the nature of their intent. When God showed Daniel the four beasts that represented the four nations that would rule up until the coming of Christ, He revealed their true identities: ravenous beasts intent on world domination. But hiding one's identity from God is a futile endeavor. He knows the heart and desires of every person. When we are trying to be someone we're not, we fool no one but ourselves.

Instead of being someone you're not, be the person God knows you are. Better yet, be the person He created you to be—one who brings honor and glory to Him.

Hypocrisy is too thin a veil to blind the eyes of the Almighty.

WILLIAM GURNALL

GET A PIECE OF THE ROCK

From everlasting to everlasting, You are God.

PSALM 90:2B

One day in 1890, an advertising agent named Mortimer Remington was traveling by rail through New Jersey to a meeting with the Prudential Insurance Company. He passed Laurel Hill, which at the time was an impressive mountain-sized rock (it has since been reduced by quarrying). Remington's mind went to the Rock of Gibraltar, and he conceived one of the greatest advertising symbols of all time. Even today, the Rock of Gibraltar is the symbol of Prudential with its slogans, "Strength of Gibraltar" and "Get a Piece of the Rock."

But even Gibraltar will one day crumble. Only God Himself is unchanging, eternal, and permanent. Some picture God almost as an elderly, white-haired Divine logo. But our God is from everlasting to everlasting, and His attributes never change. He is eternally loving, powerful, present, and omniscient; and Jesus Christ is also the same yesterday, today, and forever.

It isn't Gibraltar but Jehovah who gives us unshakable strength and unfailing hope. Our lives find stability when we get a piece of the Rock.

He who trusts in God's unchanging love
builds on a Rock that none can move.

GEORG NEUMARK, HYMNIST

LOADED LIVING

Blessed be the Lord who daily loads us with benefits.

PSALM 68:19

Joseph Leek, a 90-year-old Britisher, was a tightwad. He regularly sauntered to his neighbor's house to watch television in order to reduce his electricity bill. He shopped at secondhand clothing stores and put off home repairs. It was a shock to everyone after his death when he left almost two million dollars to an organization that provides guide dogs for the blind.

Too bad he never met the English spinster, Mary Guthrie Essame. She was a retired nurse who also wore hand-me-downs and lived in a ramshackle house. Friends were amazed when she left ten million dollars to charity upon her death.

These kinds of stories—and there are many of them—remind us of two things. First, from a material perspective, we should live simply and wisely so as to be faithful supporters of God's work. But second, in a spiritual sense, how sad to live as paupers when we're the children of the King. Our God loads us with blessings every day, and we should fully enjoy the peace and pleasure of His promises and presence.

Let's live frugally—but joyfully!

You are weak unless you are glad; you are not glad and strong unless your faith and hope are fixed in Christ.

ALEXANDER MACLAREN

TIME LOST IS NEVER FOUND

*Tell Archippus: "See to it that you complete
the work you have received in the Lord."*

COLOSSIANS 4:17 (NIV)

In *Poor Richard's Almanac*, Benjamin Franklin advised, "If time
be of all things the most precious, wasting time may be the
greatest prodigality, since lost time is never found again . . . Let us
then be up and doing, and doing to the purpose; so by diligence
shall we do more with less perplexity."

Throughout eternity, God's servants will serve Him. We'll be
worshipping around the throne in New Jerusalem and enjoying
our fellowship, work, and pursuits with endless joy. But here on
earth, we have limited time to care for our families and fulfill our
Father's will.

Let's spend time doing those things that convey God's love
to those around us. Christ had only 33 years, and in His active
public ministry He had only 42 months. But He made every
moment count; and on the eve of His crucifixion He said, "I have
finished the work which You have given Me to do" (John 17:4).

Let's be diligent today to finish the work He's assigned us
this day.

*What we must decide is how we are valuable
rather than how valuable we are.*

EDGAR Z. FRIEDENBERG

AVOID THE CONSEQUENCES

*And behold, I am coming quickly, and my reward is with Me,
to give to everyone according to his work.*

REVELATION 22:12

The National Hurricane Center at Florida International University, Miami, Florida, has a tough job: providing a balanced stream of information about approaching hurricanes—not enough to cause panic but enough to motivate people to get ready. The hurricane *is* coming and you're not going to change that fact.

The NHC folks have a tough message—the weatherman's version of tough love. Like the message of the Book of Revelation: Jesus Christ *is* coming back—and He's bringing a sword. You can prepare for His arrival now or deal with the consequences on that day. It's your choice. Call it the Bible's version of tough love. Unlike dealing with a hurricane, the way to prepare for Jesus' Second Coming is to run straight toward Him, not away from Him. And the more you read about His return in Revelation 19-20, the more likely you will be to begin preparing for His arrival.

If you're not familiar with Revelation, try reading the last two chapters to see how the story ends. It will make you want to read the whole book.

*The subject of the second coming of Christ has never
been popular to any but the true believer.*

BILLY GRAHAM

DAVID JEREMIAH

THERAPEUTIC PRAISE

*Joshua fell on his face to the earth and worshiped, and said to Him,
"What does my Lord say to His servant?"*

JOSHUA 5:14

A recent report on CNBC claimed that 1 in 5 Americans suffers
mental illness. That amounts to 62 million Americans.
Even more alarming, the highest levels of mental illness show
up among young adults. The complaints include depression,
substance abuse, thoughts of suicide, and family discord.

These are difficult times, and people around the world are
facing extraordinary levels of stress. Many need professional
help, and multitudes need a reason to be hopeful.

Try praise. One of the greatest antidotes to mental stress is
worship with thanksgiving. When we come before the Lord,
recognize His blessings, bathe our souls in His glory, claim His
promises, and sing His praises—well, it's highly therapeutic to
our souls. We don't worship Him just for what we get out of it, of
course. That would be counterproductive. Worship is all about
Him, not us. But how good of God to bless us, as we bless Him.

Joshua was worried before leading Israel into battle. But he fell
on his face, worshipped, listened to God's instructions, and rose
to conquer. We can do the same.

Worship: The spontaneous expression of the heart to the glory of God.

ANONYMOUS

OBEDIENCE

My sheep hear My voice, and I know them, and they follow Me.

JOHN 10:27

Every night of the week all across America, thousands of men and women leave their homes to spend an expensive hour or two at obedience training. They don't attend alone, and it's not their obedience they're worried about. They take Rover with them, and Benji, Buddy, or Lady and the Tramp. Dog obedience academies are big business, for pet owners want to teach their puppies not to bite, bark, dig, chew, run away, or mess up the carpet.

The Lord offers a similar program for His sheep.

As the Lamb of God was obedient to the Father, so we're to obey the Good Shepherd. It's important to ask ourselves: Have I been guilty of biting comments? Have I been barking up an unhealthy tree? Have I been digging into things I should avoid? Have I been running away from a clean conscience? Have I been messing up?

We're understudies of His obedience as we hear His voice and follow Him.

In many ways, the attitude of obedience is much more vital than the act, because if the attitude is right, the act will naturally follow. But the right action with the wrong attitude is nothing but hypocrisy.

JOHN MACARTHUR

March 12

I Now See

And when I saw Him, I fell at His feet as dead.

Revelation 1:17

It is one of the most joyous and terrifying moments of your life. Your mind races with fear, excitement, hopes, dreams, and plans. You are exhilarated and exhausted, paralyzed but purposeful. You have never known another moment that compares with this one. And as you look into the eyes of your newborn baby, you realize you never could have dreamed how amazing it truly would be.

In the same way, though John had seen the risen Lord before and had spent a lot of time with Him during His earthly ministry, nothing could prepare him for what the risen, glorified Christ would look like in all His majesty; it was terrifying and awe-inspiring.

Most of us have seen numerous images of what Jesus might have looked like during His time on earth and possibly what He looked like after the Resurrection, but just as John was paralyzed by the sight of the risen, glorified Savior, we too will find ourselves unable to comprehend the moment when we finally see what he saw.

Surrounded by Your glory, what will my heart feel; will I dance for you Jesus or in awe of You be still; will I stand in Your presence or to my knees will I fall; will I sing hallelujah, will I be able to speak at all?

MercyMe

THE MOLTEN CORE OF LOVE

Nevertheless I have this against you, that you have left your first love.

REVELATION 2:4

Imagine if your church had been founded by Paul, taught by Apollos, and led by the likes of Timothy and John? Imagine Jesus Himself saying of your church: "I have seen your hard work and your patient endurance .... You have patiently suffered for me without quitting" (Revelation 2:1-3, NLT).

Yet there was a big problem with the church of Ephesus.

As a nineteenth century British divine put it: "Not withstanding the works they had brought forth in times past, and the labor to which they had submitted, and the long-suffering patience they had displayed, and the faithful discipline they had exercised, and the false doctrine they hated and denounced there were now the symptoms of backsliding and degeneracy."[8]

The Church of Ephesus had lost its molten core of love for the Lord Jesus. It is a reminder that to keep the Church strong, as individuals we need to keep our love and devotion to Christ vibrant and strong.

Listen, Lord, to whoever now says, "Savior, I have forsaken my first love. Forgive me, cleanse my heart, fill me with Your Spirit and Your love." Thank You, Lord Jesus. Amen.

CORRIE TEN BOOM

8 Rev. J. A. Wallace, *The Seven Churches of Asia* (London: James Nisbet & Co, 1842), 36.

DAVID JEREMIAH

YOUR FINEST HOUR

Because you have kept My command to persevere,
I also will keep you from the hour of trial which shall
come upon the whole world, to test those who dwell on the earth.

REVELATION 3:10

In the 1995 film that dramatized the story of the near-disaster during the Apollo 13 mission, a member of NASA's Houston team said to Gene Kranz, mission commander, "This could be the worst disaster NASA's ever faced." Kranz replied, "With all due respect, sir, I believe this is going to be our finest hour." And it was.

We tend to think of victories as life's finest hours, but the opposite is often true. Trials and tribulations call forth faith, perseverance, prayer, and creativity in ways that victory never will. Fortunately, the Church will not be on earth during the seven years of the Great Tribulation to come. But that doesn't mean there won't be increased persecution and a need for perseverance leading up to that hour. Whether then, or in any kind of tribulation we experience, the Christian can have his finest hour by God's grace. The apostle Paul took pleasure in persecutions for Christ's sake, knowing that when he was weakest was when God's grace was strongest.

If you are experiencing trouble, ask God for the grace to make it your finest hour.

The weakness of man sets the stage for the display of God's strength.

JANET WISE

MODEL OF PATIENCE

But let patience have its perfect work, that you
may be perfect and complete, lacking nothing.

JAMES 1:4

One of the best-known idioms in the English language shows up consistently in the day's news: "the patience of Job." People are said to exhibit the patience of Job when undergoing various circumstances or in their daily vocations. But truth be told, Job was not always a patient man. Until the end of the book, Job was on an impatient mission to prove he wasn't the cause of his own suffering.

So if Job is not a good example of patience, who is? Working backward from Galatians 5:22—"But the fruit of the Spirit is . . . longsuffering [that is, patience]"—we arrive at Christ. The fruit of the Spirit represents the Spirit's manifestations of the life of Christ in us—so Christ must have been the personification of the fruit of the Spirit, including patience. But what about when Christ drove the merchants out of the temple with a whip, turning over their tables of money and cages of animals? Was that patience?

For a Christian, patience is willful and cheerful submission to the will and timing of God in one's life. Patience is not always meek and quiet—but it is God-centered, which makes it a measure by which to evaluate whether we are patient or not.

Cheerful patience is a holy art and skill, which a man learns from God.

THOMAS MANTON

DAVID JEREMIAH

BOLSTER YOUR FAITH

And we know that all things work together for good to those who love God, to those who are the called according to His purpose.

ROMANS 8:28

The disciples boarded the boat and headed for the other side of the lake, believing they would make it with no problems. But when the storm began to rage, their doubt was then revealed. It was at this point that Jesus had to rebuke the disciples for their unbelief and remind them that no matter how bad it got out there, He was with them.

When our family members are well, our finances are in order, and our health is intact, we believe we can make it through anything with unfaltering faith. But then we get an unexpected diagnosis, a pay cut, or the news that one of our children has strayed, and suddenly we begin to question just how much we truly rely upon the Lord and trust in His sovereignty and provision.

When we feel our faith needs bolstering, it's time to dig into the Word of God, spend time in prayer, and strengthen our trust in Him so that when the tough times come, as they will, we will be prepared to meet them head on, knowing no matter how bad it gets, He is always here.

A person who wholly follows the Lord is one who believes that the promises of God are trustworthy, that He is with His people, and that they are well able to overcome.

WATCHMAN NEE

STUBBED TOES

He who heeds the word wisely will find good,
and whoever trusts in the Lord, happy is he.

PROVERBS 16:20

What if you were to win an all expense paid, first-class trip around the world, but while checking your baggage at the airport you stubbed your toe? Would you say, "I wish I had never won this trip! Look! I've stubbed my toe!"?

No. You'd say, "This momentary discomfort cannot compare to the enjoyment of the trip we're about to take."

The Bible says all our earthly problems fall into that category. They aren't worth comparing to the glory that will be revealed when we get to heaven. Paul wrote, "For our light and momentary troubles are achieving for us an eternal glory that far outweighs them all" (2 Corinthians 4:17, NIV).

So we fix our eyes not on what is seen, but on what is unseen. Whatever our situation here on earth, we know that our eternal quality of life will be beyond anything we can imagine or think about. We're looking for the glory to be revealed, the eternal glory that far outweighs all the stubbed toes and broken hearts of earth.

When Christ calls me Home, I shall go with the
gladness of a boy bounding away from school.

ADONIRAM JUDSON, MISSIONARY

DAVID JEREMIAH

SURRENDER

He went away a second time and prayed, "My Father,
if it is not possible for this cup to be taken away unless
I drink it, may Your will be done."

MATTHEW 26:42 (NIV)

It's often been said of some great military leader or another: "He never asked us to do something he wasn't willing to do himself." By comparing Matthew 6 with Matthew 26, we see this is true of Christ. In the earlier passage, He taught us to pray, "Your will be done on earth." In the latter passage, He Himself prayed, "May Your will be done in Me."

Surrendering our "all" to Christ doesn't mean we're dispirited prisoners waving a white flag. It means we've come face-to-face with the King of Kings, and we are willing to defer every preference to Him. Knowing He is all-powerful, we submit as a servant to a king. Knowing He is all-loving, we yield as a child to a father. Knowing He is all-wise, we gladly choose His will over our own.

The Lord would rather have one person who is 100-percent committed than 100 people who are 90-percent yielded.

Lord, not my will, but Yours be done!

I have been before God, and have given myself,
all that I am and have, to God; so that I am not,
in any respect, my own... I have given myself clear away.

JONATHAN EDWARDS

EVERY MAN'S A BRICK!

The LORD will fight for you, and you shall hold your peace.

EXODUS 14:14

An ambassador was sent to Sparta on a diplomatic mission and was surprised to find no walls protecting the city. He exclaimed to the king, "Sir, you have no fortifications for defense. Why is this?" "Come with me...and I will show you the walls of Sparta" the king replied. He led the ambassador to where the Spartan army stood in full battle array, and pointing proudly to his soldiers who stood fearlessly in place, he said, "Behold, the walls of Sparta – 10,000 men and every man's a brick!"

We have something far greater than even the legendary, fearless Spartan army. We have God and a host of angels who stand firmly between us and the enemy. When pressure mounts, when we experience a loss of income, when we are persecuted for our values and beliefs, faithfulness to our fearless King will see us through, for though the battle is raging, He is standing watch over us, protecting us against destruction.

We have the ability to be "a brick" during the difficult and trying times in our lives. We just have to come alongside God who is already guarding us, and remain faithful and fearless.

When a train goes through a tunnel and it gets dark, you don't throw away the ticket and jump off. You sit still and trust the engineer.

CORRIE TEN BOOM

DIVINE DELAYS

*Then it came to pass, when Pharaoh had let the people go,
that God did not lead them by way of the land of the Philistines,
although that was near; for God said, "Lest perhaps the people
change their minds when they see war, and return to Egypt."*

EXODUS 13:17

Not a day goes by when our plans aren't changed by circumstances beyond our control. Natural disasters, house or car repair problems, unexpected illness, traffic jams on the freeway, a friend or neighbor with an emergency need, unforeseen time demands at work—the list goes on. The question is, "Can we trust that God is in those unforeseen delays, diversions, and distractions?"

A rarely-read, single verse in Exodus (13:17) tells how God led the newly-freed Hebrew nation into the Sinai Desert instead of around the southeast "corner" of the Mediterranean Sea into the Promised Land. Why? So the Hebrews wouldn't encounter the Philistines who inhabited that region, be attacked, and flee back to Egypt for safety. The Hebrews grumbled loud and long about the Sinai sand and sun, but at least they were alive. If they had met the Philistines, they might have been slaughtered.

Next time your path is changed unexpectedly, trust by faith that God is in it and that the change was for a good reason (Romans 8:28).

Hope is the foundation of patience.

JOHN CALVIN

THE ROPE OF PRAYER

*Then I set my face toward the Lord God
to make request by prayer and supplications...*

DANIEL 9:3A

C. H. Spurgeon once said, "Prayer pulls the rope down below and the great bell rings above in the ears of God. Some scarcely stir the bell, for they pray so languidly; others give only an occasional jerk at the rope. But he who communicates with heaven is the man who grasps the rope boldly and pulls continuously with all his might."

Daniel was a man who communicated with heaven. He prayed fervently, consistently, and for the will of God. He knew nothing of praying only before meals, at bedtime, and when he really needed God's help. On the contrary, day in and day out, and often multiple times a day, this man came before God to discover His will and obey Him in everything (Daniel 6:10).

What is the status of your prayer life? Are you scarcely stirring the bell or ringing it loudly? If you desire to actively communicate with heaven and see your prayer life come alive, study Daniel's example, set your face toward God every day, and pull the rope of prayer continuously with all your might.

*When we learn His purposes and make them our prayers,
we are giving Him the opportunity to act.*

S. D. GORDON

CALM AND QUIET

*Surely I have calmed and quieted my soul, like a weaned child
with his mother; like a weaned child is my soul within me.*

PSALM 131:2

According to medical researchers at Duke University, there is a "vicious cycle" involving insomnia, anxiety, and depression. It's sort of a "which came first: the chicken or the egg?" scenario. Perhaps it's the one that presents first; but once the cycle starts, it doesn't matter. Anxiety might cause insomnia, which might result in depression, which might lead to greater anxiety . . . and the cycle continues as the symptoms feed off one another.

There are plenty of good reasons to be anxious, depressed, and sleepless in today's world. But Christians have promises from God that should alleviate all three symptoms—promises that God rules over all the earth and knows the beginning from the end of history. Our task is to do what the psalmist David did: He didn't worry about "great matters" or things "too profound" for him. Instead, he "calmed and quieted" his soul like a "weaned child" at rest in its mother's lap—peaceful and quiet (Psalm 131:1-2).

God's job is to guide the world. Your job is to "be anxious for nothing" (Philippians 4:6), to rest in the Father's promises.

*How soon shall the present night be forgotten
in the brightness of endless day!*

HORATIUS BONAR

LIFE ON PURPOSE

*Though He was a Son, yet He learned
obedience by the things which He suffered.*

HEBREWS 5:8

If John 3:16 is the most recognizable verse in the entire Bible, then Romans 8:28 is surely next: "And we know that all things work together for good to those who love God, to those who are the called according to His purpose." Christians love this verse because it says that everything—the good and the bad—that happens in our life will be used by God for a good purpose.

While that is comforting, Romans 8:28 doesn't tell us what the good purpose is. For what purpose is God orchestrating all the events of our life? Fortunately, we are told in the next verse, Romans 8:29: "For whom He foreknew, He also predestined to be conformed to the image of His Son, that He might be the firstborn among many brethren." God's purpose is to conform us to "the image of His Son." Our lives follow the same pattern of testing that Jesus followed: "He learned obedience by the things which He suffered." As Jesus proved His Sonship by His obedience, we are conformed to His image by ours.

Whether this day is "good" or "bad" in your sight, it has moved you closer to the image of Jesus.

*God is working out his eternal purpose, not only in spite of
human and satanic opposition, but by means of them.*

A. W. PINK

AS WAS HIS CUSTOM

(Daniel) knelt down on his knees three times that day, and prayed and gave thanks before his God, as was his custom since early days.

DANIEL 6:10

Dr. L. Nelson Bell, a missionary surgeon in China, is best remembered today as the father-in-law of evangelist Billy Graham. In *A Foreign Devil in China*, John Pollock wrote: "Most important of all was Nelson Bell's discipline of devotional life. Early every morning he had a cup of coffee and went to his desk for about an hour of Bible study and prayer. He set himself to master the content and meaning of the Bible, devising such study schemes as looking up every Old Testament reference which occurs in the New Testament and typing it out. Then he turned to prayer, for friends, colleagues, and patients, praying especially for every patient listed for operation that day... This cycle of reading and prayer did not strike Nelson as formidable but vital."

Similar statements can be found in the biography of almost every effective Christian servant. Daniel prayed "as was his custom," regardless of outside influences. This example of committed prayer is a role model for all of us to follow. It must be a vital part of the daily routines of those used of Him.

It isn't the length of time I spend in my quiet time, though I usually take an hour, but there is a carry-over of the activity of prayer, the attitude of prayer, that marks the rest of the day.

STEPHEN OLFORD

OPEN DOOR POLICY

Let us therefore come boldly to the throne of grace,
that we may obtain mercy and find grace to help in time of need.

HEBREWS 4:16

The second president of the United States, John Adams (and his wife, Abigail), was the first president to occupy the White House. In his day, and for many years afterward, it was possible for average citizens to walk into the White House unannounced to attempt to see the president. Try that today! Multiple levels of security shield the president from the average citizen seeking an audience.

If it's difficult to see the president of the United States, or the leader of any modern country, think how much more difficult it ought to be to have an audience with God. But it's not difficult at all! Scripture tells us that all who have been made pure by the blood of Christ can come "boldly to the throne of grace" to "obtain mercy and find grace to help in time of need." But how many take advantage of that free access? If we don't, it's not because we don't need mercy or grace; it's not that we don't have times of need. It's more that we just can't comprehend what it means to have unfettered access to the God of the universe.

Have you entered into God's presence today? The door is open, waiting for you to walk through, if only you will.

The door is closed to prayer unless it is opened with the key of trust.

JOHN CALVIN

THE PRIORITY OF PRAISE

But You are holy, enthroned in the praises of Israel.

PSALM 22:3

When individuals find themselves at a loss for words, they fall back on tried and true excuses: "I'm just not the verbal type"; "I prefer to let my actions speak for me"; "I was never very good with words"; "I'm just not very creative." We even use those reasons when it comes to knowing how to fill our prayer time with God.

Sometimes we settle in for a time of prayer thinking we have so much to talk to God about—and find ourselves saying, ". . . in Jesus' name, Amen" after three minutes. How, we wonder, do prayer warriors pray for 10 minutes, 30 minutes, an hour—or spend a half-day in prayer? The answer is simple and biblical: by making praise the central part of prayer. Think about it: How long could you spend praising an infinite and eternal God for who He is and what He has done? You could praise Him for hours by mentioning just the things that have touched you personally. Think of all that God has done for you in the personal, spiritual, financial, emotional, and other areas of your life. In addition to what He has done, He is worthy of praise for who He is.

The next time you find yourself on your knees, make praise your priority. You may find yourself having to budget more time for prayer instead of less.

The best atmosphere for prayer is praise.

PETER ANDERSON

EXAMINE YOURSELF

Be watchful, and strengthen the things which remain, that are ready to die, for I have not found your works perfect before God.

REVELATION 3:2

Instead of saying that someone "gets cancer," cancer researchers now say that everyone "has cancer." In other words, there are always cancerous cells among the body's trillions of cells. Our health goal is to continually strengthen the body's immune system—our God-given shield of protection—so that rogue cells can be overcome and eliminated, removing their opportunity to multiply and spread.

Following the apostle Paul's practice of comparing the Body of Christ to the human body (1 Corinthians 12:12-31), we can apply the same strategy to maintain spiritual health: The spiritual body is only as healthy as its weakest part. Or, the local church is only as healthy as its weakest member. The admonition to the church at Sardis given by Jesus Christ applies: "Strengthen the things which remain." Physically and spiritually, we are on a lifelong quest to strengthen every cell of our body and every member of Christ's body.

Make today a day of self-examination. Strengthen the Body of Christ by strengthening your walk with Him.

The Christian is strong or weak depending upon how closely he has cultivated the knowledge of God.

A. W. TOZER

PERFORMANCE UNDER PRESSURE

*We are hard-pressed on every side, yet not crushed;
we are perplexed, but not in despair; persecuted,
but not forsaken; struck down, but not destroyed.*

2 CORINTHIANS 4:8-9

Pro football fans talk about DVOA (Defense-Adjusted
Value Over Average) for teams and individual players. The
quarterback with the best DVOA ranking for 2009 was Aaron
Rodgers of the Green Bay Packers. That means he was the most
productive under pressure of all quarterbacks (based on the
DVOA formula).

Pressure in sports is temporary; pressure in life is continual.
The apostle Paul talked about the pressure he faced—hard-
pressed, perplexed, persecuted, struck down—and how he
continued to bear fruit. Jesus described the pruning process in the
spiritual life that results in more fruit (John 15:1-8). And we have
the promises of God that assure us no pressure will ever be more
than we can endure (1 Corinthians 10:13). Indeed, like silver in
the refiner's fire, heat burns away the dross and reveals the true
value of Christ in us (Galatians 2:20).

How would you rate your performance under pressure in the
spiritual life? The purpose is "that the life of Jesus also may be
manifested in [your] mortal flesh" (2 Corinthians 4:11).

While the fire is hot, keep conversing with the Refiner.

F. B. MEYER

THROUGH THE OPEN DOOR

*For a great and effective door has opened to me,
and there are many adversaries.*

1 CORINTHIANS 16:9

Comedy films in the early days of movie making relied often on the "secret door" gag. In a castle or mysterious house, characters moved about a room pushing on wall panels and book cases, or pushing and pulling wall ornaments and knobs and peering behind picture frames—all in a search for the "secret door" they were sure existed—a door leading to great treasure or escape.

Too many Christians use the "secret door" approach to finding God's next opportunity for ministry or blessing. In fact, God's doors always seem to open or close when we are least looking for them. That is, God opens doors in the process of faithful ministry for Him. When Paul and his companions were in Asia Minor, they planned to go to Bithynia, but God closed the door. Within a matter of hours the reason was clear: a door opened for ministry in Macedonia. And "immediately" they left, "concluding that the Lord had called us" (Acts 16:10). Our focus should not be on searching for the open door as much as being ready to go through it when God opens it.

Make your prayer today, "Lord, prepare my eyes to see your open doors and my heart to go through them without delay."

If you can't pray a door open, don't pry it open.

LYELL RADER

DAVID JEREMIAH

WORK BY DAY; SLEEP BY NIGHT

I will bless the Lord who has given me counsel; my heart also instructs me in the night seasons. I have set the Lord always before me.

PSALM 16:7-8

Martin Luther complained, "When I go to bed, the devil is always waiting for me. When he begins to plague me, I give him this answer: 'Devil, I must sleep. That's God's command. Work by day. Sleep by night. So go away.'"[9]

It's important to get the rest we need, and a simple faith in the Lord helps us relax and rest. Remember Psalm 4:8: "I will both lie down in peace, and sleep; for You alone, O Lord, make me dwell in safety."

But when we can't sleep, we can pray. We can turn on the light and reassure ourselves with God's Word. We can meditate on Scripture. We can sing a hymn. The television is a bad friend for wee hours and is best avoided. Here's a better option: "When I remember You on my bed, I meditate on You in the night watches. Because You have been my help, therefore in the shadow of Your wings I will rejoice" (Psalm 63:6-7).

Have you noticed that if you go to sleep with the thought of Him Whom your soul loveth, you waken—at least often it is so—with some little word from Him, a verse from His Book, or a hymn, or just a simple word that tells you nothing new, but somehow helps?

AMY CARMICHAEL

9 ROLAND H. BAINTON, *Here I Stand* (NASHVILLE: ABINGDON, 1978), 284.

BEING CARRIED BY GOD

And in the wilderness where you saw how the
LORD your God carried you, as a man carries his son,
in all the way that you went until you came to this place.

DEUTERONOMY 1:31

Sometimes, when a toddler is exhausted or the path is too steep, the child will be scooped up and carried by a parent. But knowing the child might always opt for an easy ride, parents at other times insist that their child walk. Sometimes assistance is needed, other times admonishment. Sometimes carrying, other times calling.

Israel experienced both from God in her days as a "toddler" nation. Most of the time God carried Israel through the wilderness when they were just getting to know and trust Him. Moses, in recounting Israel's history to the second generation of Israelites who would enter the Promised Land, said that God "carried [Israel], as a man carries his son" until they reached the banks of the Jordan River. Like any father, God then expected Israel to do the hard work of creating a homeland out of Canaan. It is comforting to know that God is willing to carry His children when they are at their weakest.

If you are walking through your own wilderness, ask God to lift you up on His shoulders, to carry you as if on "wings like eagles" (Isaiah 40:31).

God uses men who are weak and feeble enough to lean on him.

J. HUDSON TAYLOR

DAVID JEREMIAH

APRIL

April 1

Dropped Calls

If I regard iniquity in my heart, the Lord will not hear.

Psalm 66:18

Most of us are all too familiar with the phrase "dropped call." It's the common term for a wireless phone transmission that ends abruptly, often while the caller is traveling between towers. It's odd to be talking away on the phone only to realize that no one is listening on the other end.

In a way, the same thing can happen in prayer. The old book *The Kneeling Christian* says: "No sin is too small to hinder prayer, and perhaps to turn the very prayer itself into sin."

In Daniel 9, the prophet Daniel—about whom nothing negative is said in Scripture—was praying to the Lord and making confession. He said, "We have sinned and committed iniquity...," and he prayed with deep contrition and earnestness. In response, the Lord gave him the great prediction of "seventy weeks," which is a cornerstone of biblical prophecy.

Prayer is our greatest weapon, our sweetest occupation, and our highest privilege. A tender conscience, a zeal for purity, and a habit of confession will keep the prayer lines open so that no calls will be dropped.

It is amazing that any should try to retain both sin and prayer.
Yet very many do this. Even David cried long ages ago,
"If I regard iniquity in my heart, the Lord will not hear."

From *The Kneeling Christian*

David Jeremiah

TROUBLESOME TIMES

The street shall be built again and the wall, even in troublesome times.

DANIEL 9:25

At the end of last year, the *New York Times* carried this headline: "Bad Times Draw Bigger Crowds to Churches." The story said that "bad times" were "good" for churches because when people are "shaken to the core," they become more open to the message of the Bible. The newspaper reported that the revivals that swept the United States in the nineteenth century were often triggered or touched off by economic panics. The great Fulton Street Revival (also known as the Businessman's Revival) broke out in New York City during the financial panic of 1857. And research has shown that during each recession cycle between 1968 and 2004, the rate of growth in evangelical churches jumped by 50 percent.

We aren't praying for bad news, of course, but the Lord often works wonders in troublesome times. Even in our individual lives, we often find that times of spiritual growth occur when we're pressed beyond our strength. Troubles have a way of driving us afresh to Him who said, "Let not your heart be troubled; you believe in God, believe also in Me" (John 14:1).

The Lord, who helped in troubles past, will save us to the very last.

FROM AN OLD HYMN, AN ANONYMOUS
PARAPHRASE OF PSALM 37:40

THE AUTHOR OF PEACE

But he who prophesies speaks edification
and exhortation and comfort to men.

1 CORINTHIANS 14:3

Donald Cargill was a seventeenth-century Scottish
Covenanter, a devout Presbyterian who issued a declaration
against the king of England for which he was arrested and
executed in Edinburgh. As he went to his death, he proclaimed,
"The Lord knows I go up this ladder with less fear, confusion, or
perturbation of mind than ever I entered a pulpit to preach."

How is it possible for a person who served Christ faithfully not
to be confused when his service resulted in a cruel death? It was
possible because Donald Cargill knew the prophetic Scriptures—
words like, "I go to prepare a place for you. . . . I will come again
and receive you to Myself; that where I am, there you may be also"
(John 14:2-3). The apostle Paul wrote that "God is not the author
of confusion but of peace" (1 Corinthians 14:33). Throughout
Scripture God used His prophets to speak "edification and
exhortation and comfort" to His people.

If today seems confusing, be comforted by the precious words
of assurance about your future as a child of God.

No Bible subject holds more practical
implications than the matter of prophecy.

VANCE HAVNER

THE WAY BACK

Then I will give them a heart to know Me, that I am the LORD;
and they shall be My people, and I will be their God,
for they shall return to ME with their whole heart.

JEREMIAH 24:7

Martin Luther said, "Before my conversion, had you knocked at the door of my heart and asked who lives there, I would have said, 'Martin Luther lives here.' Had you come in to see me, you would have found a monk with his head shaved, sleeping in a hair shirt.... But now if you knock at the door of my heart and ask who lives here, I will reply, 'Martin Luther no longer lives here; Jesus the Lord lives here now.'"[10]

Revelation 3:20 tells us that Jesus wants to reside and to preside in our hearts. In this verse, addressed to the lukewarm Laodiceans, the Lord Jesus offers them a way back into intimate fellowship with Him. He was knocking at their hearts; and the word "knock" is Greek present tense, signifying a persistent knocking, not a perfunctory rap.

So at the end of a discouraging passage about lukewarm hearts (Revelation 3:14-22), we have a warm and wonderful invitation. If you hear Him knocking at the door of your life, let Him in. Learn to say, "I no longer live here; Jesus lives here now!"

In Revelation 3:20, Jesus offers to reestablish fellowship with broken,
lukewarm, cultural Christians... He is the way back.

PATRICK MORLEY

10 QUOTED BY W. A. CRISWELL IN *Expository Sermons from Revelation, Vol 2* (GRAND RAPIDS: ZONDERVAN, 1966), 183-184.

HURT TO BE HEALED

*Now no chastening seems to be joyful for the present,
but painful; nevertheless, afterward it yields the peaceable
fruit of righteousness to those who have been trained by it.*

HEBREWS 12:11

One of the most famous passages in the Bible is James 1:2-5,
the passage that instructs us, when we are suffering in life, to
ask God for wisdom to understand and profit by it. Sometimes,
the answer may come back, "I am allowing you to suffer in order
to draw you closer. I am allowing you to hurt in order to heal you
at a deeper level."

The apostle Paul had that experience. In order to keep him
from being prideful and boastful, God allowed him to suffer
(2 Corinthians 12:1-10). And God also allowed some of His
chosen people to suffer for 70 years in captivity in Babylon in
order to teach them how to experience "the peaceable fruit of
righteousness." Paul writes that Israel, to this day, is dispersed
throughout the world in order that she might become jealous
enough to seek after her Messiah, Jesus Christ (Romans 11:11, 23).
We do not always suffer because we are unrighteous, but suffering
always produces deeper righteousness in those who embrace it.

If you are experiencing trouble and pain, ask God to show you
why. The very act of asking will draw you even closer to Him.

It is a rough road that leads to the heights of greatness.

SENECA

DAVID JEREMIAH

SMART MIRRORS

He who has an ear, let him hear what the Spirit says to the churches.

REVELATION 3:13

Soon we'll not have to try on that jacket. Technology wizards are working on a kind of "smart mirror" to help shoppers decide what to buy. As we stand in front of the mirror, computer images will automatically "dress" us in clothes hanging on nearby racks.

Think of Revelation 2 and 3 as God's "smart mirror" for the church. These chapters contain seven mini-epistles to seven different congregations in Asia (Turkey). Their message is perennial to the church. Every age contains churches resembling these seven. And in every church are Christians who resemble the ones in Ephesus, Smyrna, Pergamum, Thyatira, Sardis, Philadelphia, and/or Laodicea.

It's both convicting and edifying to read these passages, and to do so as if looking in a mirror. All summed up, they tell us to be heartily passionate, doctrinally sound, and zealously working for the Lord Jesus, for He is walking among His candlesticks (Matthew 5:14-16). Any failures should be confessed. All sins should be repented. All passion should be directed to Him.

Are you looking in the smart mirror of His Word?

Many Christians are like radio or television sets which are tuned in but not turned on. One of our biggest needs today is that those who have "ears to hear" shall practice "listening in" again to the Spirit.

J. SIDLOW BAXTER

Friday Faith

He said to His mother, "Woman, behold your son!"

John 19:26

Faith is the capacity to keep going between Good Friday and Easter Sunrise. It's the God-granted ability to trust God during black weekends and hard times. Without faith it's impossible to please God, but that implies hardship. Trusting God during good times is a little like riding a bike downhill; sometimes we can almost "coast." But when the path is uphill, faith has to flex its muscles, knowing sooner or later we'll arrive at the mountaintop with its far-reaching vistas.

When Gabriel visited Mary with news about the Christchild, she said, "Let it be to me according to your word." A few months later, old Simeon warned her that a sword would one day pierce her heart. No one could have foreseen how deeply the sword would pierce on that Good Friday. But approximately 39 hours later, her heaviness was lifted, her faith was fulfilled, her hope was realized, her joy was restored, and her Son was risen. Our Good Fridays aren't always so good; but they are good for our faith, and *with* faith it is very possible to please Him.

Our old history ends with the cross;
our new history begins with the resurrection.

Watchman Nee

GOD, FORGIVE "US"

In those days I, Daniel, was mourning three full weeks.

DANIEL 10:2

Imagine that the organs and limbs of the human body had hearts of their own. If the hand sinned, all the other parts would confess the hand's sins, even though they themselves had done nothing wrong. Why? Because of the interconnectedness of the parts, all bear responsibility for the whole.

Daniel must have felt some sense of that burden as well. More than once he prayed and sought God's forgiveness and guidance for sinful Israel, even though he himself had done nothing wrong. In his prayer of confession for his nation's sins in Daniel 9, the word "we" occurs 13 times—even though Daniel was not involved personally in the idolatry and disobedience that sentenced the nation in Babylon to judgment. Yet he identified with the spiritual condition of his people, his kinsmen in the flesh, and cried out to God for them.

Christians should have the same burden for the nations in which they live—for their neighbors, leaders, and friends who do not know Christ. Look around you today and see whose spiritual need you can ask God to meet.

May God pity a nation whose factory chimneys
rise higher than her church steeples.

JOHN KELMAN

STILL ONE GOD

*The king answered Daniel, and said, "Truly your God
is the God of gods, the Lord of kings, and a revealer of secrets,
since you could reveal this secret."*

DANIEL 2:47

One of the Seven Wonders of the Ancient World, the Hanging
Gardens of Babylon, was built by Nebuchadnezzar II around
600 B.C. The gardens were only one of the magnificent structures
built by a king who considered himself a deity to be worshipped
by his people. But this king discovered that there is only one true
God who alone is worthy of worship.

On more than one occasion, Nebuchadnezzar was brought
to the realization that the God of Daniel had powers that
Nebuchadnezzar and his wise men did not. God revealed to
Daniel the king's dreams and their meanings, and sentenced the
king to a period of insanity as a correction for his prideful spirit.
After each of these encounters, Nebuchadnezzar confessed that
"He does according to His will" (Daniel 4:35).

When you need wisdom, remember the king who was wise
enough to build beautiful gardens, but not as wise as the one
true God.

The heavens declare thy glory, Lord, in every star thy wisdom shines.

ISAAC WATTS

DAVID JEREMIAH

MENTORS FROM AFAR

For by it the elders obtained a good testimony.

HEBREWS 11:2

Some of our best mentors are dead people. They are the "elders" who obtained a good testimony and went on to heaven, leaving us an example to follow. We meet some of them in the pages of the Bible, such as the heroes of the faith listed in Hebrews 11 or the faithful Christians of Smyrna whom Jesus commended in Revelation 2:8-11. Others hail from the pages of church history.

Some have called Christian history the "Third Testament," for it leaves us a chronicle of faithful witnesses who, for 2000 years, have handed the Gospel down to us. In every stage of the church and in every generation, a faithful few have borne the challenges, kept the faith, and finished the work. Their biographies and autobiographies are among the most powerful books on our shelves. We learn from their lives, from their faithfulness, and even from their failures.

Now it's our turn to be faithful and to pass along a legacy to those to come. Today let's thank God for His faithful people who have gone before, and let's rededicate ourselves to obtaining a good testimony for the sake of those yet to come.

To study the lives, to meditate the sorrows,
to commune with the thoughts, of the great and holy
men and women of this rich world is a sacred discipline.

JAMES MARTINEAU

CARVED IN THE MANTEL

The Most High rules in the kingdom of men, gives it to whomever He will, and sets over it the lowest of men.

DANIEL 4:17

Visitors in Washington who tour the White House often notice the beautiful fireplace in the State Dining Room. Carved into this stone mantel, just below a painting of Abraham Lincoln, are the words: "I pray to heaven to bestow the best of blessings on this house and all that hereafter inhabit it. May none but honest and wise men ever rule under this roof." Those words were originally written in a letter by John Adams to his wife Abigail after they moved into the White House. During World War II, Franklin Roosevelt found them and had them carved into the fireplace.

We pray for honest and wise leaders, and our nation needs godly rulers. Yet the Book of Daniel gives us the example of Nebuchadnezzar, a cruel and egomaniacal man. God humbled him and used him to fulfill Divine Providence. God sometimes raises up leaders for purposes known only to Himself at the time. Yet we can rest assured that His authority is supreme and that His providence works all things together for the fulfilling of His ultimate purposes.

It is the duty of all nations to acknowledge the Providence of Almighty God, to be grateful for His benefits, and humbly to implore His protection and favor.

GEORGE WASHINGTON

BALAK

*"If Balak were to give me his house full of silver and gold,
I could not go beyond the word of the LORD."*

NUMBERS 24:13

In a wealthy culture it's easy for the rich to believe money is the ultimate resource. Not only can money buy things, it can also be used to buy people—their allegiance, their loyalty, or their protection. Some people even believe money can be used to purchase the favor of God.

A pagan king named Balak (Numbers 22–24) tried to purchase the prophetic ability of a pagan "prophet" (diviner) named Balaam. Balak wanted Balaam to speak a curse upon Israel as they approached the Promised Land. The curse was never spoken, but not for want of a misguided king trying. Much later in Israel's history, the prophet Micah reminded the people of the Balak-Balaam incident in order that they might be reminded of "the righteousness of the LORD" (Micah 6:5). In other words, God's favor cannot be purchased, nor His wrath avoided, with money. In the New Testament, others learned this truth the hard way: Ananias and his wife, Sapphira (Acts 5:1-11), and Simon the sorcerer (Acts 8:9-25).

Do you need something from God today? Follow the advice of James: "The effective fervent prayer of a righteous man avails much" (James 5:16).

Mature faith does not live by answers to prayer, but by prayer.

R. E. O. WHITE

APRIL 13

JOINING A SERVICE ALREADY IN PROGRESS

You are worthy, O Lord, to receive glory and honor and power;
for you created all things, and by Your will they exist and were created.

REVELATION 4:11

What's the most exciting worship service you've attended? Perhaps it was at your church or at a rally in an arena or stadium. Perhaps you're thinking of the service in a small country church the night Christ came into your life, or the service in which you were baptized.

If you could ask the apostle John, he'd likely talk about the service he observed in Revelation 4 and 5. Ten thousand angels surrounded the rainbow-canopied throne in heaven. The whole triumphant church was there, symbolized by the twenty-four elders. Lightning bolts and thunder booms served as pyrotechnics and percussion. Cherubim and seraphim attended the scene. A heavenly antiphonal choir sang: "Holy, holy, holy, Lord God Almighty, Who was and is and is to come!"

Whenever we gather for worship, whether in a catacomb or a cathedral, we're simply tuning in to the perpetual worship occurring in heaven. Let's not take worship casually or complain if everything isn't to our liking. It's not for us, but for Him who is worthy to receive our praise.

I'll praise my Maker with my breath; and when my voice
is lost in death, praise shall employ my nobler powers.

ISAAC WATTS

DAVID JEREMIAH

STRENGTHEN YOUR GRIP

I can do all things through Christ who strengthens me.

PHILIPPIANS 4:13

How many times have we read an account in the news like this: "When I thought I wouldn't survive, I thought of my wife and children. The thought of never seeing them again gave me the strength to hang on. I literally thought I was going to die. Once I survived and was reunited with my family, I realized that the pain and anguish was worth it."

The Book of Revelation pictures a future that is going to be painful for those on planet earth. Not the least of coming travails are those represented by the "Four Horsemen of the Apocalypse" in Revelation 6:1-8. The white horse represents a leader bent on conquering the world; the red horse, worldwide war; the black one, worldwide famine; and the pale horse, death for a fourth of humanity by violent and tragic means. For anyone who becomes a Christian after the Rapture of the Church, that is, during the Tribulation, they will have to ask themselves, "How can I survive?" And the answer will be the same as for Christians who experience suffering now: "through Jesus Christ who strengthens me."

If you are losing your grip on life today, let the promise of seeing Christ face-to-face give you new strength (1 Corinthians 13:12).

Our greatest problem in suffering is unbelief.

GEOFF THOMAS

APRIL 15

DIVINE PEACE

To everything there is a season, a time for every purpose
under heaven... A time of war, and a time of peace.

ECCLESIASTES 3:1, 8B

There has never been a generation that hasn't seen some sort of conflict or war somewhere in the world. It is evil that exists because of man's sin, and ironically, it is used as a means for providing and ensuring peace. As the late President Ronald Reagan stated, "Freedom is never more than one generation away from extinction. It must be fought for, protected, and handed on for them to do the same..."

Though we must temporarily endure the realities and tragedies of war for the sake of earthly peace and protection, there will come a day when the final battle is fought and true divine peace rests upon the earth. The Bible says, *"They shall not hurt nor destroy...for the earth shall be full of the knowledge of the LORD as the waters cover the sea"* (Isaiah 11:9). Sin will no longer provoke us to fight with one another, and freedom will belong to everyone without struggle.

Meanwhile, as we watch countries collide in battles of freedom and justice, let us stand firm in His Word as we hope and pray for that glorious day.

If you want peace, understand war.

B. H. LIDDELL HART, MILITARY HISTORIAN

DAVID JEREMIAH

APRIL 16

SQUANDERED FORTUNE

*And I saw in the right hand of Him who sat on the throne a scroll
written inside and on the back, sealed with seven seals.*

REVELATION 5:1

An interesting obituary appeared recently, announcing the death of Huntington Hartford, heir to the A&P fortune. His grandfather had helped found the Great Atlantic and Pacific Tea Company in 1859. It grew to be the world's largest retail empire, making the Hartford family one of the wealthiest on earth. But Huntington frittered his millions away on frivolous projects, misguided ventures, four marriages, and well-documented affairs. His biography was entitled *Squandered Fortune.* He died with little left.

Not so the heirs of God. According to Romans 8, if we're children of God, we are heirs of God and joint heirs with Christ. According to Titus, the "elect" are heirs according to the hope of eternal life. James says we are heirs of the Kingdom that He promises to those who love Him.

Revelation 11:15 proclaims: "The kingdoms of this world have become the kingdoms of our Lord and of His Christ." The joy of being a co-heir with Christ is beyond the limitations of our finite minds, but it should bring joy to our heart today.

*Joint heirs with Christ Jesus! I defy you to exhaust that topic, though
you should think about it all the days of the next week, nay, though you
should muse upon it till eternity commences with your soul.*

CHARLES H. SPURGEON

NO SURPRISE ENDINGS

But he who endures to the end shall be saved.

MARK 13:13B

Avid readers typically fall into one of two categories when reading a book: those who like to be surprised by the ending, and those who read the last page before even starting. Some people just love knowing what to expect so that no matter what happens in the middle, they know how it all turns out.

Sometimes Christians approach life this way as well. It can be difficult to trust God with our lives because we can't see the ending or understand the reason for everything in the middle. But in reality, though we may not know the details of how our individual life will turn out, we know that Christ will have the victory, for Scripture tells us that *"...the Lamb will overcome them, for He is the Lord of lords and King of kings; and those who are with Him are called, chosen, and faithful"* (Revelation 17:14).

Because God has already won over all earthly kings and armies, gods, Satan, death, and sin, we can rest knowing that no matter what happens between now and eternity, there are no surprise endings.

He who breathes into our hearts the heavenly hope, will not deceive or fail us when we press forward to its realization.

ANONYMOUS

TEMPORARY RESIDENTS

Peter, an apostle of Jesus Christ, to the pilgrims of the Dispersion....

1 PETER 1:1

Few Greek words have been so variously translated as the word the *New King James Version* renders *pilgrims* in 1 Peter 1:1. In other versions it is translated: *exiles, sojourners, strangers, foreigners, those who live as refugees, those away from their homes, those who reside as aliens,* and *temporary residents.*

The last is the best—temporary residents. The actual Greek word Peter used describes someone who settles down for a temporary time in a land not his own. As Christians, we're citizens of heaven and joint heirs with Christ. This world isn't our home; we're here on temporary assignment. This isn't our destination but our deployment.

The heroes of Hebrews 11 desired a better country, a heavenly one, and therefore God wasn't ashamed to be called their God, for He has prepared a city for them. The Book of Revelation ends by describing this New Jerusalem and our eternal inheritance.

This old earth isn't much of a bequest; it's too tarnished and too transient. Better things are ahead. Let's set our minds on things above, where Christ is, sitting at the right hand of God.

> *But I've been adopted, my name's written down,*
> *An heir to a mansion, a robe, and a crown.*

HARRIET E. BUELL

FAITHFUL TO THE END

*I have fought the good fight, I have finished the race,
I have kept the faith.*

2 TIMOTHY 4:7

During the 1992 Olympics, British runner Derek Redmond posted the fastest time of the first round of the 400 meter race and won his quarter-final. In the semi-final race, he started out well, but about 250 meters from the finish line, his hamstring tore, sending him to the ground in agonizing pain. When stretcher bearers came to carry him off the track, he refused their help and determined to hobble to the finish line. Soon after, his father pushed past security, joined him on the track and helped him finish the race. Despite a crushing disappointment and a dream lost, Derek Redmond, with the help of his father, finished.

Sometimes we get crippled with distraction by all that's going on in the world: injustice, sin, materialism, and war. But if we are faithful to the end, it doesn't matter what trials and tribulations the world experiences because we have a Heavenly Father who is always beside us, helping us run the race. Through Him, the race has already been won; all we have to do is remain faithful until the finish line comes into view.

*The spirit, the will to win, and the will to excel
are the things that endure. These qualities are so much
more important than the events that occur.*

VINCE LOMBARDI

DAVID JEREMIAH

JEHOSHAPHAT

O our God, will You not judge them? For we have no
power against this great multitude that is coming against us;
nor do we know what to do, but our eyes are upon You.

2 CHRONICLES 20:12

Jehoshaphat, a king whose name meant "Jehovah is judge," was one of only a few godly kings in Judah. He tore down the pagan worship sites and dispatched priests and Levites throughout the nation to teach people the laws of God (2 Chronicles 17:6-9).

Jehoshaphat is best known, however, for how he handled a crisis that could have destroyed the country he ruled. When several surrounding nations gathered against Judah to destroy it, Jehoshaphat knew he was no match militarily. So he called the people and leaders of Judah together to pray. The last sentence of his prayer summarizes his heart: "Nor do we know what to do, but our eyes are upon You" (2 Chronicles 20:12). God answered his prayer for help and gave Judah the victory—the armies against him turned on each other and destroyed themselves.

If you are facing a situation today that seems hopeless, one for which you have no answers, pray Jehoshaphat's prayer: "Lord, I don't know what to do, but my eyes are on You." Stay focused on Him until the answer comes.

It is better to meet God with tears in your
eyes than weapons in your hands.

THOMAS WATSON

WORTH IT ALL

*Well done, good and faithful servant; you were faithful
over a few things; I will make you ruler over many things.
Enter into the joy of your Lord.*

MATTHEW 25:21

Sitting atop the Mount of Olives, Jesus spoke to His disciples about the end of the age and the signs of His return. His sermon—the Olivet Discourse—is recorded in Matthew 24 and 25. There are 93 verses of text in this message. The first 31 verses are devoted to outlining the events of the Last Days. But the last 62 verses—exactly two-thirds of the whole sermon—are devoted to application. Using exhortation and illustration, Jesus warned us to stay busy until He comes, working for the Kingdom, our eyes scanning the eastern sky.

Biblical prophecy isn't written to intrigue us but to transform us. Because of His expected return, we live with anticipation, comforting others with the truths of the coming Rapture. We ought to live with holiness and purity while awaiting His return. We should be working and witnessing, watching and waiting, worshipping and walking with Him. If we're faithful in the few things assigned us by the Master, when He comes we'll hear Him say, "Well done." And it will be worth it all.

*One glimpse of His dear face all sorrow will erase,
so bravely run the race till we see Christ.*

ESTHER KERR RUSTHOI

STILL ALIVE

*Now in the place where He was crucified there was a garden,
and in the garden a new tomb in which no one had yet been laid.*

JOHN 19:41

Gardens play a significant role in the Bible's story of
redemption. Spiritual life was lost in the Garden of Eden, the
decision to redeem it was made in the Garden of Gethsemane,
and redemption was realized in the Garden of the Resurrection.
Just as new life was created in the Garden of Eden, new life was
restored when Christ left the garden tomb.

Without the resurrection of Jesus Christ from the tomb, our
preaching and our faith are "empty," and "we are of all men the
most pitiable" (1 Corinthians 15:14, 19). No one likes to think of
himself as being "pitiful," but that would be precisely the state
of our existence if the resurrection of Christ had not taken place.
Only because of the resurrection and subsequent ascension of
Christ do we serve a *living* Lord and Savior.

Whenever you question whether your prayers are being heard,
remember that a resurrected Jesus Christ is making intercession
for you at the throne of God (Hebrews 7:25).

Christianity is essentially a religion of resurrection.

JAMES S. STEWART

COUNT IT ALL JOY

For our light affliction, which is but for a moment, is working for us a far more exceeding and eternal weight of glory . . .

2 CORINTHIANS 4:17

Second Corinthians 5:7 contains a principle that flies in the face of modern human sensibility: "For we walk by faith, not by sight." Modern man says, "I'll believe it when I see it," while the spiritual man says, "I believe God's Word whether I see it or not." The biblical position is not just believing in the *absence* of evidence, it is believing *in the face of* evidence to the contrary.

Take James 1:2, for instance. How are we to have joy in the midst of trials? How are we to count suffering as a blessing when it doesn't look or feel like a blessing? Is that just a game; just an example of mind over matter? No! It's an example of walking by faith rather than by our senses. When things are difficult, we should ask first, "What has God said?" (He has said that trials are a reason for joy.) Next, we should "count it" so. That is, we should say to ourselves, "I choose to believe that the situation I'm in is a potential source of joy in my life, regardless of how it feels, because that's what God has said."

If you are in the midst of a trial right now, choose to walk by faith. Choose to "count it all joy."

To added affliction He addeth His mercy,
to multiplied trials, His multiplied peace.

ANNIE JOHNSON FLINT

THE SCARLET THREAD

*Much more then, having now been justified by His blood,
we shall be saved from wrath through Him.*

ROMANS 5:9

When kindergarten teachers need to move children from Point A to Point B—especially when it means a walk of any distance (particularly outdoors)—they sometimes take a long piece of rope and tell each child to hold on to it as they walk. The children hold on tight to the rope, keeping themselves linked to one another as they walk.

The late, great preacher Dr. W. A. Criswell once delivered a series of messages on a similar theme: the "scarlet thread" that runs through the Bible. The scarlet thread refers to the blood-bought redemption that secures the fate of the redeemed from Genesis to Revelation—first, the blood of animal sacrifices in the Old Testament, then the shed blood of Jesus Christ on Calvary's cross. Regardless of when a person is saved—past, present, or future—"without shedding of blood there is no remission" of sin (Hebrews 9:22). If you are a Christian, someday you will join that great "cloud of witnesses" (Hebrews 12:1) that are linked together by the scarlet thread of redemption.

All it takes to grasp that thread today is the hand of faith, reaching out and holding on.

Life is not worth living apart from redemption.

OSWALD CHAMBERS

SPIRITUAL BRACINGS

My soul melts from heaviness; strengthen me according to Your word.

PSALM 119:28

When designing a bridge, the engineer must take into account three different, but equally important loads: the dead load, which is the weight of the bridge itself; the live load, which is the weight of the daily traffic it must carry; and the wind load, which is the pressure of the storms that beat on the bridge. The engineer then plans for bracings that will bear all three loads.

As Christians, we need bracings for the dead load of self, the live load of daily living, and the wind load of emergencies and trials. The only bracings strong enough to withstand all three loads are found in Scripture, and they are available to us at any moment; all we have to do is open the Bible and seek the Lord.

How strong are our bracings? Every time we commit a verse to memory, read the Word of God, or ask for wisdom, we are strengthening our spiritual bracings so that during daily struggles or life-altering trials, instead of aimlessly searching elsewhere for solace and strength, we know exactly where to turn, seek wisdom, and take comfort.

Within the covers of the Bible are the answers for all the problems men face.

RONALD REAGAN

DAVID JEREMIAH

April 26

Glass Hives

There is no creature hidden from His sight, but all things are naked and open to the eyes of Him to whom we must give an account.

Hebrews 4:13

One of the best ways to teach children the genius of God's creation is with an observation hive—a glassed-in colony of bees, all organized, busy, and productive. Each bee (with a brain the size of a grass seed) works with the others as wax producer, comb builder, honey maker, floral pollinator, military guard, and hive custodian. Observant children can even detect the bees' communication patterns with the "bee dance."

Perhaps you've seen a glass hive at a county fair or science exhibition. The queen bee, worker bees, drones, and offspring bustle about, unaware that observant eyes are watching their every move. Their hive, being glass, is open and revealed to all who see it.

In the same way, the Lord looks down on our world. He sees all our actions, hears all our words, and knows all our thoughts. "A man's ways are in full view of the LORD, and He examines all his paths" (Proverbs 5:21, NIV). Remember that the Lord is watching you today. May the words of our mouths and the meditation of our hearts be pleasing in His sight (Psalm 19:14).

I trust in God wherever I may be, upon the land or on the rolling sea; for come what may, from day to day, my heavenly Father watches over me.

W. C. Martin

The Flea and the Ox

Let no one say when he is tempted, "I am tempted by God"; for God cannot be tempted by evil, nor does He Himself tempt anyone.

James 1:13

An Aesop's Fable tells of a flea who questioned an ox, saying: "Why do you, being so huge and strong, submit to the wrongs you receive from men and slave for them day by day, while I, being so small a creature, mercilessly feed on their flesh?" The ox replied: "I do not wish to be ungrateful, for I am loved and well cared for by men, and they often pat my head and shoulders." "Woe is me" said the flea; "this very patting which you like, when it happens to me, brings with it my destruction."

When we experience trials, we should be grateful because God only allows such testing in order to bring out the good...to strengthen us. But when Satan tempts us to sin, he is looking to bring out the worst in us...to bring about our destruction. We must be careful to examine every situation and discern whether it is a trial from God or a temptation from Satan, lest we get knocked down by sin when we expected a pat on the head.

Temptation may be an invitation to hell, but much more it is an opportunity to reach heaven.

Charles H. Brent

SEALED BY THE SPIRIT

And do not grieve the Holy Spirit of God,
by whom you were sealed for the day of redemption.

EPHESIANS 4:30

It would be nice to be told, when we leave on a long car trip, something like this: "I want you to know that you are going to reach your destination safely and on schedule. Regardless of what happens *en route*—you may get lost, you may encounter a fierce rainstorm, and you may have a flat tire—don't worry. I am here to promise you that you will arrive."

We have been given such a promise by God concerning our spiritual journey. And the promise comes in the form of a seal—the seal of the Holy Spirit. Paul uses language common to the ancient world. A seal affixed to documents by kings and authorities made them official and inviolable upon pain of death or punishment. No one dared to violate the terms of a document that bore an official seal. And no one in the spiritual realm would dare violate the plan God has for those He has sealed. As Paul wrote, "Who shall separate us from the love of Christ?" (Romans 8:35) The Holy Spirit, dwelling in every Christian, is God's seal.

Don't let obstacles along the road to eternity shake your confidence in God's promise. The Holy Spirit is God's seal that you will arrive.

I am packed, sealed, and waiting for the post.

JOHN NEWTON

RESISTING TEMPTATION

But God is faithful, who will not allow you to be tempted beyond what you are able, but with the temptation will also make the way of escape.

1 CORINTHIANS 10:13B

The source of one of the greatest insights about temptation is debated, though it is often attributed to the Protestant reformer, Martin Luther: "You can't stop the birds from flying over your head, but you can stop them from building a nest in your hair." If the birds are temptations, we can't prevent their presence in this world. But their presence should never be equated with the obligation to give them a place of residence in our life.

The apostle James gives the clearest description in the Bible of how temptation leads to sin: "But each one is tempted when he is drawn away by his own desires and enticed. Then, when desire has conceived, it gives birth to sin; and sin, when it is full-grown, brings forth death" (1:13-15). It's clear that we are responsible for allowing ourselves to be "drawn away" from righteousness by our own carnal desires. It is a process—temptation, yielding, birth, spiritual death—that we can stop with God's power.

It's not a sin to be tempted, but it is a sin to follow after temptation and not take the way of escape God provides.

Holiness is not freedom from temptation,
but power to overcome temptation.

G. CAMPBELL MORGAN

THE GREAT MULTITUDE

Behold, a great multitude which no one could number, of all nations, tribes, peoples, and tongues, standing before the throne and before the Lamb, clothed with white robes, with palm branches in their hands.

REVELATION 7:9

Certain Scriptures—Psalm 23, 1 Thessalonians 4, and John 11—comfort us in times of loss as if the Lord Himself were speaking to us. We seldom include Revelation 7 among those familiar passages, yet it too is full of encouragement for the grief-stricken.

Revelation 7:9-17 describes those who will be redeemed and then martyred during the Great Tribulation; but much of what it says about them is true for all Christians in eternity. These heavenly saints were clothed in white, representing the righteousness of Christ. They celebrated before the throne with palm branches, representing joy. They were of every background and ethnicity. They sang with all their hearts, serving God day and night, free from hunger, thirst, heat, and care. God was a shepherd leading them to living fountains and wiping away their tears.

It's a scene of pure eternal victory; and if our dear ones could speak to us, they'd say, "Amen! Blessing and glory and wisdom, thanksgiving and honor and power and might be to our God forever and ever. Amen!"

Surely if there is rest and peace in following Him by faith on earth, there will be far more rest and peace when you see Him face to face.

J. C. RYLE

MAY

SCULPTING THE SOUL

The fear of the Lord is the beginning of wisdom; a good understanding have all those who do His commandments. His praise endures forever.

PSALM 111:10

The *Los Angeles Times* reported some time ago about a student whose eyesight began to fail when she was seven. Later in a high school art class, she used her memory of a photograph of herself as a four-year-old to shape a sculpture of herself. Unable to see the image she was working on, she had to sculpt by feeling alone, molding herself with the benefit of nothing but her memory of that picture and her sense of touch. Her art ended up in a prestigious national competition.

When it comes to molding ourselves into what we want to be, we don't have to work blindly. We study the Bible like a mirror, discover what we should be, and then prayerfully seek to shape ourselves into the image that God desires. Meanwhile, the hands of the Master overlay our own as the Holy Spirit sculpts us into the image of Christ. When looking into the Bible, be alert for some change you can make, some improvement you can implement with His help. Sometimes the greatest growth is in the "details."

If you ask me after what fashion I mould my life, and what is the model by which I would sculpture my being, I tell you, it is Christ.

CHARLES SPURGEON

GOD'S LOVE

Now hope does not disappoint, because the love of God has been poured out in our hearts by the Holy Spirit who was given to us.

ROMANS 5:5

Our God is full of surprises. He tailor-makes every miracle; He individually designs every life. Every day is different, and His every deliverance is unique. Yet He is never capricious, changeable, erratic, or unstable. He is the same yesterday, today, and forever. Amid the complexity of His manifold ways, there is the solid foundation of His love.

We can always count on that. The Bible longs for us to understand "what is the width and length and depth and height— to know the love of Christ which passes knowledge" (Ephesians 3:18-19). According to the apostle John, the more we understand the shoreless ocean of God's love, the less we'll fear the choppy waters of life, for "perfect love casts out fear" (1 John 4:18).

If you feel your life is unpredictable and unstable right now, focus on His steady, unchanging love. Thank Him for "the love of God flooding through our hearts by the Holy Spirit given to us" (Romans 5:5, Phillips). Resting in the predictable and perfect security of God's love will bring revival to our souls.

[God's love] is shed abroad, as sweet ointment, perfuming the soul, as rain watering it and making it fruitful.

MATTHEW HENRY

MAY 3

SIGNED, SEALED, AND DELIVERED

*You were sealed with the Holy Spirit of promise,
who is the guarantee of our inheritance....*

EPHESIANS 1:13-14

Archaeologists have uncovered many ancient seals from biblical times, some of them containing names of characters mentioned in Scripture. One of them likely belonged to the infamous Queen Jezebel; others belonged to people from the Book of Jeremiah. The Bible frequently talked about the role of seals in securing information or property. If a king, for example, wrote a letter, it was sealed with wax into which his ring was pressed. This proved its ownership and authenticity. The seals in Revelation carried great authority, and only Jesus was approved to open them.

The apostle Paul said we, too, are sealed. God has taken personal possession of His people, sealing us with the Holy Spirit who is placed in our hearts as a guarantee of our future riches in Christ (2 Corinthians 1:22).

Do you ever write your name on your possessions, or put them in a lockbox, or have an important document notarized? The Lord has written His name on our hearts, secured us in the lockbox of His love, and notarized our salvation with ink drawn from the veins of Christ. We are securely His!

> *The hearts of believers are stamped with the
> Spirit as with a seal... the Spirit of Promise.*
>
> JOHN CALVIN

MAY 4

TIMES OF TROUBLE

...that the genuineness of your faith, being much more precious than gold that perishes, though it is tested by fire, may be found to praise, honor, and glory at the revelation of Jesus Christ.

1 PETER 1:7

Charles V was a teenager when he became the most powerful man in Europe, and almost immediately he faced a vexing problem. What to do with Martin Luther? He summoned Luther to the city of Worms in 1521 for a hearing on his radical teaching. Luther traveled the 300 miles to Worms expecting to be condemned there and perhaps executed. The hearing was tense and emotional, but Luther's ringing affirmation spoken that day is famous: "Here I stand," he said, "I can do no other. God help me! Amen!" Even though Charles V was a devout Catholic, he allowed Luther to leave unharmed to continue his work.

In times of stress, strain, challenge, and trouble, we have to take our stand in the truths of God's Word. Troubling times reveal in Whom our allegiance truly lies. The psalmist said: "The Lord also will be a refuge...in times of trouble.... For in the time of trouble He shall hide me in His pavilion... He is (my) strength in the time of trouble.... (Psalm 9:9; 27:5; 37:39).

In times of trouble, we can take our stand in Him—He never fails us.

A mighty fortress is our God, a bulwark never failing!

MARTIN LUTHER

LOVE LIKE GOD LOVES

But God demonstrates His own love toward us,
in that while we were still sinners, Christ died for us.

ROMANS 5:8

Some people say the world's best illustration of unconditional love is found in a dog's response to its owner. They say, "Dogs don't care if you're a good person or a bad person—they love you all the same." Without taking anything away from man's best friend, there is actually a better example. In fact, the world's only permanent example of totally unconditional love is the love God has for sinners: ". . . while we were still sinners, Christ died for us."

Paul Gossman, pastor of Peace Lutheran Church in Covington, Washington, explains his mission this way: "To establish people firmly in [God's] unconditional love for them through Christ" and then spread "His love to our local communities and beyond." Once we have experienced God's unconditional love, our mission is to manifest that same love to others: "And be kind to one another, tenderhearted, forgiving one another, even as God in Christ forgave you" (Ephesians 4:32).

If you have experienced God's unconditional love, look for the people in your world with whom that love needs to be shared.

There is nothing the Christian can do to make God love him more, or love him less. God's love for his people is infinite and unconditional.

JOHN BLANCHARD

MAY 6

WHO WILL YOU CALL?

I will say of the LORD, "He is my refuge and my fortress;
My God, in Him I will trust."

PSALM 91:2

In his book *Anticancer—A New Way of Life* (Viking, 2008), Dr. David Servan-Schreiber recounts how he responded to the news that his brain tumor had returned: "After canceling my afternoon appointments, I set out on a walk alone. My head was buzzing. I still remember the tumult that gripped me. I would have liked to talk to God. But I didn't believe in Him. I finally managed to concentrate on my breathing, calm the turmoil in my thoughts, and turn inward. In the end, it was a form of prayer . . ."

Because God has put eternity in the heart of every person (Ecclesiastes 3:11), there is an innate, unexpected inclination to cry out to Him in times of trouble. It's why someone once observed that there are "no atheists in foxholes." When people who don't believe in God are in trouble, they are forced to call out to someone or something. Revelation 6:15-16 predicts that many will call out to "mountains and rocks" to hide them from the judgment of God during the Tribulation.

If you need help today, call out to the One who knows you, loves you, and wants to help you—your Heavenly Father. Calling out to God is a sign of wisdom and strength, not weakness.

Prayer is weakness leaning on omnipotence.

W. S. BOWDEN

WHAT GOOD WORKS ARE GOOD FOR

*What does it profit, my brethren, if someone says he has
faith but does not have works? Can faith save him?*

JAMES 2:14

Scripture memory is an important discipline in the Christian
life. If there is a downside to memorizing one verse at a
time, it is that important verses lose their context. For instance,
Romans 8:28 needs verse 29 for its full effect. And Ephesians 2:8-
9 (*how* we are saved) needs verse 10 (*why* we are saved) to get the
full import of Paul's message and meaning.

Ephesians 2:8-9 are well-known verses that establish the truth
that we are saved "by grace . . . through faith." And it makes clear
that our salvation is "not of works, lest anyone should boast." But
then verse 10 makes it just as clear that we are "created in Christ
Jesus for good works, which God prepared beforehand that we
should walk in them." So, we are not saved *by* good works, but we
are definitely saved *for* good works. We are saved so we can carry
out those acts and deeds that fulfill the purpose for our salvation:
continuing the kingdom works that Jesus did in the image of
Christ Himself (Romans 8:29).

Sometimes Christians are confused about good works—but
we shouldn't be. They are the evidence, not the basis, of the
believer's salvation.

We must come to good works by faith, and not to faith by good works.

WILLIAM GURNALL

MAY 8

GOD'S COMFORT

God, who comforts the downcast, comforted us.

2 CORINTHIANS 7:6

In one of his books, Herschel Ford told about Bishop Hughes, the pastor of a Boston church of 800 members. About two years into his pastorate, Hughes was asked to preach a sermon on the subject of comfort. As he thought about it, he decided to see if such a sermon was really needed. Taking the church roll, he listed all the families who had suffered some grief or trouble during those two years, and he was astounded to find that eighty percent of his people needed this definite comfort.

The New Testament epistles are full of promises regarding divine comfort. "Blessed be the God and Father of our Lord Jesus Christ, the Father of mercies and God of all comfort, who comforts us in all our tribulation," says 2 Corinthians 1:3-4. Notice the double use of the word "all." He is the God of *all* comfort who comforts us in *all* our tribulation. He is our all *in* all.

Life is unpredictable, and in every pew sits a broken heart. But God's comfort is as certain as the rising sun, and just as enlightening and warming.

Sooner or later, sorrow comes to us all, but we have the Holy Spirit to comfort us in a way that is simply out of this world.

HERSCHEL FORD

BULLETPROOF GLASS

*And if anyone sins, we have an Advocate
with the Father, Jesus Christ the righteous.*

1 JOHN 2:1

Recently a young man in suburban Chicago tried to escape during his trial, as he'd seen done many times on television. While being led out of the courtroom, he burst free, ran across a walkway, and tried to leap through a window. But the bulletproof glass didn't break, and the man bounced off, landing on the floor where he was promptly rearrested, this time in worse trouble than ever.

There's no escaping judgment; and there's no escaping God's judgment except through the grace and pardon of Jesus Christ. He is our Advocate, our Barrister, and our Defense Attorney (1 John 2:1). The prophet Zechariah once had a vision in which he saw Israel's high priest, Joshua, standing before the Lord, dressed in filthy rags and being accused by Satan. But the Lord removed the man's filthy garments and clothed him with rich robes and a clean turban, all of grace.

The judgment that we deserve has been suspended permanently. Our Advocate provides robes of righteousness as our shame, guilt, and judgment are washed away by His blood.

*Dressed in His righteousness alone,
faultless to stand before the Throne.*

EDWARD MOTE

ENJOYING LIFE

Serve the LORD with gladness.

PSALM 100:2

When somebody is eighty-four years of age and is still able to do just a little bit of the work she loves, that is a great privilege," said the inimitable Corrie ten Boom before adding, no doubt with a smile, "but I am able to do so much!" According to her coworker, Pam Rosewell, Corrie was continually thankful to God for every opportunity to serve Him, and she went about her task with an enthusiasm hard to equal. "How she enjoyed life," Pam later recalled, "...and what a sense of humor she had! We spent a lot of time laughing; she was very young in spirit."

Proverbs 15:15 says, "He who is of a merry heart *has* a continual feast."

Every day has its share of burdens, and many of us have aches and pains. But a cheerful heart is as irrepressible as a cork in water. A joyful person just cannot be held down. What a privilege to serve the Lord with gladness and to use our gifts for His glory, doing so with a merry heart.

The future is glorious. The best is yet to be, and you and I have the privilege to help hasten the coming of Jesus.

CORRIE TEN BOOM

TALKING LESS, SAYING MORE

Set a guard, O Lord, over my mouth;
keep watch over the door of my lips.

PSALM 141:3

A recent trend in medicine suggests that a key factor in increasing human lifespan is calorie reduction—simply eating less food. This goes beyond the obvious application for reducing the growing obesity epidemic. Instead, researchers have found that the less processing of food the body is asked to do, the fewer negative side effects that lead to aging, or premature death. It's sort of like your car—the fewer hours the engine runs, the longer it will last.

The same principle applies to speech: the fewer words we speak, the less chance we have of saying something hurtful that we will regret. The Book of Proverbs establishes this principle by warning against a "multitude of words," and the apostle James says the same thing in a different way by exhorting us to be "slow to speak." We live in a world where the air is filled with words—radio, television, the Internet. Finding a person who is "slow to speak" is rare. But we should be that kind of person—one who has learned to "restrain his lips."

The next time you have the opportunity to speak, measure your words.

A sanctified heart is better than a silver tongue.

THOMAS BROOKS

GOD'S SOLUTION

*He has shown you, O man, what is good; and what
does the Lord require of you but to do justly, to love mercy,
and to walk humbly with your God?*

MICAH 6:8

We have become a society obsessed with all-natural, organic products. There are now entire supermarkets devoted to offering organic products, all-natural supplements, and other healthy alternatives. More than 47 percent of adults admit to having bought organic food in the last year.

Eating healthy and being conscientious about organic foods is good. But natural also has a darker side: the natural man. According to Scripture, "The natural man does not receive the things of the Spirit of God, for they are foolishness to him; nor can he know them, because they are spiritually discerned" (1 Corinthians 2:14). When it comes to spiritual wisdom and discernment, the natural man is dependent only on carnal impulses. And such wisdom is "earthly, sensual, [and] demonic" resulting in "envy . . . self-seeking . . . confusion . . . and every evil thing" (James 3:15-16).

"Natural" solutions fit in with the standards of this world, but they are not adequate for the kingdom of God. When you need wisdom, "Ask of God, who gives to all liberally and without reproach" (James 1:5).

There is no wisdom but that which is founded on the fear of God.

JOHN CALVIN

DAVID JEREMIAH

OH, THE HUMANITY!

*For the wrath of God is revealed from heaven against
all ungodliness and unrighteousness of men,
who suppress the truth in unrighteousness.*

ROMANS 1:18

The Hindenburg was coming in for a landing in New Jersey on
May 6, 1937. It was a thrilling sight, a zeppelin three football
fields in length, held aloft by 7 million cubic feet of hydrogen.
The blimp was luxurious, with a dining salon, lounges, and
staterooms. Gigantic Nazi swastikas adorned its fins. Suddenly a
flame appeared near the stern, and the blimp exploded in a ball
of fire, falling tail first with flames shooting out the nose. In one
moment, the wonder was turned to fiery destruction.

Without Christ we're all passengers on the Hindenburg. We
may be enjoying ourselves to the fullest, but the next moment is
going to bring the fires of God's wrath. That doesn't mean God
is mad at us in an immature or juvenile way. The wrath of God
refers to His right and necessary response to moral evil.

The good news is that we don't have to experience the judicial
wrath of God. The Bible proclaims: "Having now been justified by
His blood, we shall be saved from wrath through Him" (Romans
5:9). We don't have to go down with the Hindenburg.

*God does not throw temper tantrums or pitch fits,
but His anger against sin is intense.*

TONY EVANS

WITNESSES YOU CAN TRUST

*These are the two olive trees and the two
lampstands standing before the God of the earth.*

REVELATION 11:4

Beginning with the classic TV series featuring fictional defense attorney Perry Mason, there has been no shortage of courtroom-based dramas in recent years. People who have never set foot in a courtroom are thoroughly versed in the procedures and principles of a trial—including the role of the character witness.

A character witness is someone called to establish the believability of a defendant. But often the opposing attorney will call a witness to discredit the reputation of the character witness, hoping to make his testimony unreliable, unbelievable, or irrelevant. If the character witness cannot be trusted, neither can his testimony. God will call two witnesses to the "stand" during the Tribulation to testify for Him—and their character will be beyond reproach. Moses and Elijah will return to the prophetic stage and bear witness to God's message of judgment on the earth. They are as life-giving as the olive tree and light-giving as a lampstand.

The Bible is filled with witnesses to the words and works of God—witnesses you can trust.

*Scripture is not only human witness to God,
it is also divine self-testimony.*

J. I. PACKER

DAVID JEREMIAH

MAY 15

GOD'S PATTERN FOR LIFE

*Hold fast the pattern of sound words which you have heard
from me, in faith and love which are in Christ Jesus.*

2 TIMOTHY 1:13

The most famous center for men's custom-made suits in the
world is London's Savile Row. Napoleon III had clothes
tailored on Savile Row, as did Winston Churchill, and as does
Prince Charles today. On Savile Row, men's suits are not sewn
according to a pattern, but according to the precise size and
preference of the customer.

Custom-made may work fine when preparing a new suit, but
eternal patterns are the procedure in the kingdom of God. Those
who dwell in God's kingdom through faith in Christ must learn
that God's pattern for life and godliness is THE pattern—one size
fits all. Rather than being restrictive, we find that God's pattern
for living provides for freedom and joy. Just as a car operated
according to the manufacturer's "pattern" (guidelines) provides
the most problem-free use, so our lives are the most fruitful and
enjoyable when lived according to God's guidelines. And where is
God's pattern to be found? It is found in the pages of His Word.

The person who meditates on God's pattern "day and night"
will prosper in whatever he does (Psalm 1:1-3).

*Nothing in the world can be properly understood unless it is
understood in terms of God's design and plan.*

R. C. SPROUL

BE PERSUADED

For this reason I also suffer these things; nevertheless I am not ashamed, for I know whom I have believed and am persuaded that He is able to keep what I have committed to Him until that Day.

2 TIMOTHY 1:12

Think about the challenges faced by the early apostles—every place they went outside of Israel was virgin missionary territory. "Jesus who?" was the equivalent of the questions they were asked wherever they went. And if people had heard of Jesus of Nazareth, they had already formed a negative opinion thanks to the local Jewish community's report about this "false Messiah."

What kept the apostles going? What allowed them to be dragged out of a city, be stoned, left for dead—yet go right back into the same city to preach (Acts 14:19-20)? It was because of what Jesus had told His disciples: "All authority has been given to Me . . . ; and lo, I am with you always, even to the end of the age" (Matthew 28:18-20). Paul knew that the one he believed in was with him—and had the power and authority to keep him secure until the end.

Take courage today in your own personal mission field, to share the Gospel without fear. Be persuaded, as the early apostles were, that through Christ all things are possible.

But I know whom I have believed, and am persuaded that He is able to keep that which I've committed unto Him against that day.

DANIEL W. WHITTLE, "I KNOW WHOM I HAVE BELIEVED"

DAVID JEREMIAH

THE SAMSON SYNDROME

But (Samson) did not know that the Lord had departed from him.

JUDGES 16:20

"If Samson were alive today, he'd be a superstar athlete or an action movie star," wrote Mark Atteberry in his book, *The Samson Syndrome*. "Or he'd be a Navy SEAL or a world-champion prize fighter. He'd be on the cover of *GQ* or *Sports Illustrated*. He'd be surrounded by popping flashbulbs or adoring groupies."

Yet for all his strength and charisma, Samson was a puppet of his own desires, and not until the end of his life did he learn the biblical maxim of self-control and personal discipline. He rejected accountability, shrugged off self-denial, thought he was too tough for good advice, didn't establish personal boundaries, and didn't realize until too late that he had become a product of his own lusts.

Paul was the opposite. His very name—Paul—meant "small." But he was big for Christ. "I discipline my body," he said in 1 Corinthians 9:27, "and bring it into subjection, lest... I myself should become disqualified." Let's follow the Paul Pattern, not the Samson Syndrome.

Discipline is the ability to say "no" to what is sin, "yes" to what is right, and to say "I will" to what ought to be done.

JERRY WHITE

SUNRISE/SUNSET

Now I saw heaven opened, and behold, a white horse.
And He who sat on him was called Faithful and True,
and in righteousness He judges and makes war.

REVELATION 19:11

In Exodus 14, the same pillar of fire that provided light for the Israelites produced thick darkness to the Egyptians. In the same way, when the sun rises above the mountains of one continent, it's sinking into the horizon of another. A victory for one army means defeat for another. Even on the playground, we learn that as one child rises on the seesaw, another child descends. Life teaches us that the same event may be both positive and negative at the same time, depending on the recipients.

That's how it will be when Christ returns. The Second Coming will reward those who know the Lord Jesus while, at the same time, taking vengeance on those who don't. Revelation 19, describing the Lord's return, opens with the delight of the angels and concludes with the doom of the Beast and False Prophets.

Just as the sun setting on the horizon indicates the closing hours of another day, it should also serve as a reminder that we are one day closer to the return of Jesus Christ. It is as certain as the sun rising on the morrow—He will return!

Does your heart leap up with rapture as you know He's near?
Or do thoughts of His appearing fill your heart with fear?

ADA R. HABERSHON, HYMNIST

HEART'S LONGING

*As the deer pants for the water brooks,
so pants my soul for You, O God.*

PSALM 42:1

Christian author and speaker, Steve Maxwell, says that if we could project up onto the wall a minute-by-minute account of our day, we would see where our heart truly lies. Is it in TV? Work? Friendships? Hobbies? In and of themselves, these activities are not wrong; but when we begin to prefer sitting in front of the TV, trying to get ahead at work, spending time with friends, or participating in our hobbies, our heart's focus shifts from God to the pleasures this world has to offer, and He is no longer the resident Ruler in our heart.

The Bible says that where a man's treasure is, there his heart will be also (Luke 12:34). If you invest the treasure of your time into knowing God, your heart will be drawn to Him in everything you do. And if you invest the treasure of your finances into helping others and being a good steward of what God has given you, your heart will remain steadfast toward Him.

As we schedule our days and weeks ahead, let us ask ourselves this: "What does our heart long for?" If it is anything except God, perhaps it's time to shift our focus.

*Indeed, anything in us that denies Him full access to our souls, that
stands between our hearts and His, becomes His enemy.*

FRANCIS FRANGIPANE

MAY 20

DO NOT BE DECEIVED

I will ascend above the heights of the clouds,
I will be like the Most High.

ISAIAH 14:14

You are familiar with this brain twister: "If a tree falls in the forest and there is no one there to hear it, does it make any noise?" Here's another challenging one: "Does a deceived man know he is deceived?" While the first question is mostly for fun, the second has serious spiritual implications.

The phrase "do not be deceived" occurs five times in the New Testament, and the same warning is reiterated in other words in additional verses. The fact that Christians are warned about the possibility of being deceived means it can happen. And the fact that the warning is repeated means we have to look carefully and continually at our lives to make sure we are "[walking] in the light as He is in the light" (1 John 1:7). The best ways to avoid deception are to continually rehearse the Bible's teachings ("Is this what I believe?" Psalm 119:11), continually ask God to search our heart to see if there is any wicked way in it (Psalm 139:23-24), and be accountable to people who love us enough to correct us (Proverbs 27:6).

Take steps today to establish your defenses against deception.

The fundamental deception of Satan is the lie
that obedience can never bring happiness.

R. C. SPROUL

MAY 21

THE LOST MOTORIST

I will instruct you and teach you in the way
you should go; I will guide you with My eye.

PSALM 32:8

A lost motorist asked a farmer for directions.
"Where is the main highway to Quincy?"
"I don't know."
"Well, where is the highway to Hannibal?"
"I don't know."
"Where does this highway go?"
"I don't know."
"You don't know much do you?"
"No, but I ain't lost."[11]

Have you ever tried going on a road trip without a map? Trying to plan your life without God is just as ineffective.

If we consult God in everything, asking Him to lead and guide us on life's journey, the Bible says His footsteps shall be our pathway and His plan will be to give us a future and a hope (Psalm 85:13; Jeremiah 29:11).

When you find yourself making plans for your life, remember to first find out where God would have you go, and then map out your next move according to His will.

> *The beautiful thing about this adventure called faith*
> *is that we can count on Him to never lead us astray.*

CHARLES SWINDOLL

11 TIM TIMMONS, *Maximum Living in a Pressure Cooker World.*

PEDAL

God is our refuge and strength, a very present help in trouble.

PSALM 46:1

An unknown author once described his journey of giving God control of his life as a tandem bike ride with Christ in the front. He said, "When I had control, I knew the way. It was rather boring, but predictable. But when He took the lead, He knew delightful long trails up mountains, and through rocky places at breakneck speeds; it was all I could do to hang on!! Even though it looked like madness, He said, 'Pedal!' I was worried and anxious and asked, 'Where are You taking me?' He laughed and didn't answer, and I started to learn to trust. And I'm beginning to enjoy the cool breeze on my face with my delightful constant companion, Christ. And when I'm sure I just can't do anymore, He just smiles and says...'Pedal.'"

Though we may fear and doubt where God is taking us, when we give Him control, our life will never be the same. We'll begin to find adventure in the midst of adversity, and peace during times of pain. All we have to do is let Him steer our life while we simply pedal.

Give your life to God; He can do more with it than you can!

DWIGHT L. MOODY

ALL THESE THINGS

Your heavenly Father knows that you need all these things.

MATTHEW 6:32

The Bible is full of "all these things." Jacob once moaned, "All these things are against me" (Genesis 42:36). But Romans 8:28 says all these things work together for our good.

Referring to His teachings, Jesus asked, "Have you understood all these things?" (Matthew 13:51) Referring to the Old Testament, Paul wrote, "All these things happened" for our admonition (1 Corinthians 10:11). Referring to the events of the Nativity, Mary "kept all these things in her heart" (Luke 2:51).

When Jesus rose from the grave, the women at the tomb hurried to tell "all these things to the eleven and to all the rest" (Luke 24:9).

The Bible tells us that "in all these things we are more than conquerors through Him who loved us" (Romans 8:37). And we're commanded: "Above all these things, put on love, which is the bond of perfection" (Colossians 3:14).

He is the God of "all these things." He knows that you need all these things. And if we seek first His kingdom and His righteousness, all these things will be added to us (Matthew 6:33).

Seek first, then, your Father's kingdom and His righteousness on high.
All these things will then be given; God will not neglect your cry.

SUSAN H. PETERSON

BUNKERS AND BOULDERS

In the shadow of Your wings I will make my refuge,
until these calamities have passed by.

PSALM 57:1

Residents of Washington, D.C., were surprised in 1942 when workers started building the East Wing of the White House. During World War II, it was thought that the nation's energies should be expended on the war effort, not on enlarging the presidential residence. Only a few people knew that the East Wing was being enlarged to hide the construction of an underground bunker called the Presidential Emergency Operations Center. Originally built for Franklin Delano Roosevelt, it was designed to withstand a nuclear blast in the event of an incoming Intercontinental Ballistic Missile (ICBM).

In the days of David, a cave accomplished the same thing. While running from the armies of King Saul, David frequently found caves to be secret and secure hiding places. According to the superscription at the beginning of Psalm 57, David was hiding in such a cave when he wrote, "In the shadow of Your wings I will make my refuge...."

Everyone needs a hiding place, but our security is not found in bunkers or boulders, but under the feather protection of the Lord. He Himself is our safety. He alone is our hiding place.

Under His wings my soul shall abide, safely abide forever.

WILLIAM O. CUSHING

MAY 25

JOY IN EVERYTHING

*Blessed be the name of the Lord, from this time forth
and forevermore! From the rising of the sun to its going down,
the Lord's name is to be praised.*

PSALM 113:2-3

No small amount of harm has been done by well-intentioned Christians who misquote a particular Bible verse when attempting to comfort the grieving: "Don't forget that Scripture says to, 'Give thanks for all things.'" Actually, 1 Thessalonians 5:18 doesn't say, "*For* everything give thanks" it says, "*In* everything give thanks." And there is a world of difference between those two small words.

The Bible doesn't say we should rejoice and give thanks for the event that has caused our grief, suffering, or impatience—a lost job, the death of a loved one, or an unmet expectation. But it does say we should give thanks *in* (in the midst of) that situation. And why should we do that? Because giving thanks to God is an expression of our confident faith that He is aware of our situation and our need. The Bible is filled with expressions and promises that give us reason to trust God *in the midst of* trials and tribulations (Matthew 6:25-34; Luke 11:11-13; 2 Corinthians 9:8).

Joy in the midst of trials is another sign that we are *in*, but not *of*, this world.

Joy is the serious business of heaven.

C. S. LEWIS

THE BOILING FROG

*Be sober, be vigilant; because your adversary the devil walks
about like a roaring lion, seeking whom he may devour.*

1 PETER 5:8

Most people have heard the "boiling frog" metaphor: Drop
a frog in a pot of boiling water and it will frantically try
to climb out. But place the frog in a pot of room-temperature
water, then slowly heat the water, and the frog will get used to the
change in temperature and slowly succumb to the boiling water.
While factually incorrect, the metaphor is useful for pointing out
the danger of complacency and inattention.

This metaphor could well be used to warn residents of planet
earth about the slow rise to power of the one the Bible calls the
Antichrist. Seen first as a savior by brokering peace between Israel
and her enemies, this Man of Sin will ultimately consolidate
world power and authority by threatening to punish those who
do not acquiesce to his demands. By the time he is established on
the world stage, it will be too late. Jesus spoke often of signs of
the times (Matthew 16:3; 24:3; Mark 13:28). It behooves us to be
alert and watchful as God's end-time plans take shape.

The best way to avoid the terrible reign of the Antichrist is to
be absent from earth, safely at home with the Lord
(1 Thessalonians 4:13-18).

A wandering heart needs a watchful eye.

THOMAS WATSON

DAVID JEREMIAH

MAY 27

SHALL I PRAY TO CHANCE?

*And pray in the Spirit on all occasions
with all kinds of prayers and requests.*

EPHESIANS 6:18 (NIV)

A certain woman was crossing the Atlantic and asked a sailor one morning how long it should take them to arrive. "If it is God's will, we will arrive in Liverpool in fourteen days," said the sailor. "If it is God's will!" said the woman; "what a senseless expression! Don't you know that all comes by chance?" In a few days a terrible storm arose and the woman stood clinging to her cabin door in agony. "How long do you think it will last?" she asked the sailor. "It seems likely to last some time, madam." "Oh!" she cried, "Pray that we may not be lost!" His reply was, "Madam, shall I pray to chance?"

Oftentimes, it takes pain to get us to really pray. This is the very reason God allows us to experience difficult times, to bring us to the place where we are reminded of our great need for Him. So when God allows pain in our lives, let us not delay in falling to our knees, confessing our dependence upon Him, and establishing a consistent prayer life.

Is prayer your steering wheel or your spare tire?

CORRIE TEN BOOM

CHOOSE THIS DAY

But as for me and my house, we will serve the LORD.

JOSHUA 24:15B

Popular singer-songwriter Bob Dylan went through a public "born again" period in the late 1970s, releasing two albums of Gospel-themed songs. He even received a Grammy Award for the song, "Gotta Serve Somebody" in which he sang, "But you're gonna have to serve somebody . . . . Well, it may be the devil or it may be the Lord, but you're gonna have to serve somebody."

Moses challenged the Israelites to choose life (by obeying God's laws) or death (by disobeying God). Joshua challenged the next generation of Israelites to choose who they would serve—pagan gods or the Lord. Jesus said that no man can serve two masters: "You cannot serve God and [money]" (Matthew 6:24). Life is about nothing if not about choices. From the moment we rise until the time we go to sleep, life is all about choosing. And it's the collection of little, daily choices that eventually reveal what our "big" choices are. Choosing to follow Christ in the little things is evidence that we have given Him our whole heart.

Use today to "choose for your[self] this day whom you will serve" (Joshua 24:15). And let your actions reveal that choice to the world.

> *Most Christians salute the sovereignty of*
> *God but believe in the sovereignty of man.*
>
> R. C. SPROUL

DAVID JEREMIAH

GOD'S CHANGELESSNESS

For I am the LORD, I do not change.

MALACHI 3:6

In his book, *Knowing God*, Dr. J. I. Packer tells us that Bible study helps us because the God who interacted with the characters of Scripture is the same God who cares for us today. "The God with whom they had to do is the same God with whom we have to do," wrote Packer, "for God does not change in the least particular." His character does not change; His truth does not change; His ways do not change; His purposes do not change.

"God does not change," said Dr. Packer. "Fellowship with Him, trust in His Word, living by faith, standing on the promises of God, are essentially the same realities for us today as they were for the Old and New Testament believers. This thought brings comfort as we enter into the perplexities of each day."[12]

You can count on this—it's as predictable as God Himself: He is unchanging. Jesus Christ is the same yesterday, today, and forever (Hebrews 13:8).

All change must be to the better or the worse. But God cannot change to the better, since He is absolutely perfect; neither can He change to the worse, for the same reason.

HENRY THIESSEN

---

12 J. I. Packer, *Knowing God* (DOWNERS GROVE: INTERVARSITY, 1973), QUOTES FROM CHAPTER 7.

AMY CARMICHAEL

None of them that trust in Him shall be desolate.

PSALM 34:22 (KJV)

Like most women, missionary Amy Carmichael wanted to be married. But her work would have been impossible for a married woman, and God gave her Psalm 34:22 as a special promise. Amy's struggle was deeply personal, one she didn't divulge for years. Finally she told the story. "I went away alone to a cave in the mountain.... I had feelings of fear about the future.... The devil kept whispering, 'It's all right now, but what about afterwards? You are going to be very lonely.' And he painted pictures of loneliness.... And I turned to my God in a kind of desperation and said, 'Lord, what can I do? How can I go on to the end?' And He said, 'None of them that trust in Me shall be desolate.' That word has been with me ever since."

In heaven, we'll have no loneliness, no loss, no privation, and no painful sacrifices. But it's our joy now to yield ourselves fully to God, for no one who trusts in Him will ever be desolate.

Joy is perfect acquiescence—acceptance,
rest—in God's will, whatever comes.

AMY CARMICHAEL

MAY 31

BELONGING TO JESUS

*"Do not harm the earth, the sea, or the trees till we have
sealed the servants of our God on their foreheads."*

REVELATION 7:3

Occasionally we see a magazine article or television show that
features pets and their owners who actually look alike. Or
couples who have lived together for decades—how they finish
one another's sentences. When we see them together we think,
"Those two just naturally belong together."

That happened to some of the apostles in Jerusalem after
Pentecost. When the local Jewish authorities heard the power and
boldness of Peter's preaching, "they realized that [the apostles]
had been with Jesus" (Acts 4:13). It should be obvious to those
around us that we have been with Him as well—that we and
Jesus belong together. The world will see that happen during the
Tribulation when 144,000 Jews are saved by God to be witnesses
for Jesus during that tumultuous period on earth. They will
actually receive some sort of seal "on their foreheads" making it
obvious that they belong to God, not to the Antichrist.

When people look at you today, will they know to whom you
belong? Ask God to fill you afresh with His Spirit that you might
become more like Jesus today (Romans 8:29).

*However holy or Christlike a Christian may become,
he is still in the condition of "being changed."*

JOHN R. W. STOTT

JUNE

JUNE 1

TOY SOLDIERS

Finally, my brethren, be strong in the Lord
and in the power of His might.

EPHESIANS 6:10

You're entering a war zone when visiting the Connecticut Valley Historical Museum. The largest display of toy soldiers in the world is arranged in dramatic scenes to tell the history of war in miniature. Twenty different world battles from ancient Egypt to World War II are refought using detailed, individually-sculpted figures. It reminds us that the history of the world has repeatedly been determined by wars and their outcomes.

We're also entering a war zone when we begin the Christian life, but we aren't toy soldiers and our battles aren't miniaturized. According to Scripture, we struggle "against principalities, against powers, against the rulers of the darkness of this age, against spiritual hosts of wickedness in the heavenly places" (Ephesians 6:12).

We're to be fully aware that temptation is lurking behind every bush, demons are opposing our every step, and our "flesh" is continually making treasonous overtures trying to undercut our spiritual progress.

We're more apt to be victorious when we realize we're at war.

Our temptations can be turned into stepping stones leading to
nobility of character. By divine grace, all of us can be victors.

HERBERT LOCKYER

JUNE 2

GOT MILK?

Come out from among them and be separate,
says the Lord. Do not touch what is unclean.

2 CORINTHIANS 6:17

Midwestern newspapers are full of articles about using raw milk. Though previous generations enjoyed milk direct from the cow, health officials warn that raw milk carries increased risk for contamination. Supporters of raw milk say pasteurization destroys nutrients.

Some Turning Point readers grew up on a farm; but most of us now get our milk from stores where we have enough choices to make Betsy the Cow's head spin: standardized, whole, reduced-fat, low-fat, skim, non-fat, buttermilk, organic, acidophilus....

Grabbing that gallon of milk forces us to think about separation. After it stands awhile, fresh milk has a tendency to separate into a high-fat cream layer on top and a thinner layer below. When we grab our particular jug of choice, we're determining our degree of separation.

The processing of milk reflects a wider truth. At the Last Day, God will separate the cream from the skim, the wheat from the chaff, and the sheep from the goats. Until then, we should lead lives of separation, holy and pleasing to Him, to "come out from among them" and be separate. Perhaps there's something we need to skim off the top of our lives today.

Measure your growth in grace by your sensitiveness to sin.

OSWALD CHAMBERS

DAVID JEREMIAH

BODY ARMOR

*Put on the whole armor of God, that you may
be able to stand against the wiles of the devil.*

EPHESIANS 6:11

According to the *Richmond Times-Dispatch*, Jeff O'Dell is a
student at the University of Virginia Charlottesville with a
personal interest in his research. The biomedical and mechanical
engineering student is working on a new type of body armor for
American soldiers. Most body armor can be damaged by one shot
from an armor-piercing bullet; but the vest designed by O'Dell
and his fellow students should be able to withstand as many as 32
rounds per plate. "It could not only save American lives," O'Dell
said, "but my own life, too." That's because O'Dell is a soldier who
has served in Iraq and Afghanistan and expects to be deployed
again in the near future.

Even the best body armor won't help the soldier who
doesn't wear it. Every day we need to wear the breastplate of
righteousness, the boots of the Gospel, the shield of faith,
the helmet of salvation, the sword of the Spirit, and the other
essential pieces of soul armor in the arsenal of our God.

We have the best armor in the universe, if we'll just wear it.

You live in that armor. You wear it like a T-shirt.

JEFF O'DELL

JUNE 4

UNIVERSAL REFLECTION

For since the creation of the world His invisible attributes are clearly seen, being understood by the things that are made, even His eternal power and Godhead, so that they are without excuse.

ROMANS 1:20

The heavens declare the glory of God! By looking into the stellar sky, we can learn many facts about God. Since the universe appears almost limitless in extent, the First Cause—God—must be virtually infinite. Since the universe appears almost endless in duration, He must be virtually eternal. Since the universe pulsates with energy, He must be omnipotent. Since the universe is phenomenally complex and contains intelligent life, God must be omniscient. Since the universe contains feeling and emotions and love and human relations, its Creator must be personal. Since the universe contains goodness and righteousness and love and justice, He must be moral.[13]

A cornerstone of the Christian faith is belief that God is the Creator. During the last days, those who deny His rightful role as Creator will separate themselves from Him forever.

Marvel at what He has made today!

A man can no more diminish God's glory by refusing to worship Him than a lunatic can put out the sun by scribbling 'darkness' on the wall of his cell.

C. S. LEWIS

13 HENRY MORRIS, *Many Infallible Proofs* (SAN DIEGO: CLP PUBLISHERS, 1974), 101-104.

DAVID JEREMIAH

GOD OUR REFUGE

He who dwells in the secret place of the Most High
shall abide under the shadow of the Almighty.

PSALM 91:1

In the 1950s, at the height of the Cold War, many families built underground fallout shelters in their back yards as a defense against a nuclear attack. Not many people know that the United States government built a massive bunker beneath the famous Greenbrier Resort in White Sulphur Springs, West Virginia, large enough to house the entire Congress so the government could continue to function in case of attack. It was a secret for 30 years, only revealed to the public in 1992—and was never used.

There's nothing wrong with taking precautions against approaching dangers. But a time of danger is fast approaching against which no human defense will be able to stand. During the coming Tribulation, judgments from heaven will be released more powerful than any nuclear attack. But there is a refuge: God Himself. Those who belong to God through faith in Christ will be removed from earth before the Tribulation. Make Him your "dwelling place" and "no evil shall befall you" (Psalm 91:9-10).

How do you make God your refuge and hiding place? By trusting in His Son, Jesus Christ, through faith.

> *Only he who can say, "The Lord is the strength of my life"*
> *can say, "Of whom shall I be afraid?"*

ALEXANDER MACLAREN

PRAYER

He went a little farther and fell on His face, and prayed,
saying, "O My Father, if it is possible, let this cup pass from Me;
nevertheless, not as I will, but as You will."

MATTHEW 26:39

While there is no agreement about the origin of the phrase, there is no disagreement about its meaning: "There are no atheists in foxholes," or, "There are no atheists in the trenches." We don't know who said it first, but sources date the idea back as far as World War I.

Crying out to God for protection in times of heated battle is nothing to be ashamed of. Jesus Christ Himself, on the night of His arrest and trial for blasphemy, fell on His face before God and prayed that God might spare Him from the pain He knew was coming. But He ended His prayer with these all-important words: "Not as I will, but as You will." We know what God's will for Jesus was—it was for Him to die for the sins of the world. When we need to hear from God about our own future—when Scripture does not speak directly to our situation—the first thing we should do is pray. God has promised to hear us when we pray according to His will, and to answer (1 John 5:14-15).

When we pray for God's will to be done, we can be assured it will be as we rise submissively from our knees.

The spirit of prayer is the fruit and token of the Spirit of adoption.

JOHN NEWTON

WHY GOD IS WORTHY

Great and marvelous are Your works, Lord God Almighty!
Just and true are Your ways, O King of the saints!

REVELATION 15:3

Our English word "worship" is derived from the Old English *weorthscipe*, or "worthship." It was a word that meant "worthiness" or an "acknowledgement of worth." People today have ascribed worth to all sorts of things and people, thereby worshipping them: gold, wealth, appearance, position, and talent—among other things. But throughout Scripture, God is worshipped for two reasons: His perfection (who He is) and His ways (what He has done).

It's possible for the term "worship" to be loosely applied in Christian circles. There is a need to keep worship focused on the object of the Christian's love: the triune God—Father, Son, and Spirit. Whenever the apostle John caught a glimpse of worship in heaven, the songs were always about who God is and what He has done. For instance, in Revelation 15:3-4, God is called "Lord God Almighty," "King," and "holy." He is praised for His "works," "ways," and "judgments."

In your personal worship this week, remember to praise God for who He is and what He has done in your life—a simple outline for ascribing worthiness to Him.

What or whom we worship determines our behavior.

JOHN MURRAY

JUNE 8

INDECENT EXPOSURE

I put on righteousness, and it clothed me.

JOB 29:14

None of us wants to be indecently exposed; we make sure we're dressed when we leave home. But what of our spiritual clothing? The Bible uses the command "put on" in telling us how to prepare for every day. Job said that every day he put on the garment of righteousness and it clothed him. Isaiah tells us to put on strength and the breastplate of righteousness (Isaiah 51:9; 59:17). Peter said that rather than putting on costly apparel, we should wear the beauty of a gentle and quiet spirit (1 Peter 3:4). Paul wrote, "Put on the armor of light...put on the new man...put on tender mercies, kindness, and humility...put on love...put on the breastplate of faith...put on the whole armor of God."

It's summed up in Romans 13:14: "Put on the Lord Jesus Christ, and make no provision for the flesh, to fulfill its lusts."

The process of preparing our minds and hearts for each day is as important as putting on our clothes in the morning. Never let your soul be indecently exposed.

> *The best earrings that a woman can wear are*
> *the earrings of hearing the Word with attention.*
>
> CHARLES SPURGEON

DAVID JEREMIAH

A SURPRISE ON EVERY PAGE

For you yourselves know perfectly that the day
of the Lord so comes as a thief in the night.

1 THESSALONIANS 5:2

A well-known Florida mystery writer recently published his twelfth book, and critics gave it two thumbs-up. One reviewer said that readers would find "a surprise on every page."

That may or may not be true of our favorite writers, but it's certainly true of the Bible. Those who love God's Word find surprises on every page.

That's also true of the way God is writing the pages of history. Time is swiftly flying by, and pages are blowing off the calendar like leaves in the wind. The last days will be full of surprises, and the coming of Christ will be like a thief in the night. The apostle Peter said, "The day of the Lord will come as a thief in the night, in which the heavens will pass away with a great noise, and the elements will melt with fervent heat" (2 Peter 3:10).

Those who know Christ are not in darkness that the Day should overtake us as a thief. We see the warning signs and read the prediction of Scripture. We're watching, waiting, working, and ready!

In an hour to us unknown, as a thief in deepest night, Christ shall
suddenly come down, with all His saints in light.

CHARLES WESLEY

LOOKING IN WRONG PLACES

Narrow is the gate and difficult is the way
which leads to life, and there are few who find it.

MATTHEW 7:14

If you've ever lost your cell phone, diamond ring, or the remote control to your television, you know there's only one simple thing that can keep you from finding it: looking in the wrong places. For every lost item, there are potentially hundreds of wrong places to look, but only one right place. Once we find the right place, our problem is solved and our loss is restored.

Millions of people today are looking for inner strength and mental peace. They're looking for ultimate purpose and meaningful relationships. They're searching for spiritual fulfillment and eternal life. There are thousands of wrong places to look, but only one right place—in the Lord Jesus Christ.

At the beginning of His ministry in the Sermon on the Mount, Jesus said, "Difficult is the way which leads to life, and there are few who find it." At the end of His ministry, He said, "I am the way" (John 14:6). When we find Christ, we find all we want and all we need. He is our All-in-All.

Oh, it is madness to choose any other road; it is stark madness
to think you will get adequate help anywhere in the universe apart
from this divine Savior and Lord.

GEORGE W. TRUETT

JUNE 11

A WAFER-THIN LINE

Every prudent man acts with knowledge...

PROVERBS 13:16

There is a "wafer-thin line between success and failure," writes Stuart Crainer in *The 75 Greatest Management Decisions Ever Made.* The difference is the quality of decisions we make. He cites the example of Reuben Mattus, a Polish immigrant and ice cream producer. When Mattus had trouble marketing to supermarkets, he created an expensive variety made from fresh cream and real fruit, and he decided to give it a sophisticated Euro-sounding name—Häagen-Dazs. That decision made the difference.

Christians have an advantage when it comes to decision-making. The Word of God gives us the grid of truth with which to evaluate circumstances and think wisely. We not only *think through* situations, we *pray through* them. We have the character of God and the truth of Scripture as compass needles. We have the promise of His guidance as a safeguard.

The Bible says, "The wisdom of the prudent is to give thought to their ways.... A prudent man gives thought to his steps" (Proverbs 14:8, 15, NIV).

May God make us wise decision makers in matters large and small.

Only as we walk in close and constant fellowship with the Lord...
can He communicate the knowledge of His will to us.

G. CHRISTIAN WEISS

CALLED OUT, CALLED TO

*To the church of God which is at Corinth, to those
who are sanctified in Christ Jesus, called to be saints . . . .*

1 CORINTHIANS 1:2

The word "church" in the original Greek language was
ekklesia—a compound word from *kaleo* (to call) and *ek* (out).
So *ekklesia* meant "called out ones," both concepts appearing in
1 Corinthians 1:2: The "church of God" is made up of those who
are "called [out] to be saints."

But called *out* of where, and called *to* where? The idea of
calling has its roots in the great redemptive event in Jewish
history, the calling of the Hebrews out of bondage in Egypt. Israel
was called *out* of Egypt and *to* a personal relationship with God.
They were God's chosen people. Likewise, Peter says the Church
has been called to be "a chosen generation, a royal priesthood, a
holy nation, His own special people" (1 Peter 2:9). We have not
been called out of slavery in Egypt but out of slavery to sin in
the world (John 8:34; Romans 6:16). It would have been a long
walk for the Israelites to return to Egypt, but the world is always
around us—just a decision away.

If you are being tempted by the world out of which God has
saved you, ask Him for grace and strength today to "walk worthy
of the calling with which you were called" (Ephesians 4:1).

We are called to an everlasting preoccupation with God.

A. W. TOZER

JUNE 13

ONE SIZE FITS ALL

And having shod your feet with the preparation of the gospel of peace.

EPHESIANS 6:15

Shoes serve an important role—protecting our feet. We wear galoshes to protect our feet from water. Snow boots guard our feet from frostbite and cold. Depending upon your occupation, there may be very specific footwear that you are required to wear to protect your feet while doing your job. While many unique situations call for a different type of shoe, there is a single pair that fits every believer.

The apostle Paul wrote that the feet of every Christian should be "shod with the preparation of the gospel of peace." Just as every other part of our body is to be clothed in armor from God—the belt of truth, breastplate of righteousness, shield of faith, helmet of salvation, and sword of the Spirit—so our feet are also to be "clothed." But what does it mean to have our feet "shod" with the Gospel of peace? Paul is playing off the words of Isaiah 52:7, a description of a warrior who brings back news of a great victory in battle. Everywhere our feet take us, we are to proclaim the victory of Jesus Christ on the cross— a victory that brings us peace with God and will one day bring peace to the world.

When was the last time you announced to someone that the victory has been won? Good news is meant for sharing!

He that is not a son of peace is not a son of God.

RICHARD BAXTER

SCRIPTURE

Now all these things happened to them as examples,
and they were written for our admonition,
upon whom the ends of the ages have come.

1 CORINTHIANS 10:11

It's easy for Christians to focus solely on reading the New Testament, thinking the Old Testament "was for Israel." But the apostle Paul discounted that notion when he wrote that, "All Scripture . . . is profitable" (2 Timothy 3:16). And remember: He was referring to the Old Testament since the New Testament was only coming into existence in his day.

A good example of Paul practicing what he preached is in 1 Corinthians 10:1-13 which contains warnings for Christians in Corinth from Israel's history. When we are seeking guidance from God, we can find principles to inform our decisions from all parts of Scripture. Paul warns the Corinthians about idolatry, sexual immorality, testing the Lord, and grumbling by citing instances of the same in Israel's history. By seeing how swiftly God dealt with Israel in these areas of life, we are warned—and guided—to err on the side of safety. Even the "appearance of evil" (1 Thessalonians 5:22, KJV) should serve as a warning: Flee!

If all Scripture is profitable, we will profit from guidance gleaned in all 66 books.

Never mind the scribes—what saith the Scripture?

MARTIN LUTHER

FULL-BODY FAITH

Above all, taking the shield of faith with which you will
be able to quench all the fiery darts of the wicked one.

EPHESIANS 6:16

Roman soldiers used two kinds of shields in battle. There was a small, round shield used in close-quarter combat, and a large, door-sized shield used when troops were advancing across an open plain. When the enemy fired a barrage of arrows, Roman soldiers linked their shields together and crouched behind them—total protection from the incoming barbs.

It is the latter shield—the large, body-sized one—that Paul says Christians are to take up as part of our spiritual armor. And that shield is a metaphor for faith. It is the Christian's faith that is our best "full-body" defense against the attacks of Satan. Here's why: Satan's primary objective in spiritual warfare is to discredit God in the eyes of believers. If he can make us believe God is not to be trusted, then we become easy prey for his circumstantial attacks against us. Therefore, faith—unshakeable, undeniable, impenetrable faith in the goodness of God—is our number one shield against Satan's attacks.

If you have any thoughts today about whether God is good and faithful, cast them aside! Take up your shield of faith and protect yourself from the enemy's attacks.

Our assurance is only as strong as our faith.

R. C. SPROUL

REACHING FOR PEARLS

Alas, alas… for in one hour such great riches came to nothing.

REVELATION 18:16-17

Someone once said, "The trouble is that too many people are spending money they don't have for things they don't need to impress people they don't like." The Methodist writer, Clovis Chappell, once wrote about excavators in ancient Pompeii who found a body that had been suddenly entombed when Mount Vesuvius had erupted. Her feet were turned toward the city gate, but her face was turned backward and her hand was stretched out, as if reaching for something. It was a bag of pearls. She had perhaps dropped them and, in turning to pick them up, met instant entombment.

It's easy to get caught up with the pearls in life. And our struggle with materialism becomes even more difficult as God blesses us more and more. We have to work hard to stay humble, to enjoy the simple life, to be generous, and to have our hearts fixed on our Master instead of our money. The Book of Revelation warns that all the wealth of the coming Babylon will be vaporized by the wrath of Tribulation Days. In one hour, great riches will come to nothing.

But the riches of Christ belong to us forever.

The fellow that has no money is poor.
The fellow who has nothing but money is poorer still.

BILLY SUNDAY

How Much Longer?

"Where is the promise of His coming? For since the fathers fell asleep,
all things continue as they were from the beginning of creation."

2 Peter 3:4b

Impatience is part of every child's emotional "DNA." What
parent, while on a family road trip, hasn't been asked multiple
times, "How much longer?" Unfortunately, impatience can often
turn to skepticism in adulthood—like when skeptics ask, "How
much longer until Jesus returns? I thought you said He was
coming back to earth."

If people were asking that question in the first century (and
they were; see 2 Peter 3:4), how much more cynically do they
sometimes ask it after an additional 1,900 years? How should we
respond when people question the fact of the Second Coming
of Christ? When the prophets predicted His first coming (Micah
5:2), it was hundreds of years before He appeared. But He did
appear. And since the same prophets predicted His Second
Coming (Zechariah 14:4), we have no reason not to take them at
their word, regardless of the passing of time.

Jesus' own words are our reason for certainty in the face of
skepticism: "Let not your heart be troubled . . . I will come again"
(John 14:1-3). Be certain today of His return one day.

Lord, keep my spirits up, my courage strong,
my zeal inflamed, and my eyes on Christ alone.

Anonymous

SHARPEN YOUR WEAPONS

So He Himself often withdrew into the wilderness and prayed.

LUKE 5:16

A wild boar stood under a tree and rubbed his tusks against the trunk. A fox passing by asked him why he was doing this when there was no danger from either hunters or hounds. He replied, "I do it intentionally; for it would not be wise to have to sharpen my weapons just at the time I ought to be using them."

As Christians, we should be sharpening our spiritual tusks every day through Bible reading and prayer because attacks from the world will come at us at all times, and as the boar so aptly pointed out, it would not be wise for us to prepare for battle just at the time it begins.

The Bible says to *"Be ready in season and out of season,"* and Jesus set the example of how to do this by consistently getting alone to spend time with His Father and using Scripture to fight against Satan (2 Timothy 4:2). If our sinless Savior placed such importance on preparing in order to protect against spiritual attack, we can be sure it should be a priority for all of us.

The purpose of Christianity is not to avoid difficulty, but to produce a character adequate to meet it when it comes. It does not make life easy; rather it tries to make us great enough for life.

JAMES L. CHRISTENSEN

AN HOUR OF YOUR TIME

And you fathers, do not provoke your children to wrath,
but bring them up in the training and admonition of the Lord.

EPHESIANS 6:4

A man came home late from work to find his 5-year-old son waiting for him at the door. The first thing out of the child's mouth was, "Daddy, how much money do you make in an hour?" "If you must know, I make $50 an hour" said the man. "Well, can I borrow $25?" the boy asked. "For what?" replied the man. Without saying a word, the little boy went to his room, removed some crumpled money from under his bed and added it to the money his dad gave him. He came back and said, "Daddy, now I have $50. Can I buy an hour of your time?"

Sometimes, balancing the responsibilities of providing for our children and making time to invest in their lives can become overwhelming. Being a godly father is a huge responsibility. But it is also one of life's greatest joys. As we raise our children in the love of the Lord, may we not become discouraged as the pressures mount; rather, let us look to our own Heavenly Father for the strength, love, courage, and discipline needed to carry out this high calling.

A good father is one of the most unsung, unpraised, unnoticed,
and yet one of the most valuable assets in our society.

BILLY GRAHAM

WARNING! DANGER AHEAD!

Him we preach, warning every man and teaching every man in all wisdom, that we may present every man perfect in Christ Jesus.

COLOSSIANS 1:28

Secret intelligence networks exist to warn of impending terrorist attacks. Radar systems warn of approaching missiles. Deep-water buoys warn of approaching tsunamis. And Doppler radar warns us to hide from approaching tornadoes.

Why do we invest so many resources—money, technology, people—in warning systems? Because of the innately felt desire to protect and save human life, the most valuable part of God's creation. There is one warning system that no government or agency can implement; it can only be carried out by those who know the Lord Jesus Christ and His Word. The warning is this: "God intends to judge the world in which we live; His righteousness requires it. All who have not repented of their sins and found forgiveness through God's Son, Jesus Christ, will find themselves caught up in God's judgment and consigned to an eternity separated from Him." Every Christian is to warn those nearby of this coming judgment.

You would warn your neighbors of an approaching tornado. Have you pointed out to them the gathering storm clouds that portend God's judgment?

If you are not seeking the Lord, judgment is at your heels.

C. H. SPURGEON

THE BEST OFFENSE

And take . . . the sword of the Spirit, which is the word of God.

EPHESIANS 6:17B

Depending on whom you talk to, in which sport, "The best defense is a good offense" or "The best offense is a good defense." Perhaps they both have value in different situations. But when it comes to living the Christian life, it appears the apostle Paul is going with "the best offense is a good defense."

In Paul's discussion of the Christian's spiritual armor, all of the elements of armor he mentions are defensive in nature—the belt, breastplate, protection for the feet, the shield, and the helmet—except for one: "the sword of the Spirit, which is the word of God." The Bible is the only offensive weapon we have at our disposal among the armor of God. Because Christians are constantly subjected to the "fiery darts" of the evil one, it makes sense that our ability to stay spiritually alive is a function of our defensive armor. But there are times for offense as well—for going on the attack. And our weapon is the same one that Jesus used to defeat Satan: the promises of God (Matthew 4:4, 7, 10).

How sharp is the edge of your sword? How quickly can you access a promise of God when you are under attack? Don't be caught off guard in the midst of the battle.

The Bible is a rock of diamonds, a chain of pearls,
the sword of the Spirit.

THOMAS WATSON

Paper Cuts

For I consider that the sufferings of this present time are not worthy to be compared with the glory which shall be revealed in us.

Romans 8:18

Imagine that your friend called you and complained, "My business card was drawn out of a fish bowl at the convention and I've won an all-expense paid trip to Paris, but I suffered a paper cut when I opened the envelope announcing the prize. I'm very upset."

You'd say, "Why be upset? A little paper cut isn't worth considering, compared to the excitement of a trip to Paris."

That's the argument God makes in Romans 8:18. Granted, our trials and troubles in life are often more than paper cuts. But our coming trip to New Jerusalem and the glories to follow are a lot greater than any trip to Paris. The apostle Paul, who wrote these words, had been shipwrecked, flogged, bound in stocks, beaten with rods, chained, stoned, and treated like a dog. Yet he said his sufferings weren't worth comparing with coming glory.

Whatever we're going through today, we can live in Romans 8:18. For our light and momentary affliction is working for us a far more exceeding and eternal weight of glory.

One second of glory will outweigh a lifetime of suffering.

Arthur W. Pink

JUNE 23

ALWAYS

Praying always with all prayer and supplication in the Spirit.

EPHESIANS 6:18

*A*lways means *in all ways* and *at all times*. It's not a word to use carelessly; it's an absolute. Yet some *always* are ours by perpetual promise. The Lord tells us to a*lways* keep His commands and to fear the Lord our God for our good *always* (Deuteronomy 5:29, 6:24). Psalm 16:8 says, "I have set the LORD *always* before me." Proverbs 28:14 says, "Happy is the man who is *always* reverent." Paul testified, "I myself *always* strive to have a conscience without offense toward God and man" (Acts 24:16).

Jesus promised to be with us *always*; and we're to be *always* abounding in the work of the Lord (Matthew 28:20, 1 Corinthians 15:58). We ought *always* to pray and not to lose heart (Luke 18:1), and to *always* do what pleases Him (John 8:29).

The Bible says: "Now may the Lord of peace Himself give you peace *always* in every way," for He "*always* leads us in triumph in Christ" (2 Thessalonians 3:16; 2 Corinthians 2:14). So we're *always* confident, *always* having sufficiency in all things (2 Corinthians 5:8, 9:8).

That's why we can rejoice *always*! (1 Thessalonians 5:16)

Take my voice, and let me sing always, only, for my King.

FRANCES HAVERGAL

MAKING THE PORT OF HEAVEN

Prepare to meet your God, O Israel.

AMOS 4:12

The steamship *London* sank off the Land's End in the English Channel on January 11, 1866, amid a terrible storm. Only one lifeboat was launched before the great ship sank, and only three passengers survived. Among the dead was Daniel Draper, a Wesleyan Methodist preacher. In the hours before the ship was lost, he reportedly went from person to person, evangelizing the passengers and crew, and he led virtually the whole ship to faith in Christ. The last words anyone heard him utter were these: "Those of you who are not converted, now is the time; not a moment to be lost, for in a few minutes we shall all be in the presence of the Judge."

Our world is in a storm, and many are sinking in life's alarms. Revelation 20 vividly describes the coming judgment at the Great White Throne of God at the end of history. If you don't know Christ as Savior, there's not a moment to be lost. Prepare to meet God by confessing Christ as Lord of your life today.

The captain tells us there is no hope; that we must all perish. But I tell you there is hope, hope for all. Although we must die, and shall never again see land, we may all make the port of heaven.

DANIEL DRAPER, ABOARD THE *London*

DAVID JEREMIAH

CANDY FOR BREAKFAST!

Ask, and you will receive, that your joy may be full.

JOHN 16:24

Have you ever wondered why children never hesitate to ask for anything? They have the audacity to ask if they can eat candy for breakfast, buy a toy every time they are in a store, and stay up past bedtime on a school night. And on a more practical level, they ask for something to drink when they are thirsty, help with their homework when they are struggling, and new shoes for gym class. The reason they come to their parents so freely is that they are dependent upon them, and they understand that without asking, they won't receive.

God's purpose in instructing us to ask Him for anything is to remind us to be dependent upon Him and give Him the glory when He provides for us. So often we rob Him of the glory and ourselves of joy when we become self-sufficient. The Bible clearly states that we do not have because we do not ask (James 4:2).

Whenever we have a need, let us try going to the Lord first. We should ask without hesitation, keep our motives in check, and expect God to provide.

He is your Shepherd, and has charged Himself with the care and keeping of you...for with such a Shepherd how could it be possible for you ever to want any good thing?

HANNAH WHITALL SMITH

THE SADDEST WORDS

And then I will declare to them, "I never knew you;
depart from Me, you who practice lawlessness."

MATTHEW 7:23

Suppose you had been living on a piece of property for twenty years and you decided to sell. When it was time to have an updated survey of the property prepared, the surveyor gave you bad news: You are not the registered owner of your property! Somehow, your name was never entered in the county's book of deeds and registrations. You know you own the property, but the county registrar does not.

The absence of a name in a deed book can usually be remedied with supporting documentation. But there is one book of names that, once it is opened by God, cannot be changed. And that is the Lamb's Book of Life (Revelation 21:27). In that book are the names of all who have placed their faith in Jesus Christ for the forgiveness of sins. For Jesus to say, "I never knew you; depart from Me" will be the saddest words anyone could ever hear. The only thing that could be as bad would be for a Christian to hear those words spoken to a person he had the opportunity to influence toward a decision for Christ. What will Jesus say to such a person?

If you know someone to whom Jesus will one day say, "I never knew you," tell that person how to avoid that sad day.

Every single believer is a God-ordained agent of evangelism.

R. B. KUIPER

CIRCUMSTANCES

*After they had come to Mysia, they tried to go
into Bithynia, but the Spirit did not permit them.*

ACTS 16:7

Multiple times in a day things happen that influence or
change our plans. Yet how many times do we say, "Thank
you, Lord. I trust that this change is from You." How often
should we say that? Is every single circumstance, large or small, a
message from God?

When the apostle Paul and his coworkers were intent on going
in one direction in their missionary journey, they were stopped.
We don't know how they were stopped; we only know that Luke
attributed the circumstance to the Holy Spirit's intervention.
Writing in hindsight, Luke realized they were stopped from going
to Mysia so they could go into Macedonia (Acts 16:8-10). If we
really believe God is sovereign, that He has ordained our days
(Psalm 139:16), then a strong case can be made for circumstances
being signposts from God: either a new direction, a new correction,
or a lesson in patience, submission, or seeking God's will.

At the very least, we know God is guiding us toward at least
one goal in every circumstance, good or bad: conformity to Jesus
Christ (Romans 8:28-29).

*The Holy Spirit loves so to arrange men's circumstances that
they are brought within the sphere of God's influence.*

MAURICE A. P. WOOD

BROCHURE OF HEAVEN

*I know a man in Christ who fourteen years ago—whether in the body
I do not know, or whether out of the body I do not know, God knows—
such a one was caught up to the third heaven... into Paradise and heard
inexpressible words, which it is not lawful for a man to utter.*

2 CORINTHIANS 12:2-4

The apostle Paul was caught into heaven where he saw glorious
things, but he wasn't allowed to describe them. Perhaps
that was because he was the apostle of salvation, a man with one
message—we are saved by grace through faith. Later, however,
John was also caught into heaven and he, too, saw God's Paradise,
the New Jerusalem. To John was given the privilege of closing
God's Book with a two-chapter travel brochure of New Jerusalem.

He described the descent of this capital city from a distance,
then up close. He gave us its measurements in human terms.
He described the walls, gates, foundations, and streets. He went
inside and saw the throne in the city's center, from which flowed a
river, a golden boulevard, and the verdant Tree of Life Park.

Do you have your place reserved in God's city? Our
reservations are held under the name of Jesus, and He alone is
our ticket there. Make sure your name is written in the Lamb's
Book of Life.

*The best moment of a Christian's life is his last one,
because it is the one that is nearest heaven.*

CHARLES SPURGEON

DAVID JEREMIAH

FOLLOW THE LEADER

*I say then: Walk in the Spirit, and you
shall not fulfill the lust of the flesh.*

GALATIANS 5:16

Every child grows up learning to play the "Follow the Leader" game. Unknown to children, it's really an instinctive tendency on the part of humans. As much as we might not like to admit it, we are all followers of something or someone.

As his logical, deductive mind did so often, the apostle Paul boiled down the "following" tendency into two major categories: We can follow the flesh (energized by Satan, the enemy of God) or we can follow the Spirit of God. To follow one means we are not following the other (Luke 16:13). And we are never in the "neutral" zone where we are not following one or the other. From the point in life at which we develop the conscious ability to make moral and spiritual choices, we are in a following mode. The "flesh," in Paul's terminology, is our natural (fallen) human instincts, oriented to self-serving and self-gratification. That's what we follow if we are not following the leading of the Holy Spirit. The only way not to follow the desires of the flesh is to follow the desires of the Spirit.

Live in the choosing mode today, and choose wisely: Follow the Spirit of God.

*The wisdom of the flesh is always exclaiming
against the mysteries of God.*

JOHN CALVIN

HEAVENLY OCCUPATION

He who overcomes shall inherit all things,
and I will be his God and he shall be My son.

REVELATION 21:7

Everyone who uses the Internet has mistakenly believed errone-ous information received in an unsolicited email. Such false in-formation gets forwarded from user to user until, after years or even months, it attains the status of "urban legend"—a fictitious body of information accepted as truth. There are even websites dedicated to identifying urban legends—separating fact from fiction.

Urban legends aren't only on the Internet—they exist in Christendom as well, or at least among those who have a faulty understanding of the faith. One of the myths is about heaven—that it will be boring; that the redeemed will float around in white robes, perch on clouds, and play harps for eternity. That whole idea is wrong. While the Bible doesn't say exactly what the daily activities in heaven will be, we know that they will be characterized by Adam and Eve's short life in Eden: activity, responsibility, accountability, and productivity.

Heaven is not a vacation resort. It is where redeemed human beings will manifest the potential and destiny for which they were created—to the glory of God.

Wisdom opens the eyes both to the glories
of heaven and to the hollowness of earth.

J. A. MOTYER

JULY

BEGGAR OR CHILD?

Yes, I have loved you with an everlasting love.

JEREMIAH 31:3

In one of Dr. J. Wilbur Chapman's meetings, a man stood up and gave his testimony: "For one year I begged the streets as a tramp and one day I tapped a man on the shoulder and said 'Mister, could you please give me a dime?' As soon as I saw his face, I realized it was my father. He threw his arms around me and said 'I have found you. All I have is yours!' I had stood there begging my father for ten cents while he had been looking for me to give me all he had."

So often, Christians approach God like a stranger on the street, begging Him just to help them get by. But when we have accepted Christ as our Savior, He is no stranger to us; He is our Father, waiting with open arms, ready to embrace us in love and offer us everything He has.

Do we approach God from a beggar's perspective or as His cherished child? If we have any difficulty seeing Him as our loving Father, we need to ask Him to help us develop a healthy Father/child relationship.

God is still on His throne and man is still on His footstool.
There's only a knee's distance in between.

JIM ELLIOT

DAVID JEREMIAH

JULY 2

TRAVELING LIGHT

Therefore, beloved, looking forward to these things,
be diligent to be found by Him in peace.

2 PETER 3:14

Seasoned travelers enjoy packing for trips; it's part of the anticipation. But we're also learning to travel light because of increased costs and security complications. It's helpful to have wrinkle-proof clothing made from modern micro-fibers that can be washed out at night. Some travel companies even make garments you can wash and put right on with the assurance they'll dry on your body within an hour. That may be going too far, but planning and packing for a big vacation increases our eagerness.

No weekend getaway or overseas odysseys can compare to the reservations being held for us in heaven's *hotel de ville*. The Lord Jesus is preparing a place for us in the diamond-like city of New Jerusalem, and one day we'll walk alongside the Crystal River, gaze on the towering walls, visit the Tree of Life Park, and worship by the Throne of God.

Traveling light is a good philosophy for life. This world isn't our home; we're just passing through. Today pack your mind with God's Word and anticipate your eternal home.

Alas! how we forget that we are but strangers and pilgrims
on the earth; that we are journeying to our eternal home,
and will soon be there!

OCTAVIUS WINSLOW

JULY 3

STRIPPING A GEAR

You also be patient. Establish your hearts,
for the coming of the Lord is at hand.

JAMES 5:8

Someone quipped that patience can be defined as idling your motor when you feel like stripping a gear. It's hard to be patient in an instant-gratification world. We like fast food and fast-paced fun. We want high-speed Internet and the ability to instantly manage our accounts. We want money from ATMs at a moment's notice, expedited resolutions to problems, entertainment on demand, express lanes on our freeways, and quick replies to our questions.

Those of us who know the Lord Jesus are standing on tiptoe, waiting every moment for the trumpet call. Each morning we watch the sun rising through the clouds, wondering if Jesus might come today, remembering His words in Revelation 22, "Surely I am coming quickly." But we must wait patiently, and we must work faithfully as we wait. In James 5, the Lord tells us to learn a lesson from farmers who wait for the rain and for the harvest. Let's mix our anticipation with patience, our expectation with labor, and our hope with endurance. Let's work till Jesus comes, then we'll be carried home.

We could never learn to be brave and patient
if there were only joy in the world.

HELEN KELLER

ABUNDANCE!

The Lord is longsuffering and abundant in mercy.

NUMBERS 14:18

As we thank God today for America, it's a good time to recall a speech given by President Franklin Roosevelt on December 6, 1933, as the Great Depression had the nation in its grip. Roosevelt spoke that day on the need for American families to be economically secure. He called his address: "The Right to a More Abundant Life."

Jesus Christ once gave a speech on the same subject, saying in John 10:10, *"The thief does not come except to steal, and to kill, and to destroy. I have come that they may have life, and that they may have it more abundantly."*

The Bible teaches that God gives us abundant mercy (Numbers 14:18), abundant provision (2 Chronicles 11:23), abundant kindness (Nehemiah 9:17), abundant pardon (Isaiah 55:7), and abundant peace (Psalm 37:11).

It's a serious thing to neglect the abundant life God offers, as Moses warned in Deuteronomy 28: *"Because you did not serve the Lord your God with joy and gladness of heart, for the abundance of everything, therefore you shall serve your enemies"* (verses 47-48).

On this Fourth of July, enjoy the abundant life He gives!

To be a follower of Jesus, to know who He is and what He means, is to have a superabundance of life.

WILLIAM BARCLAY

No Condemnation!

God did not send His Son into the world to condemn the world,
but that the world through Him might be saved.

John 3:17

Our word "condemn" comes from a Latin term combining the prefix *con* (*together with*) and the biblical verb to *damn*. It means to pronounce judgment, to declare unfit, or to doom. It's one of the harshest words in the English language, and it occurs seventy-five times in the Bible.

Many of these references, however, are joyful, for they tell us that Jesus saves us from condemnation. How wonderful to read: *"None of those who trust in Him shall be condemned . . . He who believes in Him is not condemned. . . . There is therefore now no condemnation to those who are in Christ Jesus. . . .* (Psalm 34:22; John 3:18; Romans 8:1). No wonder Charles Wesley wrote:

No condemnation now I dread;
Jesus, and all in Him, is mine;
Alive in Him, my living Head,
And clothed in righteousness divine.

Are you certain that you've invited Jesus Christ to be your personal Lord and Savior? If not, come to Him today in simple faith and discover the eternal relief of an uncondemned life.

Will you not prize and love Him who has done so much for you?

Christopher Love

David Jeremiah

JULY 6

GOD'S CLOCK IS NEVER WRONG

And He said to them, "It is not for you to know times
or seasons which the Father has put in His own authority."

ACTS 1:7

There is a story told of a man who rushed into a suburban railroad station one morning and, almost breathlessly, asked the station agent: "When does the 8:01 train leave?"

"At 8:01, sir" was the answer.

"Well," the man replied, "it's 7:59 by my watch, 7:57 by the town clock, and 8:04 by the station clock. Which am I to go by?"

"You can go by any clock you wish," said the agent, "but you can't go by the 8:01 train, for it has already left."

It is easy for us to be tempted into one of two errors concerning time. The first is to believe that things just happen when they happen, totally random without rhyme or reason. The other is to suppose that we can schedule and manage—and thus control—every detail of our lives. God, our sovereign Lord, stands outside of time and controls it. This realization can either make us fatalistic or incredibly confident and patiently trusting. Everything in our individual lives occurs, when it occurs, because our loving Lord commands or allows it. Therefore, we can go into the future, knowing history has a purpose and that God awaits us there.

> *Work as if you were to live a hundred years.*
> *Pray as if you were to die tomorrow.*
>
> BENJAMIN FRANKLIN

Saul

So Saul disguised himself . . . . And he said,
"Please conduct a séance for me . . . ."

1 Samuel 28:8

As a young man, Saul was a natural-born leader whose charisma was obvious, whose calling was noble, and whose career was promising. His character, however, was flawed; and as a result, his crown was lost. In the end, Saul longed for the advice of the mentor he had rejected—Samuel—and, in despair, he was reduced to seeking guidance from black magic, ghosts, goblins, and witches.

Warren W. Wiersbe, in his little book *Don't Lose Your Crown*, wrote, "Isn't it a tragedy that Saul realized too late how much he needed Samuel? He had ignored Samuel when he was there to help. . . . Do you have someone—a pastor, a parent, a friend—who wants to guide you in the right direction, but you aren't paying any attention? I want to warn you: One day that person may be gone, and you will wish you had his or her wisdom. Appreciate the people who are trying to help you."

Saul disguised himself, but he couldn't hide from the God whose Word He had rejected. Don't seek in the darkness the guidance that only comes from walking in the Light.

The Scriptures tell us that Saul "disguised himself." In one sense,
Saul . . . revealed himself! The darkness of his soul was coming out.

Warren W. Wiersbe

SIMPLE, BUT NOT SIMPLISTIC

For God so loved the world that He gave His only begotten Son, that
whoever believes in Him should not perish but have everlasting life.

JOHN 3:16

The physics equation explaining one of the deepest areas of
man's knowledge—the relationship between time and space
in the universe—is expressed in very simple terms: E=mc2. When
Albert Einstein proposed this theory in a 1905 scientific paper,
he probably didn't realize how simply he had expressed such a
complicated set of realities.

John 3:16 is the spiritual equivalent of Einstein's theory of
relativity. John 3:16 explains in simple words the most profound
truth in the universe: the Gospel of Jesus Christ. The Gospel is
simple, but not simplistic. The truth of the Gospel is beyond
human comprehension—how a holy God could sacrifice His
own Son to redeem a race of creatures who had rebelled against
Him. Nothing in the universe is more profound, yet the Gospel is
expressed in terms that the simplest of persons can understand.
We don't have to understand God's thoughts and ways. It is
enough to believe that He loves us and forgives us.

Why not pause today and thank God for making the world's
most profound truth simple enough for you to act on by faith.

The gospel is the clear manifestation of the mystery of Christ.

JOHN CALVIN

DAILY BREAD

Give us this day our daily bread.

MATTHEW 6:11

One of the lines of demarcation between poor and wealthy people in the world has to do with food. If you have food for the day at the beginning of the day, you could be called wealthy. If you have no food at the beginning of the day and are forced to find food for the day, you could be called poor. In other words, the concept of "reserves" or "ready supply" moves one from the category of poverty to non-poverty.

There is nothing official about that classification; it serves only to highlight the temptation to trust in reserves rather than trust in God. It is not wrong to have reserves; the Bible is filled with illustrations of the wisdom of preparing for the future (Genesis 41:46-49; Proverbs 6:6-11). But it is interesting that when Jesus taught His disciples to pray, He taught them to ask God for daily—not weekly, monthly, or yearly—bread. Why? Because it reminds us who the source of bread (and everything) really is. Even if we have food at the beginning of the day, asking and thanking God for daily bread reminds us of His blessing, reminds us that "all things come from [Him]" (1 Chronicles 29:14).

God is committed to caring daily for "the birds of the air... Are you not of more value than they?" (Matthew 6:26)

A piece of bread with God's love is angels' food.

THOMAS WATSON

HEAVEN ON EARTH

My help comes from the Lord, Who made heaven and earth.

PSALM 121:2

The economic downturn that began in 2008 has provided a corrective for this modern conviction: We can have anything we want, whenever we want it. That erroneous concept gets transferred to the spiritual life, especially when Christians read Bible verses that suggest we can ask for whatever we want "in Jesus' name" and receive it.

In the prayer Jesus taught His disciples (and us) to pray, there is a needed corrective to that cultural conditioning. Praying for God's will to be done "on earth as it is in heaven" is a way of aligning us with God's will, not God with our will. God's will is obviously done in heaven. If we pray for His will to be done on earth, it means that we will need to align ourselves with (conform to) His will. That means praying like this: "Father, I want Your will to be worked out on earth. If that means I need to change my life to have 'heaven on earth,' then I am willing to change. Please give me the grace and the power to make those changes." The apostle John wrote that when we pray according to His will (not our will), we know God hears and answers (1 John 5:14-15).

When you pray today, ask God to enable you to be conformed to His will so that it might be done on earth just as it is in heaven.

To obey God's will is the way to have our will.

THOMAS WATSON

GRACE UNDER STRESS

*Therefore I take pleasure in infirmities, in reproaches,
in needs, in persecutions, in distresses, for Christ's sake.
For when I am weak, then I am strong.*

2 CORINTHIANS 12:10

Stress testing, fatigue testing, performance testing, load testing, destruction testing—they all mean the same thing: pushing something beyond its designed capability to measure its capacity to withstand pressure and to discover its breaking point. If it breaks before reaching designed limits, it's back to the drawing board.

God allows his children to undergo stress testing—like a treadmill cardiac stress test. Cardiac tests are not designed to induce a heart attack resulting in a "breaking point," but they are designed to discover weaknesses in "the system." When God allows us to undergo stress in our life, it is not to kill us, but to help us see our own human weaknesses—and turn to Him. The apostle Paul had a "thorn in the flesh" that caused him great weakness and it forced him to avail himself of the grace of God (2 Corinthians 12:7-10). In fact, he said he now took pleasure in stress because "When I am weak, then I am strong."

If you are experiencing stress in your life, embrace it as an opportunity to receive the grace of God.

Christian doctrine is grace, and Christian conduct is gratitude.

J. I. PACKER

LEAVE JUDGING TO THE JUDGE

Therefore judge nothing before the time, until the Lord comes,
who will both bring to light the hidden things of darkness
and reveal the counsels of the hearts.

1 CORINTHIANS 4:5A

In a 1993 *Christianity Today* article (April 5, p. 17), Stephen Brown recalled the words of the British preacher F. B. Meyer concerning judging others. Meyer pointed out that when we see a brother or sister in sin, there are two things we do not know: First, we don't know how hard he or she tried not to sin; second, we don't know the strength of the force that assailed him or her. Brown added a third unknown: We don't know what we would have done in the same situation.

To those three wise observations, we can add a fourth from the apostle Paul: The true Judge, Jesus Christ, is coming; and He will bring to light everything that is now hidden to the eyes and heart of man. Therefore, since the true Judge is coming, we should *"judge nothing before the time, until the Lord comes."* When we judge another, we usurp the role given by God to Christ alone (John 5:22). Next time you're tempted to judge another, remember these four reasons not to judge—especially the last one.

The only person we are qualified and authorized to judge is ourself (1 Corinthians 11:31).

If you judge people, you have no time to love them.

MOTHER TERESA

MORE SOLID THAN GIBRALTAR

Heaven and earth will pass away,
but My words will by no means pass away.

MATTHEW 24:35

The Rock of Gibraltar is a massive limestone mountain on the southernmost tip of Europe's Iberian Peninsula, standing guard over the entrance to the Mediterranean Sea. For three centuries it has played a key role as a military fortification, its base honeycombed with tunnels. "Solid as the Rock of Gibraltar" is used to describe something that cannot be moved, and the motto of the Royal Gibraltar Regiment is *Nulli Expugnabilis Hosti*—"Conquered by No Enemy."

The Rock of Gibraltar may never have been overcome by bombs and bullets, but it will be moved one day according to the Bible: *"The elements will melt with fervent heat; both the earth and the works that are in it will be burned up"* (2 Peter 3:10). Mount Everest, Mount Rushmore, the Rock of Gibraltar—as impregnable as these seem, there is something yet more dependable: The Word of God. If you are looking for something to grasp hold of forever, let it be the teaching of Jesus.

Since man is created to be eternal, only a Word that will never pass away is sufficient.

[The Bible] outlives, outloves, outlifts, outlasts,
outreaches, outruns, and outranks all books.

A. Z. CONRAD

AVOIDING PAIN

*Flee also youthful lusts; but pursue righteousness, faith,
love, peace with those who call on the Lord out of a pure heart.*

2 TIMOTHY 2:22

Once there was a man who prayed that God would protect him from evil. His prayer was like the prayer Jesus taught His disciples except that he went further. He expressed a specific reason for wanting not to be led into temptation: "Oh, . . . that You would keep me from evil, that I may not cause pain!" (1 Chronicles 4:10) The man was Jabez, an Old Testament saint who displayed mature wisdom in his prayer.

Whenever we yield to temptation or succumb to evil, we are not the only ones who are hurt. There is usually a friend, a spouse, a child, or some other person who is caused pain by our choice. Even if our choice to sin is purely internal, in the realm of our thoughts, we diminish our future impact on others by the loss of energy and spiritual vitality needed to deal with our sin. Therefore there are always three reasons not to sin: Pain to ourselves, pain to others, and pain to God. No parent likes to witness the failure of his or her children, and God certainly takes no pleasure when we fail.

When you pray, "Lead me not into temptation," keep Jabez's insight in mind: that you might not cause pain in anyone's life.

Each temptation leaves us better or worse; neutrality is impossible.

ERWIN W. LUTZER

DELIVERANCE FROM DESPAIR

*Why are you cast down, O my soul? And why are you
disquieted within me? Hope in God, for I shall yet praise
Him for the help of His countenance.*

PSALM 42:5

Many new Christians are surprised to discover that some of the greatest saints in history suffered from moments of despair, even depression. The prophet Jeremiah cursed the day of his own birth (Jeremiah 20:14), and the prophet Elijah pleaded with the Lord to take his life (1 Kings 19:4). And no one could fault Job for his lament that he had ever been born (Job 3).

The single most encompassing verse in Scripture about despondency is found three times in Psalms (42:5, 11; 43:5). In the first half of the verse, the psalmist acknowledges that his soul is "cast down" and "disquieted" within him. Being honest about one's condition is an important first step. But the psalmist doesn't end there. He immediately tells himself, "Hope in God." He looks to the future and says, "I shall yet praise Him for [His] help." Identifying the problem is good, but moving to God's solution—hope—is better.

If you are downcast today, admit it to yourself and God. And then confess your hope in Him and praise Him for his help.

*The Christian's chief occupational hazards
are depression and discouragement.*

JOHN R. W. STOTT

JULY 16

WHEN TROUBLE COMES

*For we do not want you to be ignorant, brethren, of our trouble which
came to us in Asia: that we were burdened beyond measure, above
strength, so that we despaired even of life.*

2 CORINTHIANS 1:8

Some people grow depressed during the holidays or during the
light-shortened days of winter. For others, it's the anniversary
of the death of a loved one. Perhaps a single person dreads
spending the weekends alone. Identifying the "triggers" that
promote discouragement can be healthy.

Not long after beginning his missionary career, the apostle
Paul learned when trouble was likely to come to him—when
he entered a new area and began to preach the Gospel. He said
that at one point in Asia, he and his coworkers "despaired even
of life." But his troubles did not take his life. He later said he
was "not crushed . . . not in despair . . . not forsaken . . . not
destroyed." Indeed, it was the weakness of their "human vessels"
that allowed "the life of Jesus" to be manifested through them to
the world. When we despair, we do not despair about the ability
of Jesus to see us through.

When you see troubles coming your way, know that you will
not be crushed, forsaken, or destroyed as long as Jesus lives in
and through you.

You may despair of yourself as much as you like, but never of God.

FRANÇOIS FENELON

USEFUL VESSELS

For I say, through the grace given to me, to everyone who is among you, not to think of himself more highly than he ought to think, but to think soberly, as God has dealt to each one a measure of faith.

ROMANS 12:3

Bertoldo de Giovanni is likely an unknown name, even amongst art lovers. He was the teacher of Michelangelo. Michelangelo was only fourteen years old when he came to Bertoldo, but it was already obvious that he was enormously gifted.

One day he came into the studio to find Michelangelo toying with a piece of sculpture far beneath his abilities. Bertoldo grabbed a hammer and smashed the work into tiny pieces, shouting this unforgettable message, "Michelangelo, talent is cheap; dedication is costly!"

How easy it is to envy those in God's kingdom with very visible talent, wishing we, too, had our share of the limelight. Likewise, it is easy for those with such talent to believe their gift is more important than those of other believers. God, by His Holy Spirit, gives the church, in the form of differing spiritual gifts imparted to every believer, everything it needs to prosper. Every gift is vital. So, it's not the gift, but what you do with it that counts.

Find a need right now and fill it . . . . Do it in the name of the Lord Jesus, and you're doing it as unto Him.

DAVID JEREMIAH

Y I E L D

Now do not be stiff-necked, as your fathers were,
but yield yourselves to the LORD.

2 CHRONICLES 30:8

Every week on our motorways, cars plow into each other because drivers fail to yield right-of-way at busy intersections. By nature, we don't like to yield. The word itself means "to give up, to relinquish, to surrender, to give way to." That goes against our nature; but it's for our good on the highways. Learning to yield can save our lives and those of others.

Route 66 is also lined with YIELD signs. The Bible tells us we're to yield ourselves to the Lord. James 3:17 says that the wisdom that is from above is first pure, then peaceable, gentle, and willing to yield.

Hannah Whitall Smith said, "In order to mold you into entire conformity to His will, He must have you pliable in His hands, and this pliability is more quickly reached by yielding in the little things than even by the greater. Your one great desire is to follow Him fully. Can you not say then a continual 'yes' to all His sweet commands, whether small or great?"

Yes, we can YIELD at all God's intersections.

You become stronger only when you become weaker.
When you surrender your will to God, you discover
the resources to do what God requires.

ERWIN LUTZER

FROM POINT A TO POINT B

Blessed is the man who endures temptation;
for when he has been approved, he will receive the crown of life,
which the Lord has promised to those who love Him.

JAMES 1:12

If you see a large brown truck with yellow lettering in your neighborhood, you know why they are there. They're delivering. Delivery is the process of moving something or someone from point A to point B in the physical world. And it means almost the same in the spiritual world.

The members of the "deliver" family of words appear 553 times in the *New King James Version* of the Bible. It would not be unfair to say that the Bible is all about deliverance. In the largest sense, every Christian has experienced the ultimate form of moving from point A ("the power of darkness") to point B ("the kingdom of the Son of His love") (Colossians 1:13). But think of all the other ways we continually need God's deliverance after being saved: deliverance from enemies, disease, Satan's attacks, temptation, the world, lethargy, carnality. That's why Jesus taught His disciples to continually pray for deliverance from Satan and all his attempts to derail our walk with Christ.

When was the last time you prayed for God to deliver you from the evil one? If it wasn't today, you may want to stop and pray.

Salvation is not deliverance from hell alone, it is deliverance from sin.

CHARLES H. SPURGEON

WORDS OF GLORY

For Yours is the kingdom and the power and the glory forever. Amen.

MATTHEW 6:13C

Many liturgical churches sing the *Gloria Patri* (Latin for the first two words, "Glory be to the Father") at the end of a church service. Other less formal churches sing what is simply called "The Doxology" or "The Common Doxology": "Praise God from whom all blessings flow..." Both are Christian doxologies (Greek *doxa* = glory, *logos* = word), short hymns of praise to God.

Jesus taught His disciples to conclude their prayers with a doxology: "For Yours is the kingdom and the power and the glory forever. Amen." Even though this doxology is omitted from many ancient manuscripts and may not be part of the original text, its theological value is undiminished. Concluding a prayer with words of praise to God is a way of saying, "It is Your kingdom resources, Your power, and Your glory that determine when and how You will answer. I trust You, Lord." That's really the purpose of prayer—to bring us into an ever-deepening and more-trusting relationship with God.

Consider creating your own doxology—or use the one Jesus created—to affirm your commitment to God's kingdom, power, and glory when you pray.

The Christian ought to be a living doxology.

MARTIN LUTHER

KNOW THYSELF

O LORD, You have searched me and known me.

PSALM 139:1

The ancient philosopher said, "Know thyself," but that's hard to do. Jeremiah 17:9 says, "The heart is deceitful above all things, and desperately wicked; who can know it?" The apostle Paul cautioned us against being too quick to approve ourselves or condemn others, saying, "I care very little if I am judged by you... indeed, I do not even judge myself. My conscience is clear, but that does not make me innocent. It is the Lord who judges me" (1 Corinthians 4:3-4, NIV).

We must be careful about being overly self-introspective, and about being too quick to criticize others. As fallen creatures, we're capable of wounding ourselves and others with misguided judgments.

Yes, be discerning about right and wrong, and be willing to properly admonish someone when the Spirit leads; but remember there's only One who can actually read the heart. How much better to say with the psalmist, "Search me, O God, and know my heart; try me, and know my anxieties; and see if there is any wicked way in me, and lead me in the way everlasting."

The best of (us) are too apt to judge rashly, and harshly, and unjustly; but (God's) judgment is always according to truth.

MATTHEW HENRY

DAVID JEREMIAH

THE SACRIFICES OF STEWARDSHIP

And let us not grow weary while doing good,
for in due season we shall reap if we do not lose heart.

GALATIANS 6:9

The pastor of a small Baptist church in Texas wrote to an oil millionaire, requesting a donation for his congregation's building fund campaign. The tycoon declined, and added this to his letter of refusal: "And as for this Christianity thing, it seems to me to be nothing but give, give, give." The pastor wrote the oilman back and thanked him for articulating the best definition of Christianity he had ever heard.

Often, when we hear the word *stewardship,* our minds race immediately to thoughts of money. Stewardship includes returning a portion of the financial blessings God has given us, but that doesn't exhaust its true meaning. Genuine stewardship involves the deliberate and faithful caretaking of the Master's resources for the furtherance of His kingdom and His ultimate glory.

It also entails risk: the risk of loss, the risk of vulnerability, and the risk of possible criticism by others. But the rewards for being a faithful steward far outweigh any risk involved. Besides the joy we experience from giving of ourselves in this life, we are promised the recompense of our Lord when He says, "Well done, thou good and faithful servant."

For it is in giving that we receive.

FRANCIS OF ASSISI

A WORKING FAITH

Show me your faith without your works,
and I will show you my faith by my works.

Ask the average man or woman on the street what the prerequisite is for a person to go to heaven, and the response you are likely to receive is that he or she must "be a good person." This view might be termed the "merit system" of salvation. On a practical level, this belief is untenable because it is impossible to know in this life how many good works are sufficient to win paradise. But more importantly, the "merit system" of salvation is contrary to the clear teaching of Holy Scripture.

The Bible says that "all have sinned" (Romans 3:23), and that a man is justified—that is, has had his sins forgiven and has established a right relationship with God—by faith alone in Jesus Christ (Galatians 2:16) apart from good works.

But have good works no role to play in our salvation? Yes, they validate and make manifest to others that the faith we profess is indeed a saving faith in Jesus Christ. And because this kind of faith produces good works, those who view our actions will also see the light of Jesus and glorify God the Father (Matthew 5:16). So let your faith be revealed in your actions today.

We are justified by faith alone, but by a faith that is not alone.

JOHN CALVIN

JULY 24

BRINGING IN THE SHEAVES

Do the work of an evangelist.

2 TIMOTHY 4:5

Fritz Kreisler (1875-1962), the world-famous violinist, earned a fortune with his concerts and compositions, but he generously gave most of it away. So, when he discovered an exquisite violin on one of his trips, he wasn't able to buy it. Later, having raised enough money to meet the asking price, he returned to the seller, hoping to purchase that beautiful instrument. But to his great dismay, it had been sold to a collector. Kreisler made his way to the new owner's home and offered to buy the violin. The collector said it had become his prized possession, and he would not sell it. Keenly disappointed, Kreisler was about to leave when he had an idea. "Could I play the instrument once more before it is consigned to silence?" he asked. Permission was granted, and the great virtuoso filled the room with such heart-moving music that the collector's emotions were deeply stirred. "I have no right to keep that to myself," he exclaimed. "It's yours, Mr. Kreisler. Take it into the world, and let people hear it."

We have a message to share. Our heavenly Father created us as exquisite instruments, and the beautiful music we are to make is the Good News of salvation through faith in Jesus Christ. We were made to be played.

The church has many tasks but only one mission.

ARTHUR PRESTON

JULY 25

ELOQUENT SILENCE

In the multitude of words sin is not lacking,
but he who restrains his lips is wise.

PROVERBS 10:19

The nineteenth-century French playwright, Victor Hugo, once wrote, "Tomorrow, if all literature was to be destroyed and it was left to me to retain one work only, I should save Job." Writers love Job's literary beauty, but the average reader, after just a few of the book's 42 chapters, begins to wonder if the speakers were being paid by the word. Eloquent as they may be, their words go on forever.

It is not until Job encounters God Himself that light begins to invade Job's dark confusion. And therein lies an illustration of Proverbs 10:19 (generally, the fewer words spoken, the better) and James 1:19 (be swift to listen, slow to speak). Man's wisdom is limited. There is only so much we can say about life's mysteries before we begin, at best, to repeat ourselves, and, at worst, to speculate—both of which Job's friends (and Job himself) were guilty. But when we accompany the suffering to God's throne of grace, there is where new light can be found (Hebrews 4:16).

When ministering to the suffering, Job's friends' first act may be our best: sitting silently and empathetically as the Spirit of God in us reaches out to a hurting heart.

Eloquent silence often is better than eloquent speech.

UNKNOWN

DAVID JEREMIAH

DAILY INVESTMENT

If anyone desires to come after Me, let him deny himself,
and take up his cross daily, and follow Me.

LUKE 9:23

All over the country, people are suffering the consequences of desiring rewards without investment. Many bought houses and cars they couldn't afford; and because finance companies were willing to fund those bad loans, they ignored good judgment and only saw the rewards they could have with little to no sacrifice. Those rewards they thought they could have so easily are in jeopardy or gone completely; and the reality that we can't have something for nothing is here to stay.

In the same way, we must invest our time, our thoughts, and our prayers into time with God if we desire the indescribable blessings He has to offer us. We so often live on the fringe of an amazing life with God, never quite reaching our full potential because we fail to invest in knowing God's will and His way.

The Bible says, *"Blessed is the man who listens to me, watching daily at my gates"* (Proverbs 8:34). Are we listening and watching daily? Are we investing now for a future of promised blessing?

To place ourselves in range of God's choicest gifts,
we have to walk with God, work with God, lean on God,
cling to God, come to have the sense and feel of God,
refer all things to God.

CORNELIUS PLANTINGA, JR.

THE HEART OF CHRIST

So we, being many, are one body in Christ,
and individually members of one another.

ROMANS 12:5

If a person walks into any church in any town across America on any given Sunday, they will most likely find something they don't like about it. Whether it's the worship style, what version of the Bible they use, the décor of the sanctuary, or how many people attend, someone is bound to have a problem with something in the church because we're all different.

The good news is that God doesn't focus on those minor issues within a church. He's more interested in whether or not a church can look beyond its members' differences and become united in its effort to carry out His purpose in the world. Whatever church is prepared to do that will get the honor of being involved in His work.

There are a lot of amazing things happening through churches right now, including providing for those displaced by the failing housing market, mobilizing thousands to help those dying of AIDS, and holding job fairs for those who have been victimized by the declining economy.

Look around. Christ's heart is shining through these acts for all to see and witness His love.

It does not take a perfect church
to introduce a man to the perfect Christ.

RICHARD WOODSOME

A HUMBLE SPIRIT

Better to be of a humble spirit with the lowly,
than to divide the spoil with the proud.

PROVERBS 16:19

In his book on humility, Andrew Murray wrote, "There is nothing so divine and heavenly as being the servant and helper to all. The faithful servant, who recognizes his position, finds a real pleasure in supplying the wants of the master or his guests."

Because we're infected with the blood disease of pride, it's easy to take offense when we encounter haughty friends. We live in a highly competitive society, and there are a thousand subtle little ways of signaling our self-importance. When others do the same, we inwardly resent it. Oh, what a tangled knot it becomes. Only the knife of true biblical humility can cut through it.

One of the best ways to practice Christlikeness is to start each day saying, "Who can I serve today? To whom can I minister?" Remember that Jesus Christ never ministered to a perfect person, for He was the only one of those in sight. He came to serve imperfect people like us; and He bids us do the same.

The humble man feels no jealousy or envy. He can praise
God when others are preferred and blessed before Him.

ANDREW MURRAY

PERCEPTION VERSUS REALITY

Why do the wicked live and become old, yes, become mighty in power?

JOB 21:7

Most people agree that perception is (at least) 90 percent of reality. In other words, perception is more influential than reality; what we perceive to be true influences us more than what is true.

Take the perception many Christians have of the wealthy and worldly. It appears that everything they touch turns to gold, that they have more than enough money to smooth out life's daily inconveniences, and to do whatever they want without the limitations experienced by the average person—especially the average Christian. Is that really true? Does the external appearance of abundance and carefree living mean those without God are truly happy? Asaph, the psalmist, thought so until he contemplated the end of those without God: "Until I went into the sanctuary of God; then I understood their end" (Psalm 73:17b). The true test of human contentedness is not wealth, but the answer to the questions, "Why am I here?" and, "What happens when I die?"

If you are ever prone to envy those in the world, pray for them while thanking God that you know why you are here and where you will spend eternity.

> *The humble Christian is far happier in*
> *a cottage than the wicked in a palace.*

A. W. PINK

JULY 30

FOLLOWING DIRECTIONS: ONE WAY

I will give them one heart and one way, that they may fear Me forever.

JEREMIAH 32:39

Arecent study from the Pew Forum on Religion & Public Life found that large numbers of people now engage in multiple religious practices, mixing features of various faiths. Many blend Christianity with elements of Eastern and New Age beliefs, such as reincarnation, astrology, and even the occult. Because of this politically-correct pluralism, many Christians are questioning whether Jesus Christ is really the only way to God.

If pollsters could ask Jesus that question, they would get a clear-cut answer: "I am the way, the truth, and the life. No one comes to the Father except through Me" (John 14:6).

If they asked the apostle Peter, they would be told: "Salvation is found in no one else, for there is no other name under heaven given to men by which we must be saved" (Acts 4:12, NIV).

Going the wrong way down a one-way street is deadly. It doesn't matter how sincerely intentioned the driver is, or how educated, or how broad-minded—it can still get him killed. Don't try to paint over the one-way signs of Scripture. Just make sure you're going the right way.

Jesus is not one of many ways to approach God,
nor is He the best of several ways; He is the only way.

A. W. TOZER

JOURNEY   223

THE REAL McCOY

*But he who looks into the perfect law of liberty
and continues in it, and is not a forgetful hearer
but a doer of the work, this one will be blessed in what he does.*

JAMES 1:25

Elijah McCoy invented a cup that automatically dripped oil and it was installed on locomotives. Soon, everyone wanted a "McCoy Cup" because it greatly increased engine efficiency. Because of its popularity, there were many inferior copies made; so many in fact, that train engineers had to demand "the real McCoy" in order to get the genuine article.

On the surface, many people appear to have a blessed life. They have the house, the car, the vacations, and the career. But as we have all witnessed during the recent economic downturn, those things are not the mark of a blessed life; they are merely an inferior copy of "the real McCoy."

A genuinely blessed life is one that is lived in the obedience and direction of God despite circumstances and regardless of material possessions. It is experiencing blessings in ways the world cannot understand or offer, and it's only available to those who seek His will and His way.

If you desire to have a life that is truly blessed by God, don't settle for an imitation. Ask God to lead you to "the real McCoy."

God's commands are designed to guide you to life's very best.

HENRY BLACKABY

AUGUST

HANG IN THERE

Hezekiah gave encouragement to all the Levites
who taught the good knowledge of the Lord.

2 CHRONICLES 30:22

Motivational expert Ron White tells of being in Navy boot camp. He was tired, intimidated, scared, and hungry. Another sailor who was about to graduate passed him in the hallway and, seeing his fatigued expression, whispered out of the side of his mouth, "Hang in there. . . . You can do it."

Ron never learned the sailor's name, and he never saw him again. But those words shot through him like electricity, and he replayed them each night before going to bed. They revamped his attitude, and Ron persevered until he finished the program.

On graduation day, Ron saw three sailors leaning against the wall. They were tired, intimidated, scared, and hungry. Walking over to them, he whispered, "Hang in there. . . . You can do it." From the expressions on their faces, he knew his words had hit home.

In 2 Chronicles 30, Hezekiah encouraged the Levites who went on to encourage the people to whom they ministered. Encouragement isn't just a shot in the dark. It's a chain-reaction that passes from person to person until it travels far beyond its point of origin. Has someone encouraged you recently? Pass it on.

The best way to cheer yourself up is to cheer everybody else up.

MARK TWAIN

PATIENT OR PEEVISH?

Then the LORD said, "Is it right for you to be angry?"

JONAH 4:4

Newspapers recently reported about a Chicago murder suspect who attacked his own attorney. The lawyer had advised the plaintiff to stop "mouthing off" during jury selection, but the alleged murderer didn't like the advice. He punched his defender in the face. Now the plaintiff comes to court with his hands, feet, and head strapped to a chair and his mouth covered. He also has a new lawyer.

It's odd how irritable we can be at others when the fault lies purely with us. We often resent those who try to help us. We may really be angry at ourselves; but our frustration erupts toward our husband, wife, coworker, teacher, or church worker. Sometimes we can even be angry at God, as Jonah was when God spared Nineveh. But whenever we lash out, it's wise to listen to the Lord, who has a way of asking: "Is it right for you to be angry?"

He is our advocate who works for our good, and our friends seek our welfare. Be patient today rather than peevish, and thankful rather than resentful.

Anger never made anybody the happier.

JOHN BOWRING IN AN 1834 BOOK,
Minor Morals for Young People

AUGUST 3

ENERGIZED

*Why are you cast down, O my soul? And why are you
disquieted within me? Hope in God; For I shall yet praise Him,
the help of my countenance and my God.*

PSALM 43:5

A man flying home from a mission's project was weary.
He worried that his overseas trip had been only partially
productive, and dreaded coming home to his desktop of work.
Pulling out his Bible, he began thumbing through it; and, like
a flash, certain verses about joy came to mind. He reached for a
pen and paper and began writing them down: *In Your presence is
fullness of joy. . . . These things I have spoken to you, that . . . your joy
may be full. . . . The joy of the Lord is your strength. . . .*

By the time he finished, he had a list of fifteen "Joy Verses"
from the Bible, and those verses energized him like a divine tonic.

We often need a jolt of energy to make it through the day,
and the power of God's Word applied by God's Spirit gives us
the continual strength we need. He energizes us. Perhaps that's
what Paul had in mind when he spoke of God's *"energy, which so
powerfully works in me"* (Colossians 1:29 NIV).

Do you need renewed strength today? Remember that
spending time with Jesus energizes the soul.

God helping me, I will not rest until endued with power from on high.

D. L. MOODY

DAVID JEREMIAH

AUGUST 4

CHECK YOUR BALANCES

Therefore take heed to yourselves.

ACTS 20:28

A bank recently advertised its services with the words: "Check your balances." Using online tools, customers can instantly check the balances on any and all of their accounts.

Perhaps you need to take a moment today to check your balances in another sense. There's the private you and the public you, and one of the secrets to good mental health is keeping the two balanced. Jesus ministered to the multitudes, and then He withdrew to the wilderness to be alone. Few of us want to be alone, but if we're always surrounded by noise and people, we'll not have the necessary quiet to recharge our batteries.

Our need for independence is balanced by our need for interaction, and our craving for solitude is matched by a need for society.

If you're alone too much, do something about it today. Volunteer. Make a phone call. Invite someone to tea. Get out and go to church.

If you're too rushed and busy, slow down a little. Take time for Bible reading. Take a little stroll through the park with this book in hand, and find a sunny bench to sit and read awhile. Take heed to yourself—and check your balances.

Lord, grant me the blessing of a balanced life!

UNKNOWN

THE TOUCH OF THE MASTER

Then Jesus put out His hand and touched him.

MATTHEW 8:3

In his book, *How to Really Love Your Child,* Dr. Ross Campbell extols the power of touch. Hugging is important, of course, but so are pats on the back, gentle pokes in the ribs, tousling their hair, and appropriate rough-housing or high-fiving. One of the ways parents convey love for their children is by appropriate physical contact.

That's true for us all. The next time you read through one of the four Gospels, notice how often Jesus touched people. His power and love were conveyed through the touch of the Master's hands.

There are few things more loving or affirming than the right physical contact with another human being. We have a biblical warrant through the example of Jesus.

Have you hugged your husband or wife today? Have you given your child a friendly tussle? Have you warmly greeted a friend by an outstretched hand and a hearty handshake? Have you rested your arm around the shoulder of someone needing cheer? Have you given a few pats on the back along the way?

Remember—you can't give a hug without receiving one in return. Today reach out and touch someone!

A hug is a handshake from the heart.

ANONYMOUS

DAVID JEREMIAH

THE KING ETERNAL

And He has...a name written:
KING OF KINGS AND LORD OF LORDS.

REVELATION 19:16

There aren't many kings left anymore. Monarchies—a form of government in which power resides with an individual until death, then passes to the heir—saw steep declines in the last century. Much of the world was ruled by royalty in 1900. Today only forty-four nations have monarchs, sixteen of which are commonwealth realms recognizing Queen Elizabeth as their head of state.

Citizens living in a monarchy have a better understanding of the word "sovereign" than those who don't, but few live in a realm where the monarch possesses absolute sovereignty. An absolute sovereign has unlimited right to control everything and everyone within his or her territory. In politics, this creates reigns of terror. In the divine realm, it gives unlimited peace when we accept the absolute sovereignty of Jesus Christ. He is the King of the Jews (Matthew 2:2), the King of Israel (John 1:49), the King of righteousness (Hebrews 7:2), the King eternal (1 Timothy 1:17), and the King of Kings (Revelation 19:16).

Let His absolute reign comfort you today.

My choice is King Jesus; He's reigning above,
His service is gladness, His banner is love.

E. E. HEWITT

WISDOM FROM ABOVE

*The wisdom that is from above is first pure,
then peaceable, gentle, willing to yield, full of mercy and
good fruits, without partiality and without hypocrisy.*

JAMES 3:17

Last spring, local newspapers in St. Cloud, Minnesota, reported that a laptop computer fell out of a medical helicopter and tumbled through the air, hitting the ground with a crash that sounded like a gunshot. It landed inches from a ten-year-old boy. The little fellow ran to his aunt, crying, "Something just fell out of the sky and almost hit me!"

That's not what the Bible has in mind when it talks about the "wisdom from above." No matter how much data is on a laptop, it can't crash into your brain. Only God's wisdom can descend from the sky and change your thinking.

The Bible speaks of two kinds of wisdom—wisdom from below and from above. God's wisdom has little to do with age, and spiritual maturity isn't determined by experience. It is a matter of having an open heart toward the Lord and an open Bible on your desk. The books of Proverbs and James are great places for those wanting to understand the wisdom from above. Why not scan one of those books and find a verse to memorize today?

No chain of pearl you wear so adorns you as wisdom.

THOMAS WATSON

Living on Purpose

*May He grant you according to your heart's desire,
and fulfill all your purpose.*

Psalm 20:4

When big cities swelter under the summer sun, sometimes a fire hydrant is opened to provide a soaring fountain of water to cool off children. But attach a fire hose to that same hydrant and the water turns from a spray to a laser that would send a child tumbling.

It's all about focus—and focus is at the heart of life and ministry as well. Christ's apostles were able to turn their world "upside down" (Acts 17:6) because they were focused on Christ's purpose for their lives: go into all the world, preach the Gospel, and make disciples in every nation (Matthew 28:19-20). Paul was focused. When writing to the Corinthians he said he "determined not to know anything among [them] except Jesus Christ and Him crucified" (1 Corinthians 2:2). And he also wrote that he had only one goal (purpose) in life: to win "the prize of the upward call of God in Christ Jesus" (Philippians 3:14). Paul was nothing if not focused, living his life on purpose.

Does any purpose in your life supersede that of living a life pleasing to God? Purpose today to "walk worthy of the Lord, fully pleasing Him" (Colossians 1:10).

Velocity is no substitute for direction or purpose.

John Blanchard

AUGUST 9

MEMORIES BITTER AND SWEET

Oh, that I were as in months past, as in the days when God watched over me.

JOB 29:2

America in the 1950s is what some people refer to as the "good old days." In fact, a popular television sitcom that aired from 1974 to 1984 captured the era with its title: *Happy Days*. History's largest war was over, American factories were producing baby strollers instead of bullets, a hero-general was president, and the revolutionary 1960s had not even been thought of.

Job and his family enjoyed their own *Happy Days* before their lives were crushed by adversity. And from that point on, Job had two kinds of memories: the sweet and the severe. And he longed for his happier days: "When my steps were bathed with cream, and the rock poured out rivers of oil for me!" (Job 29:6) But it was his adversity and suffering that ultimately allowed Job to create even better memories—memories of an encounter with God that changed his life forever and for the better.

Every person has both kinds of memories. But we live in the present, not the past. Ask God for grace to find His lessons in every event and every memory, to let go of the past, rejoice in the present, and reach for the future—"the prize of the upward call of God in Christ Jesus" (Philippians 3:13-14).

Meditation is the best help to memory.

MATTHEW HENRY

The Barnabas Committee

*Joses . . . was also named Barnabas by the apostles
(which is translated Son of Encouragement).*

Acts 4:36

Popular conference speaker Jeanne Zornes has frequently told of a low point in her life. She was thirty and single, attending Bible college, struggling with finances, fighting sickness, facing constant car repairs, and watching her parents battle life-threatening illnesses.

One morning, her professor surprised the class by admitting he was facing some overwhelming burdens in his own life. He asked the students to pray for him. Jeanne and her friends formed a "Barnabas Committee" to encourage him; and throughout the semester, they sent him notes and little tokens of their concern and prayers.

As she did so, Jeanne discovered the truth of Proverbs 11:25: Those who encourage others will themselves be encouraged. "Even though my problems didn't go away," she wrote, "my reaching out to others helped keep my focus on God's love and power."

Why not think of yourself as a one-person Barnabas Committee, devoted to encouraging others. Multitudes need a word of encouragement today, especially young people. They are big bundles of potential who can do great things for the Lord if spurred on by our encouragement. See who you can "Barnabize" today.

Encouragers see potential where others only see problems.

David Jeremiah

AUGUST 11

MARK THIS!

*Now Barnabas was determined to take with them John called Mark.
But Paul insisted that they should not take with them the one who had
departed from them in Pamphylia.*

ACTS 15:37-38

When we read the Gospel of Mark, we're reading an inspired account penned by a man whose prior fickleness and failure had caused the breakup of the greatest missionary team in history. Paul and Barnabas parted ways because of John Mark, who had deserted them on an earlier mission. Paul was fed up with the young man, but Barnabas wanted to give him another chance.

Well, the Lord certainly gave him another chance. In the end, John Mark learned from his mistakes and became so valuable to the Kingdom that even Paul changed his mind about him. "Get Mark and bring him with you, for he is useful to me for ministry," wrote Paul at the end of his life (2 Timothy 4:11). And it was this man—John Mark—who later, apparently aiding Simon Peter, wrote the second Gospel.

Learning from past failures leads to future success. God doesn't easily give up on us. Remember that when you fumble and fail. A failure is often the back door to success.

*Our failures can be stepping-stones
to a more meaningful relationship with God.*

ERWIN W. LUTZER

THE ALMOST FORGOTTEN BEATITUDE

And remember the words of the Lord Jesus, that He said,
"It is more blessed to give than to receive."

ACTS 20:35

*T*his verse gives us an almost forgotten beatitude. It was spoken by
Jesus, but not recorded by Matthew, Mark, Luke, or John. The
apostle Paul knew of it, however, and recalled it in Acts 20, thus
preserving it for us in Scripture.

This verse gives us a super-beatitude. There are many beatitudes
in the Bible when a sentence begins with the words *Blessed is .
. .* or *Blessed are . . . .* But only once in the Bible does the phrase
"more blessed" occur. This verse tells us how to go beyond
blessing to greater blessing.

This verse gives us a double blessing. First, there is the blessing
of receiving, which is a very me-like thing. God created us as
recipients. He is the Source, the Supply, the Endless Provider who
gives universal blessings, daily blessings, and spiritual blessings.

But there is one blessing greater than receiving. It's the blessing
of giving. Why is it more blessed to give than to receive? When
we receive, we're acting like ourselves; but when we give, we're
acting like God. Receiving is me-like. Giving is Christ-like.

Never forget that at the very heart of the
Gospel is the whole principle of giving.

STEPHEN OLFORD

To Have and to Hold

And the Lord God said, "It is not good that man should be alone;
I will make him a helper comparable to him."

Genesis 2:18

Comedian Red Skelton once explained the secret of his happy marriage. "Two times a week, we go to a nice restaurant, have a little beverage, good food, and companionship," he said. "She goes on Tuesdays, I go on Fridays."

He was joking, of course, but his words remind us that companionship and partnership are essential to good marriages. Healthy couples focus on the three "Hs" of Home.

They engage in *holy* pursuits—praying with one another and working together for the Lord. If your wife is working in a children's Sunday school class, why not join her and make it a joint ministry?

Healthy couples also forge some joint *hobbies*, things they enjoy doing together as friends, like sports, gardening, traveling, cooking, or collecting.

Healthy couples also *hold* each other—to have and to hold, says the traditional marriage vows. A happy marriage enjoys an abundance of physical embracing and affection.

Holiness, hobbies, and holding—couples who cultivate these things grow stronger as the years go by.

We always hold hands. If I let go, she shops!

Red Skelton

David Jeremiah

A TUNIC FOR JOSEPH

Now Israel loved Joseph more than all his children, because he was the
son of his old age. Also he made him a tunic of many colors.

GENESIS 37:3

Jacob, grandson of Abraham, had twelve sons of his own. The
next to youngest was Joseph, a son of Jacob's old age. For some
reason (it couldn't have been only Jacob's old age since there was
another son, Benjamin, born after Joseph) Jacob loved Joseph
more than all the others. And to show his love, Jacob made Joseph
a "tunic of many colors."

Jacob's choice of Joseph for reasons known only to himself is
not unlike God's choosing of believers in Christ: *"He chose us in
[Christ] before the foundation of the world"* (Ephesians 1:4). And as
the many colors of Joseph's coat represented the many blessings
that would come to Joseph, so God has *"blessed us with every
spiritual blessing in the heavenly places"* (Ephesians 1:3). Joseph's
beautiful coat was a coat of grace—undeserved, unexpected,
unexplainable. So the blessings of the believer in Christ are
"according to the riches of His grace" (Ephesians 1:7).

Are you wearing the coat of grace—the tunic of God's
blessings—every day? Don't try to earn it. Just receive it with
gratitude for the gift it is.

Grace is the good pleasure of God that inclines
Him to bestow benefits upon the undeserving.

A. W. TOZER

AUGUST 15

UNSEARCHABLE

Great is the LORD, and greatly to be praised;
and His greatness is unsearchable.

PSALM 145:3

Our God is too big to be contained in facts, formulas, or finite minds. Trying to explain Him is like a child trying to lecture about quantum physics to his classmates at nursery school. If we could comprehend the infinite God and pack Him up within our soggy brains, He would not be eternal, illimitable, and transcendent. If we could remove the mystery of God, He would not be God after all. As theologian Wayne Grudem wrote, "It is spiritually healthy for us to acknowledge openly that God's very being is far greater than we can ever comprehend."

Another scholar, Henry Morris, adds an important point. Speaking of the person of God, he said, "We cannot really comprehend this with our minds, but we can believe it and rejoice with our hearts." We can sing praise to God who reigns above, the God of all creation, the God of power, the God of love, the God of our salvation. The characteristics of God cannot be fully known by our limited understanding; we just know He is mighty, merciful, and full of majesty.

If God were small enough to be understood,
He would not be big enough to be worshipped.

EVELYN UNDERHILL, QUOTED BY ELIZABETH ELLIOT IN
Secure in the Everlasting Arms.

EMPTY CUPS

*For My people have committed two evils: they have forsaken Me,
the fountain of living waters, and hewn themselves cisterns—
broken cisterns that can hold no water.*

JEREMIAH 2:13

In his seventeenth-century devotional classic, *A Serious Call to a Devout and Holy Life*, William Law described a thirsty man who kept holding up one empty cup after another to his lips. No matter how beautiful the cups were, Law observed, and no matter how glittery and golden they seemed, the poor man only grew thirstier while lifting them to his mouth—for empty cups cannot quench the thirst.

Many people today are seeking inner fulfillment and emotional peace by lifting one empty cup after another to their lips. But Jesus said, *"If anyone thirsts, let him come to Me and drink. . . . Out of his heart will flow rivers of living water"* (John 7:37-38).

Without the risen Christ in our homes and hearts, we're missing the kind of encouragement we need to keep going. He is the true source of encouragement; and as we partake of the living waters of His grace, we'll overflow with true encouragement into the lives of others.

Put down your empty cups, and drink richly of Christ!

*Awaken your soul into a zealous desire of that solid happiness
which is only to be found in recourse to God.*

WILLIAM LAW

FIRES AND FLOODS

When you pass through the waters, I will be with you; and through the rivers, they shall not overflow you. When you walk through the fire, you shall not be burned, nor shall the flame scorch you.

ISAIAH 43:2

Anyone who has seen a rampaging river or a burning house knows the terror of flood and flame. The destructive power of fire and water is dreadful to see. Yet these are the dramatic images Isaiah uses to describe our own trials and troubles in life.

The Lord hasn't promised to keep us out of hardship, but He has given us two great promises to sustain us when we're in it: He will be with us, and our troubles will not overwhelm us. *I will be with you… They shall not overflow you.*

Remember how the Lord brought the Israelites through the waters of the Red Sea in Exodus 14, and how He stood with Shadrach, Meshach, and Abed-Nego in the fiery furnace of Daniel 3? If a problem is pressing down on you today, claim Isaiah 43:2. Picture the Lord as though He were really beside you, for He is. Trust Him to keep you from being swept away or consumed by your circumstances, for He has promised that His grace is sufficient.

When through fiery trials, thy pathway shall lie, my grace, all sufficient, shall be thy supply.

JOHN KEITH

Making Deposits

I have no greater joy than to hear that my children walk in truth.

3 John 1:4

Bill Cosby once quipped, "If the new father feels bewildered and even defeated, let him take comfort from the fact that whatever he does in any fathering situation has a fifty percent chance of being right."

You can increase the odds! In 1 Thessalonians 2:11-12, the apostle Paul tells the Thessalonian Christians that he dealt with them as a father deals with his own children, *"encouraging, comforting, and urging you to live lives worthy of God"* (NIV).

Those are the three things we must do for our children if we're to have the joy of seeing them walk in truth. Children need our encouragement. Have you told your child today that you're proud of him or her? Pointed out a strength? Thanked them for a task well done? Given them a high-five?

Children need our comfort. Take time to hold, reassure, and gently share a verse of comfort with your child in a moment of disappointment or discouragement.

Children need to hear us urging them to live God-worthy lives, directing them to Christ and to His Word. What can you do today to encourage, comfort, and urge your child?

*Each day of our lives we make deposits
in the memory banks of our children.*

Charles Swindoll

THE REFINER'S FIRE

*... you have been grieved by various trials, that the
genuineness of your faith, being much more precious
than gold that perishes, though it is tested by fire, may be
found to praise, honor, and glory at the revelation of Jesus Christ.*

1 PETER 1:6-7

Most people think a goldsmith's furnace is used to extract gold from its ore and burn away the dross and impurities, purifying the metal. That's only half right. It also makes the gold pliable. Alexander of Neckham, a twelfth-century Englishman, wrote of a goldsmith who plunged the gold into the fire to soften it. As Neckham watched, the metal was molded into the required form using tools to mold, smooth, and polish the surface.

As Christians, it's not hard to see the analogy. We become more sensitive to God during hard times. We fall to our knees in helpless dependence on His grace. We rediscover the power of prayer, and we claim promises in the Bible hitherto neglected. In the process, the fire eliminates those things that might be obscuring our vision of our Heavenly Father, and we are molded into the image of our Lord.

The Refiner's fire is always for His glory and our good.

*When God puts us in the furnace, His hand is on
the thermostat and His eye is on the clock.*

AUTHOR UNKNOWN

DAVID JEREMIAH

FIVE-STAR RESTORATIONS

He who has begun a good work in you will complete it....

PHILIPPIANS 1:6

If you have a lot of money and like to travel, check into five-star hotels that have the word "restored" in their descriptions. There's a hotel in Venice, for example, in a masterfully restored fourteenth-century residence filled with Murano glass chandeliers, carved pink marble columns, stained glass, and gilded ceilings. In Amsterdam, a luxury hotel was created when a series of seventeenth-century canal houses were restored and turned into 239 unique rooms.

Most of us don't have the money for five-star travel, but we can all appreciate the craft of restoration. It happens when something broken down is renovated. Somehow the architects and builders manage to make it more magnificent than it was originally. Restoration is more than restoring. It is improving.

That's what God does with us. We're under construction, and we may have broken-down areas in our lives. His aim isn't simply to restore, but to edify, improve, and perfect that which concerns us. When God restored Job's life, for example, He left him better than before. He can do the same with you.

If your progress seems slow while it appears those around
you are engaged in remarkable success, just remember:
Patience! God is not finished with you yet!

TED W. ENGSTROM

CHERISHING THE WORD

The grass withers, the flower fades,
but the word of our God stands forever.

ISAIAH 40:8

We occasionally read stories—perhaps it has happened to you—of people who find a box of letters in an attic, letters long since forgotten or thought lost, that provide a window into the world of departed loved ones. The words immediately create memories and images of those precious to us—we can hear their laughter, feel their touch, even taste their tears. Once in hand, we vow never to let treasured words escape us again.

When blessings are committed to writing, they can be savored and enjoyed time after time. No wonder archaeologists and linguists treat ancient biblical manuscripts like they are made of gold. Indeed, they are more precious than gold (Psalm 19:10)! The Bible has been called God's love letter to mankind. If we cherish letters from family members and friends, how much more ought we to cherish the love letter we've received from God? It's one thing to honor the Bible in a place of safekeeping, but it's an even better thing to read and commit its words to heart and mind.

The frequency with which we read and reread a letter from someone is an indication of its importance to us.

When you read God's Word, you must constantly
be saying to yourself, "It is talking to me, and about me."

SØREN KIERKEGAARD

Night Fear

*The LORD will command His lovingkindness in the daytime,
and in the night His song shall be with me.*

Psalm 42:8

Research shows that newborn babies have no fear of the dark. After all, they've just spent nine months in the darkness of the womb. We put nightlights in the nursery so we can see them, not so they'll be unafraid. But a strange thing happens as we start growing. Many children develop night fears, imagining creatures outside their windows or monsters under their beds. As we age, those nighttime fears become more sophisticated. Many of us struggle every night with letting go of our worries so we can sleep.

Listen to what the psalmist wrote: *The day is Yours, the night also is Yours.... He who keeps (you) shall neither slumber nor sleep.... I will both lie down in peace, and sleep, for You alone, O Lord, make me dwell in safety... You will light my lamp; The LORD my God will enlighten my darkness... I meditate on You in the night watches.... He gives His beloved sleep.* (Psalm 74:16; 121:4; 4:8; 18:28; 63:6; 127:2).

As Spurgeon said: "They slumber sweetly whom faith rocks to sleep. No pillow so soft as a promise."

*If the Lord's going to stay awake all night,
I'm going to sleep! There's no use in us both staying up!*

Anonymous

Promises Aweigh? Never!

This hope we have as an anchor of the soul, both sure and steadfast,
and which enters the Presence behind the veil.

Hebrews 6:19

Most people are familiar with the fight song of the United States Naval Academy, "Anchors Aweigh." Fewer are familiar with the meaning of "aweigh." An anchor is "aweigh" when it has been lifted off the seabed and is suspended in midwater. The call, "Anchors aweigh" is given to signal that the ship is free to move; it is no longer tethered to the seabed.

One phrase you will never hear—or *should* never hear—called out from a biblical pulpit is, "Promises aweigh!" That would mean that our spiritual anchor—the hope we have in the person and promises of God through Jesus Christ—was changing position. The writer to the Hebrews said that our hope is "an anchor of the soul, both sure and steadfast." And what is our hope? It is two-fold: the promise and oath of God Almighty (Hebrews 6:17). In other words, our hope is in God's character and His Word. Because God is true, His Word is true and can never be broken—so said Jesus Christ in John 10:35.

Regardless of how circumstances move about you, you will never hear, "Promises aweigh!" God's promises are "both sure and steadfast," an anchor for your soul.

Let thy hope of heaven master thy fear of death.

William Gurnall

GOD'S R&R

And [Jonah] said, "I cried out to the Lord because of my affliction,
and He answered me. Out of the belly of Sheol I cried,
and You heard my voice."

JONAH 2:2

Remember old Jonah? He had his personal plans made the day God approached him and asked him to go to Nineveh to preach to the Assyrians. Jonah thought better of that idea and jumped on a ship heading to Spain. Because this was not acceptable behavior for a prophet, the Lord allowed Jonah a few days of "R&R" (Rest and Regurgitation) to reconsider. After that, Jonah saw the light and also saw things God's way.

The very fact that God would set Jonah aside in an uncomfortable place in order to get his attention ought to be a warning for us. That doesn't mean that every time we disobey God He's going to do the same to us. But it apparently is an option. The psalmist David said, after he spent a number of months incapacitated because of sin, *"Do not be like the horse or like the mule . . . which must be harnessed with bit and bridle"* (Psalm 32:9). Instead, just do what you know you should. Is there anything God has asked you to do to which you still haven't said "Yes"?

Going where God wants you to go might not be nearly as unpleasant as the alternative.

It hurts when God has to PRY things out of our hand!

CORRIE TEN BOOM

OUR RÉSUMÉ

Your servant has killed both lion and bear; and this
uncircumcised Philistine will be like one of them.

1 SAMUEL 17:36

That was David's entire résumé for the job of giant slayer, but it was enough. As a lad, he had taken his flocks to picture-postcard sites—green pastures and still waters. But along the fringes of the wilderness lurked hidden dangers—ferocious animals, prowling, hungry for defenseless lambs. David had to remain vigilant; and on several occasions, he tossed down his harp and grabbed his slingshot, flying into action and saving his flock.

It was those wilderness experiences that taught David to aim with precision and to trust the Lord with conviction. It was a time of faith-building.

Whatever your circumstances right now, the Lord wants to use them as a training ground to prepare you for future tests. Life seldom gets easier with time. If we learn to trust God today, our faith will be stronger tomorrow.

Are you developing a résumé of faith?

When David was young in years, he was old in experience because he
had watched the hand of the Lord in its dealings with him. . . .

CHARLES SPURGEON

SATISFACTION GUARANTEED

You will show me the path of life; in Your presence is fullness of joy;
at Your right hand are pleasures forevermore.

PSALM 16:11

Legend says that a Nordstrom department store in Alaska—a clothing retailer—refunded cash to a man who insisted he bought snow tires at Nordstrom but wanted to return them. A cofounder of Home Depot claims one of his stores did the same thing. Supposedly, both stores wanted to prove that "the customer is always right."

As amazing as those claims are, no doubt even the best retailer has a limit to what it will do to satisfy a customer. But no such limits exist with God's plan to satisfy His children in eternity. The psalmist wrote that God plans to provide "fullness of joy" and "pleasures forevermore" for those who inherit the eternal kingdom of God. Not a single promise of God has ever been found to be untrue, and there is no reason to doubt God's guarantee of total satisfaction. It's possible to be jaded about such promises, but the policies of modern companies that don't back their guarantees should not make us suspicious of God's promises.

If you long for total satisfaction in this life, take God at His Word today. And prepare to be satisfied forever.

The enjoyment of God is the only happiness
with which our souls can be satisfied.

JONATHAN EDWARDS

BTS

*What I am doing you do not understand now,
but you will know after this.*

JOHN 13:7

Each week a popular television show takes viewers behind the cameras to show them how a movie was made, how the special effects were done, and what happened during the course of filming. It's titled *BTS: Behind the Scenes,* and it satisfies a certain curiosity felt by many movie-goers who ask, "How did they do that?"

If only we could see behind the scenes of our lives! The hidden hand of God's providence is directing and producing events in life that will result in our good and His glory. His hidden angels are watching over us in more ways than we know. His hidden Spirit is refreshing us with daily joy and strength. His Word, hidden in our hearts, is keeping us from sin.

Much of what God does in our lives is almost imperceptible. He works in ways we cannot see, and someday we'll understand.

You're in the starring role of your life. Make sure the Lord Jesus is writer, producer, and director of the story.

*I am not skilled to understand
What God hath willed, what God hath planned;
I only know that at His right hand
Is One Who is my Savior!*

DOROTHY GREENWELL

DAVID JEREMIAH

AUGUST 28

STORM WATCHING

My grace is sufficient for you,
for My strength is made perfect in weakness.

2 CORINTHIANS 12 :9

A woman was once asked what one of her favorite childhood memories was, and without hesitation she responded by saying, "Being woken up out of a sound sleep by my dad to sit at our bay window and watch the lightning crawl across the sky during a big thunderstorm." Watching storms was fascinating for her because she was in a safe, familiar place.

When storms arise in our life, it is comforting to have those around us who are familiar and safe—a spouse, children, or close friends. But when we are alone and facing uncertainty, we must remind ourselves that God controls not only the wind and the waves created by nature, but those created by life as well. We are never truly alone and facing the elements by ourselves; God will always walk through the storm with us.

During the uncertain and frightening storms of life, let us do as the psalmist "...in the shadow of Your wings I will make my refuge, until these calamities have passed by" (Psalm 57:1).

In the greatest difficulties, in the heaviest trials, in the deepest
poverty and necessities, He has never failed me.

GEORGE MULLER

ALL THINGS

*...predestined according to the purpose of Him who works
all things according to the counsel of His will.*

EPHESIANS 1:11

Our Lord's overruling providence not only works all things
for our good (Romans 8:28), but He works all things
according to the counsel of His will. His sovereign power can
even transform our faults, failures, and mistakes into tapestries
that bring Him glory. That doesn't give us an allowance to sin,
but it does invite us to bring our "goofs" to Jesus and place them
under His blood.

One evening just before an outreach service, evangelist
D. L. Moody lost his temper at a man who insulted him. Moody
actually shoved the man. "This meeting is killed," thought
a friend. "The (audience) will hardly be in a condition to be
influenced by anything Mr. Moody may say tonight." But Moody
rose with trembling voice; and his humble apology and tender
confession so moved the crowd that the tide turned, and the
meeting was touched with divine power.

This isn't an excuse for losing our tempers; but isn't it
wonderful to know that our Lord works all things—even our
faults—for our good and His glory?

*Our God is a God who not merely restores, but takes up our mistakes
and follies into His plan for us and brings good out of them.*

J. I. PACKER

AUGUST 30

DARE TO LIVE

Do not quench the Spirit.

1 THESSALONIANS 5:19

There was a very cautious man
    Who never laughed or played;
He never risked, he never tried,
He never sang or prayed.
And when he one day passed away
His insurance was denied;
For since he never really lived,
They claimed he never died![14]

We are told that in order to have an amazing life we should go sky diving, travel the world, and experience all that we can. But the real secret to an extraordinary life is heeding the call of Christ and following Him wherever He leads.

When we put off the invitation of salvation through Christ Jesus, tell the Lord we'll start serving Him tomorrow, or ignore the Holy Spirit's prompting to live a more godly life, we are missing out on really living.

Let us not miss one more moment. Choose to live life to its fullest with Him!

All of God's people are ordinary people who have been made extraordinary by the purpose He has given them.

OSWALD CHAMBERS

14 HTTP://WWW.SERMONILLUSTRATIONS.COM/A-Z/R/RISK.HTM

WHEN LESS IS MORE

Now may the God of hope fill you with all joy and peace in believing,
that you may abound in hope by the power of the Holy Spirit.

ROMANS 15:13

"Less" plays a significant role in our lives. On the one hand, it's good to be fearless, ceaseless, ageless, cordless, errorless, guiltless, painless, and odorless. On the other hand, we don't want to be jobless, friendless, homeless, penniless, fruitless, shiftless, spineless, aimless, careless, feckless, or lifeless—especially lifeless! But of all the things we don't want to have less of, none is as important as hope. We definitely need to have less hopelessness.

In Romans 5:3-5, the apostle Paul had a way of explaining why hope is an ultimate value to grasp in life. And how it derives from an unlikely source: tribulations. "Tribulation," he wrote, "produces perseverance; and perseverance, character; and character, hope. Now hope does not disappoint, because the love of God has been poured out in our hearts by the Holy Spirit who was given to us." When we lose hope in the face of tribulation, it means we have lost sight of God's love that was poured out in our heart. And to lose touch with God's love—to be loveless—is to lose touch with the greatest thing of all (1 Corinthians 13:13).

Hope, then, is a measure of our realization of God's love. Grasp His love today, and you will grasp hope as well!

Christianity knows nothing of hopeless cases.

ALEXANDER MACLAREN

September

NO STATUES FOR CRITICS

I have become the ridicule of all my people—
their taunting song all the day.

LAMENTATIONS 3:14

The story is told of a young musician whose concert was roundly criticized by the music critics of his day. The famous Finnish composer Jean Sibelius consoled him by patting him on the shoulder and saying, "Remember, son, there is no city in the world where they have erected a statue to a critic."

Well, there might be such a statue somewhere. But there are surely more statues erected to remember champions and heroes than critics. Yet critics will always be the stone in the champion's shoe—and they may be found close to home. When the teenaged David wanted to go down and confront the Philistine giant Goliath, his own older brother, Eliab, was his biggest critic. David was accused of being prideful and insolent, of not taking the cost of war seriously. What happened to David can happen to anyone who wants to be a champion for Christ. Others who are fearful of stepping out in faith and obeying God will try to make themselves feel better by criticizing you. But if God is calling you to step out and trust Him, there is no safer place you can be.

Far better to be criticized by God's opponents than to disappoint God by not heeding His call.

Any fool can criticize, condemn, and complain, and most fools do.

BENJAMIN FRANKLIN

DAVID JEREMIAH

CALLED OUT

To the church of God which is at Corinth, to those who are sanctified in Christ Jesus, called to be saints, with all who in every place call on the name of Jesus Christ our Lord, both theirs and ours.

1 CORINTHIANS 1:2

The English word "church" in the New Testament is based on the Greek word *ekklesia*, a compound word derived from *ek* (out of) and *kaleo* (to call). So the church is that group of people who have been "called out" of the world to be God's people.

When we were in the world, we had no ultimate sense of purpose. But in Christ, called to be saints of God, the church's mission and purpose comes from God. "Saint" means "holy one"—therefore, the church is a group of unholy people who have been declared to be holy in Christ and who represent their holy God in the world. That is the church's defining purpose, its reason for existence. If the church loses sight of its "called out" place in the world, it will begin to be more like the world than like God. The church's greatest challenge is to remember her identity: called to be holy.

As you make your way through the world this week, stay aware of your place in the church as one called out of the world to be holy in Christ.

We don't go to church; we are the church.

ERNEST SOUTHCOTT

THE OPPOSITE OF FAITH

But He said to them, "Why are you so fearful?
How is it that you have no faith?"

MARK 4:40

In grammar school language studies we learned about opposites. Some were simple to understand like directions (up versus down), but others had shades of meaning that required more careful thinking (nice versus not-nice). When we come to opposites in the spiritual life, we move even further away from simple meanings. For instance, what is the opposite of faith? The easy answer is "unbelief." If we have faith, we believe; if we don't have faith, we don't believe.

But when Jesus called His disciples to account for their lack of faith, He suggested the opposite was fear instead of unbelief: "Why are you so fearful? How is it that you have no faith?" Why is fear the opposite of faith? In the setting where Jesus chastised His disciples, the issue at hand was the future. They were in the middle of a storm on the Sea of Galilee and the disciples didn't think they would make it to shore. So when we approach the future, we can approach it one of two ways: with faith or with fear.

If you are in the midst of a storm, choose to have faith in Christ to see you through.

The beginning of anxiety is the end of faith,
and the beginning of faith is the end of anxiety.

GEORGE MULLER

DAVID JEREMIAH

MONEY MATTERS

The blessing of the Lord makes one rich,
and He adds no sorrow with it.

PROVERBS 10:22

A wealthy American textile buyer told a lengthy but amusing joke at a luncheon in Seoul, Korea. When his translator repeated it in just a few phrases, the audience laughed uproariously and applauded. The rich American asked the translator how he was able to translate the story with so few words. "It was not a problem," the translator said. "I told them, 'Rich American with big checkbook has told a joke. Do what you think is appropriate.'"

Why is everyone so fascinated with wealth? Is wealth always a blessing from God? True, everything comes from Him ultimately. But for every person whose wealth is a blessing, we can probably find one for whom it is a curse. For every person whom God has blessed with riches, we can probably find one who has fought tooth and nail to accumulate them. Wherever you are on the wealth scale, make sure you received it and are spending it as a blessing from God: God's wealth has no sorrow attached to it.

Money is neutral. Whether it becomes a blessing or curse is a function of how it is used.

God divided the hands into fingers so that money could slip through.

MARTIN LUTHER

THE WORD OF POWER

Preach the Word!

2 TIMOTHY 4:2A

Whenever the Word of God is soundly and seriously taught or preached, it invariably does good. In every pew there's a hurting heart, and in every audience there's a hungry soul in need of a morsel of God's unchanging truth. Often it's the Scripture text itself or a quoted verse that heals the heart.

The respected British expositor Dr. D. Martyn Lloyd-Jones pointed out that the Puritans considered their sermons to be the means by which God solved the personal, individual problems of those who listened. Puritan preachers often spent less time in counseling and more time in preparing biblical, practical messages for the lectern and pulpit.

Counseling and personal interaction are vital, as we see from the ministry of Christ. But if you are a teacher or preacher, don't underestimate the power of the public reading and proclamation of the Scriptures rightly divided. If you're a listener, pray for God to speak through your pastor. Bow your head before every sermon and ask the Lord to speak to your own heart.

The preaching of the Gospel from the pulpit, applied by the Holy Spirit to individuals who are listening, has been the means of dealing with personal problems of which I as the preacher knew nothing . . .

D. MARTYN LLOYD-JONES

WHO APPROVES OF YOU?

Know and see that there is neither evil nor rebellion in my hand,
and I have not sinned against you. Yet you hunt my life to take it.

1 SAMUEL 24:11

The human soul seeks approval. It's as if every descendant of Adam and Eve spends his life trying to replace the disapproval God showed his forebears in the Garden of Eden. We know "we" did wrong in disobeying God, and we latch on to whomever we think can pat us on the head and tell us everything will be okay.

Even when we hear God pronounce us forgiven, our old need for approval still kicks in. That's what happened to David, the teenager God chose to succeed Saul as king of Israel. God looked at David's heart and was pleased (1 Samuel 16:7). But when King Saul saw that God was with David instead of with him, Saul began persecuting his young successor. David did everything he could to win Saul's approval instead of resting in God's approval of his life. David was so focused on Saul's disapproval that he made a series of terrible decisions that marked his life forever. If you are a Christian, your search for approval should be over.

Accepting God's opinion of you in Christ is the first step toward self-acceptance.

Jesus loves you the way you are,
but loves you too much to leave you that way.

LEO VENDEN

KNOWING WHAT TO DO

Come to Me, all you who labor and are heavy laden,
and I will give you rest.

MATTHEW 11:28

Cultural rebels have always waved the "Me Against the World" banner. It's one thing to choose to stand alone, but entirely another thing to find yourself standing alone when it is none of your doing. That's what happened to one of the kings of Israel. His solution is worth imitating today. He stood before God, then stood against his enemy.

Jehoshaphat was a godly king of Judah. When word came to him that the armies of Moab, Ammon, and Edom were coming to attack Judah, he was humanly helpless. Judah had no military resources sufficient to repel such an invasion. He gathered the people of Judah and led them in prayer in the temple, and concluded with these famous words: *"We [don't] know what to do, but our eyes are upon You."* In answer to his prayer, a prophet of the Lord brought a word from God (20:15): *"Do not be afraid . . . for the battle is not yours, but God's."* The next day, God gave them victory when the invading forces turned on each other. The next time you don't know what to do, pray Jehoshaphat's prayer to God: "My eyes are on You."

Focus your eyes on the Solution instead of the problem.

Faith isn't faith until it's all you're holding on to.

UNKNOWN

NEVER ALONE

For He Himself has said, "I will never leave you nor forsake you."

HEBREWS 13:5B

One of the most well-known folk-pop songs from the 1960s was Paul Simon's "I Am a Rock." In this sad song Simon wrote, "Hiding in my room, safe within my womb. I touch no one and no one touches me. I am a rock, I am an island. And a rock feels no pain; and an island never cries." Loneliness wasn't a symptom just of the tumultuous Sixties. Most modern societies today are called collections of intimate strangers.

One of the benefits of knowing God is the reality that we are never alone. Not only is God omnipresent, but Christ lives in believers by the presence of the Holy Spirit (John 14:26-27; 16:8-11; Galatians 2:20). That means that we can never escape God's presence (Psalm 139:5-12). Whether we are literally alone or just feel alone in the midst of a crowd, the fact is that He is always near. God is only a prayer away.

Whether you are alone or lonely—you are actually neither. God is with you and will never leave you. And where God is, there is also His peace. As the bumper sticker says, "No God, no peace. Know God, know peace." You can't be an island when surrounded by Him.

*Walking with our divine Lord we should
never feel lonely and never feel lost.*

FRANK FARLEY

CAPTIVATED BY GRACE

For if I preach the gospel, I have nothing to boast of, for necessity is laid upon me; yes, woe is me if I do not preach the gospel!

1 CORINTHIANS 9:16

A homeless pit bull now named Eisenhower "captivated audiences with two days worth of activity on the Eisenhower Expressway" in Chicago. He dodged traffic for two days before being rescued by an animal protection charity. How does a homeless dog "captivate" a city? It means people's attention was riveted as they watched the news reports; they became fans of the dog, pulling for him to stay safe. They devoted time to talking about the dog and expressing concern.

The same could be said about the apostle Paul when he was captured and captivated by the grace of God. He had been a persecutor of Christ and His church, but the very One he persecuted reached out to him with love and forgiveness. Paul never got over being a recipient of the grace of God; he remained a "captive" of God's grace the rest of his life. He said, "Woe is me" if I do not fulfill the purpose for which grace was extended to me.

Are you captivated by God's grace? Give thought this week to what God has done for you and how evident your "captivity" is to those around you. God's grace becomes irresistible over time.

Christian doctrine is grace, and Christian conduct is gratitude.

J. I. PACKER

GOD IS ALWAYS BIGGER

Then Caleb quieted the people before Moses, and said, "Let us go up at once and take possession, for we are well able to overcome it."

NUMBERS 13:30

In Russia they are known as *matryoshka*. In the West we know them as "nesting dolls." They are the most popular and well-known of all Russian souvenirs—the gradually-decreasing-in-size wooden dolls that "nest" inside one another.

It helps for us to see God as the one in whom all the affairs of our life "fit." For instance, when the twelve spies went up from Kadesh Barnea to check out the Promised Land, ten of them saw only the size of the giants in the land. They didn't see God looming larger than the giants. David, on the other hand, when he saw the giant Goliath, wasn't afraid of being smaller than the giant because he saw the giant as being smaller than God. If we look hard enough in this life, we'll always find a problem bigger than our current one. But if we look with spiritual eyes, we'll always see that God is bigger than them all. If you're facing a problem right now that is bigger than you are, look again. That problem "nests" inside God's purposes for your life. The problem is larger than you, but God is larger than the problem.

Keep stepping back until God, not your problem, fills your vision.

In the church we seem to have the vision of the majesty of God.

JOHN R. W. STOTT

FRIENDS HAVE FRIENDS

A man who has friends must himself be friendly,
but there is a friend who sticks closer than a brother.

PROVERBS 18:24

Though they didn't know it at the time, the original disciples of Jesus enjoyed a status that many today would relish: being the personal friend of Jesus Christ. On the night before His arrest, trial, and crucifixion, Jesus told His disciples, "No longer do I call you servants . . . but I have called you friends, for all things that I heard from My father I have made known to you" (John 15:15).

Jesus and His disciples epitomized the relationship pictured in Proverbs 18:24: "a friend who sticks closer than a brother." Another real-life example of that kind of friendship in the Old Testament was David and Jonathan, the son of Saul. They formed a covenant relationship by which they shared their possessions, their needs, and their future welfare. Jesus even experienced his own brothers being distant from Him (John 7:5). In the end, it was His disciples—His friends—who stayed closest to Him. Jesus was first close to them and they became close to Him.

If you would like more close friends, you'll first need to be a close friend. Be available, be loyal, be present, be forgiving—be a friend who sticks closer than a brother.

Friendship flourishes at the fountain of forgiveness.

WILLIAM A. WARD

TAKING REFUGE

The eternal God is your refuge,
and underneath are the everlasting arms.

DEUTERONOMY 33:27A

John Elliott had logged many miles through the deep snows of the mountain passes of the Rockies in southwestern Alberta. As dusk and exhaustion overcame him, he decided to rest. He made it wearily to his cabin, but was so tired that it didn't cross his mind to light a fire or put on warm clothes. Outside the blizzard continued to thrash the old cabin walls, but Elliot fell silent, paralyzed by the lure of sweet sleep.

Suddenly, his dog, a St. Bernard, sprang into action and, with unrelenting whines, finally managed to rouse his near-comatose master. "If that dog hadn't been with me, I'd be dead today," Elliott said. "When you're freezing to death, you actually feel warm all over and don't wake up because it feels too good."

This moving story illustrates the spiritual condition of many people today. They are cold spiritually and oblivious of their true condition. But God is close by to arouse such sleepers. He sends messengers to nudge them awake. If you're feeling sleepy, don't ignore God's prodding. Instead, thank Him for His loving disturbances which will save you from an eternal death.

Conscience tells us that we ought to do right, but it does
not tell us what right is—that we are taught by God's Word.

H. C. TRUMBULL

WHO CARES FOR YOU?

And Jesus answered and said to her, "Martha, Martha,
you are worried and troubled about many things."

LUKE 10:41

If you could wear a tape recorder around your neck for one week—one that recorded every word you spoke for seven days—how many times would it record the word "worry"? *"I'm worried about you—what's wrong?" "I've been worrying about her for weeks and haven't known what to do." "I worry that we won't be able to pay for John's medical bills since we don't have insurance."*

A 1996 book by Richard Carlson was titled *Don't Sweat the Small Stuff—and It's All Small Stuff*. A point biblically taken. That doesn't mean there aren't important issues in life and serious decisions to be made. It's just that worrying about them (sweating them) does not make any impact on the outcome. As Jesus said in Matthew 6:27, "When did worrying ever add anything to your life?" (paraphrase) Answer: never. Worrying is a form of stress, and stress is bad for you. Instead of worrying, do something that is good for you: Commit all your concerns to the Lord in prayer and let His peace guard your heart and mind in Christ Jesus (Philippians 4:6-7).

When we are in difficult moments in life, it's easy to forget: God cares more than we care (1 Peter 5:7).

Worry is an indication that we think God cannot look after us.

OSWALD CHAMBERS

DAVID JEREMIAH

SEPTEMBER 14

THE CAUSE OF TROUBLE

When a man's way please the Lord,
He makes even his enemies to be at peace with him.

PROVERBS 16:7

Dale Carnegie once told of a young man whose mind was riddled with anxiety like honeycomb. On the verge of a nervous breakdown, he moved to Florida; but his dad, in a letter, told him bluntly: "Son, you are 1500 miles from home, and you don't feel any different, do you? I knew you wouldn't because you took with you the one thing that is the cause of all your trouble, that is, yourself."

The enraged young man stalked down the street like a pouting lion. Passing a church at service time, he went in. The pastor was speaking from Proverbs 16:32: *"He who . . . rules his spirit (is better) than he who takes a city."*

It was the turning point, for the man suddenly realized he could change. He could control his own thoughts and emotions with the help of Scripture. He could let the Lord rule over his spirit. He could manage his emotions instead of letting them manage him. Returning home, his life took on new meaning.

Are you ruling your emotions or are they ruling you? Claim Proverbs 16:32 as God's Word for you today.

The greatest part of our happiness depends
on our dispositions, not our circumstances.

MARTHA WASHINGTON

THE WHISTLE

Wisdom is the principal thing; therefore get wisdom. And in all your getting, get understanding.

PROVERBS 4:7

When Benjamin Franklin was seven years old, his mother gave him several pennies—the first money he'd ever owned. He ran into the street and met a boy blowing a whistle. Giving all his coppers for the whistle, young Benjamin ran home to show his treasure to his brothers and sisters. Imagine his chagrin when they laughingly informed him his whistle was worth only one penny at best. Throwing himself on the floor, he cried with vexation. But the lesson wasn't lost. "Afterward...," he wrote, "when I was tempted to buy some unnecessary thing, I said to myself, 'Don't give too much for the whistle.'"

If even children can learn from their mistakes, God's children can do the same. When we pay too much for the whistle (or foul up in any way), it's important to take responsibility for our actions, to repent, and to learn from our mistakes. By confessing our sins, we're removing guilt and allowing ourselves to learn the lessons of grace and growth.

A day is never lost if a lesson is learned.

After crosses and losses men grow humbler and wiser.

BENJAMIN FRANKLIN

DAVID JEREMIAH

STRATEGIC AVOIDANCE

Avoid it, do not travel on it; turn away from it and pass on.

PROVERBS 4:15

When professional athletes are arrested during brawls at places like night clubs and dog fights, we say, "How stupid! Why would they risk their millions of fans—and million-dollar contracts—by deliberately putting themselves in the wrong place at the wrong time?"

Yet every one of us is doing the same thing whenever we go anywhere that exposes our own hearts to needless temptation. For each person, the temptation might be something different— the availability of various forms of media alone can present temptations that you know you need to avoid. The Bible says plainly, "Avoid every kind of evil" (1 Thessalonians 5:22, NIV). Our sinful natures are drawn like magnets to the things of this world; they seem attractive to us. One significant way to slay temptation is by not placing ourselves in an environment where we'll be tempted.

Call it Strategic Avoidance.

Proverbs 16:17 says, "The highway of the upright avoids evil; he who guards his way guards his life" (NIV).

It's easier to avoid temptation than to resist it.

BILL SHANNON

SPECKS AND PLANKS

Hypocrite! First remove the plank from your own eye, and then you will see clearly to remove the speck from your brother's eye.

MATTHEW 7:5

Early in the film version of the near-disastrous *Apollo 13* space flight, astronaut Jim Lovell is in his backyard, looking up at the moon that hangs small in the night sky. He holds up his thumb and it blocks out the entire moon from his sight. How could something so large be obscured from view by something so small?

It's all a matter of perspective. Things often aren't as they seem; sometimes a small thing can obscure something larger and more important. For instance, we may see a sin in the life of another person but fail to see our own giant, judgmental attitude. The small sin of another has blocked our view of our own larger problem. Jesus put it this way: Don't worry about the speck in another's eye until you've removed the plank from your own eye. Until our own eye is clear from a judgmental spirit, we are unqualified to judge the sins of another. Yes, the other person may have sinned, but God has not appointed us the judge of him.

Of all the sins in the world, God calls us to be concerned about only one before any other: our own. Once we have removed our plank, we can help our brother remove his speck.

No man's conscience is to be a judge for another.

C. H. SPURGEON

David's Sorrow

So David said to Nathan, "I have sinned against the Lord."

2 Samuel 12:13

David's life was characterized by victory, both on the battlefield and in the chaotic world of ancient Israeli politics; and though he had many enemies, he triumphed over them all. The one foe who almost defeated him, however, was the most dangerous one of all. It was himself.

David lost his personal struggle against lust and passion, committed adultery with Bathsheba, then arranged for the death of Uriah and a subsequent cover-up of the scandal. But Nathan the prophet confronted David regarding his sin. The Bible says that godly sorrow produces repentance (2 Corinthians 7:10), and David's sorrow and tender repentance led him back to God and restored his victory in life.

None of us likes being confronted and rebuked; but how wonderful of God to send us warnings and to give us a tender conscience. Has sin crept into your life and stolen your victory in Christ? Do you feel the Holy Spirit reproving you in your heart? Is a godly friend concerned about your behavior?

Godly sorrow and genuine repentance lead to spiritual victory.

Unconfessed sin is unforgiven sin, and unforgiven sin is the darkest, foulest thing on this sin-cursed earth.

D. L. Moody

ALL SUFFICIENCY

And God is able to make all grace abound toward you,
that you, always having all sufficiency in all things,
may have an abundance for every good work.

2 CORINTHIANS 9:8

Are you worried about a need in your life right now? Perhaps you've forgotten how often God promises to meet all our needs as we trust Him.

Your heavenly Father knows that you need all these things—Matthew 6:32.

I have been young, and now am old; yet I have not seen the righteous forsaken nor his descendants begging bread—Psalm 37:25.

God has dealt graciously with me . . . I have enough—Genesis 33:11.

My God shall supply all your need according to His riches in glory by Christ Jesus—Philippians 4:19.

Oh, fear the Lord, you His saints! There is no want to those who fear Him...Those who seek the LORD shall not lack any good thing—Psalm 34:9-10.

Seek first the kingdom of God and His righteousness, and all these things shall be added to you—Matthew 6:33.

Your heavenly Father is the great provider, and in Christ we have all His promises and all our provision. Today, don't worry. Trust.

We need to remember that our extremity
is always the Lord's opportunity.

H. EDWIN YOUNG

DAVID JEREMIAH

SEPTEMBER 20

FRIDGE FAILINGS

Your words were found, and I ate them,
and Your word was to me the joy and rejoicing of my heart

JEREMIAH 15:16

Last summer, a worker at the AT&T office in San Jose tried to clean out an old refrigerator. She couldn't smell the stench due to allergies, but the smell from the rotten food was so noxious it prompted someone to call 911, and firefighters evacuated the building. Seven coworkers were taken to the hospital, and it took a hazmat team to clear out the mess.

Our lives, like refrigerators, can suffer spoilage if we don't keep them cleared out and cleaned up. Things can go bad quickly when lukewarm (Revelation 3:16). Make sure the sincere milk of the Word is on a shelf you can reach every day, along with solid food for the soul (1 Peter 2:2; Hebrews 5:12). Treasure the words of His mouth more than your daily bread, and make sure the manna of daily Bible study doesn't become stale and wormy (Job 23:12; Exodus 16:20). Keep the oil of joy fresh (Psalm 45:7). Throw out anything that doesn't contribute to your overall spiritual well-being, and beware of anything rotten. Stay plugged in to the current of heaven through prayer, and you'll be a source of nourishment to others.

We can never give out spiritual nourishment
until we have first taken it in ourselves.

KENNETH OSBECK

PRECIOUS BIBLE PROMISES

*He did not waver at the promise of God through unbelief, but was
strengthened in faith, giving glory to God, and being fully convinced
that what He had promised He was also able to perform.*

ROMANS 4:20-21

On January 19, 1750, Isaac Watts, the brilliant London pastor
who is today remembered as the "Father of the English
Hymn," sat down and wrote the foreword to a new edition of
Samuel Clarke's book, *Precious Bible Promises.* In describing
biblical promises, Watts called them "the constant food of a
living Christian, as well as his highest cordials (medicines) in a
fainting hour."

He wrote, "In such a world as this, where duties perpetually
demand our practice, and difficulties and trials are ever
surrounding us, what can we do better than to treasure up the
promises in our hearts? Here are the true riches of a Christian,
and his highest hopes on this side of heaven."

If depression, discouragement, or disappointment is settling
down on you like a cold fog, warm up to the sunbeams of a
promise of Scripture. Search through the Bible until you find the
very promise God has for you today. Be like Abraham who did
not waver at the promise, but was strengthened in faith, fully
persuaded that God had the power to do as He had promised.

Lord, I believe! Help Thou mine unbelief.

THE GOSPEL ACCORDING TO MARK

278   DAVID JEREMIAH

The Holiness Habit

Get rid of every filthy habit and all wicked conduct. Submit to God and accept the word that He plants in your hearts.

James 1:21 (GNT)

Holiness is a habit. It's much more than that, of course. It's a characteristic of God himself, displayed perfectly in Christ and imputed to our accounts by grace through faith. But in practical terms, holy living means daily discipline. We form habits, then they form us.

That's why we must weed out bad habits regularly, just as we weed our yards. An untended garden soon deteriorates into a weed patch, and an untended life does the same. It requires the discipline of the hoe to produce hollyhocks in our fields and holiness in our lives.

In his book *How to Say No to a Stubborn Habit,* Erwin Lutzer writes: "We are responsible for our own sin—including those sins 'which so easily beset us.' The fact that we do something wrong habitually does not relieve us of responsibility. On the contrary, it may make the sin all the worse. So we must take personal responsibility for our own habits and not shrink from calling them sin."

Ask the Lord to help you identify "weeds" in your life, and replace them with holy habits that produce a crop of righteousness.

The Christian must see that bad habits are ultimately spiritual issues.

Erwin Lutzer

THE ANGER VIRUS

A wrathful man stirs up strife,
but he who is slow to anger allays contention.

PROVERBS 15:18

Fears of a global flu pandemic have rekindled memories of the terrible 1918 epidemic in which a virulent strain of influenza infected a third of the world's population and killed an estimated 50 to 100 million people. Some researchers believe the flu spread so quickly that year because of soldiers who, already weakened from fatigue, were traveling across national and geographical boundaries during the waning months of World War I.

Studying the communicable effects of disease teaches us something about spiritual illness, too. Spiritual viruses and emotional maladies spread person to person just like germs and viruses. According to Proverbs 15:18, angry people spread their anger wherever they go. The words *influenza* and *influence*, after all, come from the same root word.

But the cure spreads person-to-person, too! We can reverse the anger of those around us by staying cool and calm, gentle and patient. Whatever our emotions—joy, anger, depression, anxiety—they infect those near us. This is one of the Christian's great secrets. When we're filled with the calming strength of the Spirit, we can improve whatever environment we find ourselves in.

Your lifestyle is your most powerful message.

JOHN MACARTHUR

Deal-making (In a Sense)

*And whenever you stand praying, if you have anything
against anyone, forgive him, that your Father
in heaven may also forgive you your trespasses.*

Mark 11:25

The Latin phrase *quid pro quo* doesn't have a very positive
reputation in modern America. Literally, it means
"something for something" and is most often heard in the realms
of law and politics: "I'll do this for you if you'll do that for me."

There is a *quid pro quo* of sorts in the Bible. Jesus stated that
the condition for having God forgive us of our sins is that we
forgive others of their sins (Matthew 6:14-15). But isn't the
forgiveness of sin a gift of grace based on Jesus' death on the
cross? Definitely. Jesus was talking about fellowship with God,
not eternal salvation. If we want to maintain our intimacy with
God (if we want Him to forgive our sins), we have to maintain
intimacy with others (we must forgive those who have wronged
us). This is what Jesus taught the disciples (us) to pray: "And
forgive us our debts, as we forgive our debtors" (Matthew 6:12).

If there is someone who has wronged you and you're having a
hard time forgiving them, think of what happens when you do:
God forgives you. That's a good deal to make.

*Everyone says forgiveness is a lovely
idea until he has something to forgive.*

C. S. Lewis

NOT DROPS OR DRIBBLES

If you . . . know how to give good gifts to your children, how much more will your heavenly Father give the Holy Spirit to those who ask Him!

LUKE 11:13

Recently a newspaper ran a column describing the world's greatest cheapskates. One man, for example, went grocery shopping with his wife. As she filled the cart with goods, he strolled over to the card section and selected a beautiful birthday card for her. Finding her among the pickles and relishes, he gave her the card, watched with joy while she read it, gave her a little hug—then returned the card to the rack!

That's not the way the Lord gives.

Take the Holy Spirit, for example. The moment we receive Christ as Savior, the Father pours His Spirit into our hearts. It isn't a drop or a dribble. Jesus compared the Holy Spirit to rivers of waters flowing from our hearts (John 7:38-39). We're born again by the Spirit, indwelled by the Spirit, empowered by the Spirit, illumined by the Spirit, comforted by the Spirit, taught by the Spirit, filled with the Spirit, and sanctified by the Spirit.

How grateful we should be that God has given us His Spirit, and that Jesus—by His Spirit—will never leave or forsake us (Hebrews 13:5).

Jesus, fill now with Thy Spirit hearts that full surrender know
That the streams of living water from our inner self may flow.

MARY MAXWELL

THE UNEXPLAINABLE

"For My thoughts are not your thoughts,
nor are your ways My ways," says the Lord.

ISAIAH 55:8

There are some things in life that just do not make sense, such as the placebo effect, a round earth with a flat horizon, and the Bermuda Triangle. Though scientists constantly search to understand these mysteries, for the majority of us, they are so far beyond our comprehension that we just accept them as a part of the universe we will never understand.

In the same way, there are things about God that even the greatest minds will never be able to comprehend. For those that need to have the answer for everything in life, this is difficult and can be an obstacle to fully accepting God's love and authority. For others, it is comforting to know that while we may not fully understand everything, the One who holds everything in His hands does.

We cannot allow doubt to creep into our thoughts when we don't understand something; this is exactly what the enemy wants. Instead, we must ask God to help us accept that some things are perhaps hidden from our understanding for a purpose, and we must trust Him regardless.

God has wisely kept us in the dark concerning future events and reserved for Himself the knowledge of them, that He may train us up in a dependence upon Himself and a continued readiness for every event.

MATTHEW HENRY

GOOD PLANS

I know the thoughts that I think toward you,
says the Lord, thoughts of peace... to give you a future and a hope.

JEREMIAH 29:11

A reporter in Alaska, working on an article about caregivers, interviewed a woman who was caring for her husband as he battled chronic obstructive pulmonary disease. She was afraid to leave his side, but the strain was wearing her down. "It's sort of a helpless and hopeless feeling," she said. "You quickly become exhausted."

Perhaps you're a caregiver who can relate to those feelings. Or perhaps other factors in your life are producing helpless, hopeless, exhausted feelings. Sometimes we forget that God knows the plans He has for us—and that they are good plans. He'll give you needed strength for each day, and His purposes will prevail in your life.

Take a moment right now to remind yourself that, though you may not understand it all, God is working out His plan for you in Christ Jesus, working all things together according to the good counsel of His will (Ephesians 1:11). You can trust His guidance.

In heavenly love abiding, no change my heart shall fear.
And safe in such confiding, for nothing changes here.
The storm may roar without me, my heart may low be laid,
But God is round about me, and can I be dismayed?

ANNA WARING

A CAPITAL "T"

If you abide in My word, you are My disciples indeed. And you shall know the truth, and the truth shall make you free.

JOHN 8:31-32

In John's gospel, the words *true* and *truth* occur forty-five times. Jesus is the true light (1:9), the true bread from heaven (6:32), and the true vine (15:1). He is full of grace and truth (1:14). His witness is true (8:14). When He speaks, He tells the truth (8:40), for He himself was the Truth (14:6). When He stood before Pilate, He bore witness to the truth (18:37-38).

Yet Pilate said, "What is truth?"

Today we call that philosophy by a name—moral relativism. Our society has rejected transcendent truth and moral absolutes, choosing instead to craft their laws and govern their lives by personal opinion and societal consensus.

But God's Word is truth between two covers. It is absolute, inerrant, infallible, unshakable, timeless truth; and it enables us to live our lives with certainty, having all the God-given facts, promises, and explanations we need from Him who created us.

That Bible in your hands—it's the truth with a capital "T." Not one word will fail, nor will a single promise be forgotten. You can trust it—with a capital "T."

If we understood what happens when we use the Word of God, we would use it oftener.

OSWALD CHAMBERS

FAILING TO SUCCESS

*The steps of a good man are ordered by the LORD,
and He delights in his way. Though he fall, he shall not be
utterly cast down; for the LORD upholds him with His hand.*

PSALM 37:23-24

The literal definition of the word "failure" is: *a lack of success in or at something.* In reality though, you cannot achieve success in anything without failures along the way. No one is born with the ability to do anything successfully on the first attempt. Babies fall when learning to walk; pianists hit sour notes when trying to master a composition; athletes come in second and third while building up what it takes to place first. But there is a common thread among them all: they never let fear of failure stop them from striving for success.

A lot of us have a fear of failure; but if we desire to be used by God to further His kingdom and bring glory to His name, we must ask Him to help us overcome this. Imagine the amazing things we could do in God's name if we never let fear hold us back! We might stumble along the way; but in the end, God's name would be glorified, and we would set an example for those around us that it's okay to try big things for God, even if we fail along the way to success.

Success comes in cans; failure comes in can'ts.

UNKNOWN

NEVER-ENDING GRACE

But where sin abounded, grace abounded much more.

ROMANS 5:20B

Water from an artesian well flows to the surface without pumping. Often, the head of an artesian well is surrounded by hills containing water tables higher than the wellhead. The resulting water pressure causes the water in the aquifer to flow up and out in a steady stream—as long as the supplying water tables remain full.

The grace of God is, in some ways, like an artesian well. God's grace flows continually and requires no "pumping," no effort, on the part of recipients who need to drink deeply of its soul-sustaining provision. Even when we sin, the flow of God's grace is uninterrupted to all who seek it. That does not mean grace is never interrupted by discipline. But even God's discipline is fueled by measures of grace, mercy, and love as the heavenly Father acts with His children's long-term best interests in mind. Christians are not punished by God, but disciplined, corrected, and trained. And even correction is an aspect of God's grace.

When you quench your body's thirst with water today, think of the grace that quenches your soul—and thank God for its uninterrupted flow.

Grace . . . turns counters into gold, pebbles into pearls, sickness into health, weakness into strength and wants into abundance.

THOMAS BROOKS

OCTOBER

What "All" Means

You who fear the Lord, trust in the Lord;
He is their help and their shield.

Psalm 115:11

A preacher, known for his diligent and exhaustive study of Scripture in the original languages of the Bible, stood in his pulpit to explain part of Ephesians 6:16 to his congregation: ". . . you will be able to quench all the fiery darts of the wicked one." He began by saying, "I have studied this word 'all' in the Hebrew and Greek languages. I have consulted the finest authorities who have written on this text. And I have discovered what Paul was really saying when he spoke of 'all the fiery darts of the wicked one.' 'All' in this verse means . . . ALL!"

Now that we know that "all" means "all," perhaps every Christian should spend time contemplating how much of one's life can actually be protected by the shield of faith Paul describes as the defense against Satan's fiery darts. Satan has a large armory of various types of darts: He might fire a dart of discouragement, of frustration, of anger, of envy or jealousy, of confusion, of unforgiveness, of bitterness, of doubt, of worry or anxiety—the list goes on. But whatever kind of dart Satan fires, it is covered by "all."

The shield of faith will protect you from every temptation and attack from the evil one—if you will make faith your shield.

Faith begins where man's power ends.

Unknown

WHAT GRACE PROVIDES

*And now for a little while grace has been shown
from the LORD our God, to leave us a remnant to escape,
and to give us a peg in His holy place . . . .*

EZRA 9:8

Some things in life come in pairs: socks, pant legs, gloves, a bird's wings, scissors' blades, and a coin's sides. Mercy and grace are in that same category. Mercy is not receiving a negative outcome we deserve, while grace is receiving a positive outcome we don't deserve. Every negative outcome averted is itself a positive outcome; and every positive outcome is a negative outcome averted. If God was a coin, grace and mercy would be His two sides.

Mercy spares us from hell while grace delivers us to heaven. The nation of Israel had been shown mercy many times until God finally sent them into captivity. But then, after 70 years, grace intervened and a remnant of Israel returned to the homeland, the Holy Land. Just as grace gave Israel a place in the temple's Holy Place, so grace gives us a place in God's Holy City, the New Jerusalem. Mercy prevents, and grace provides—the two sides of God's love.

Thank God today for His mercy and grace—the hell you have avoided and the heaven you have attained.

*When we've been there ten thousand years, bright shining as the sun,
we've no less days to sing God's praise than when we first begun.*

JOHN NEWTON

OCTOBER 3

DEVOTED FOR LIFE

Then He said to them, "Follow Me."

MATTHEW 4:19

Missionary Adoniram Judson said, "The motto for every missionary, whether preacher, printer, or schoolmaster, ought to be 'Devoted for Life.'"

Judson certainly lived by his motto, but "Devoted for Life" isn't a slogan limited to missionaries and ministers. All Christians are called to a life of discipleship, and the decision to follow Jesus is that of being devoted totally to Him for both life and eternity.

The problem, of course, is that commitment is an abstract word. We may agree, in general, to total commitment. But does it show up on the stubs of your checkbook? In your daily planner? In the letters you send, the calls you make, the sins you avoid, and the witness you bear? In the way you treat your spouse?

Someone once asked: If you were on trial for being a Christian, would there be enough evidence to convict you? Well? Hymnist Leila Morris put it this way: *Fully surrendered, to go or to stay, just where He needs me, His will to obey.* We must commit ourselves to follow God's leading at all times and in all circumstances.

Are you *Devoted for Life?*

> *If Jesus Christ be God and died for me,*
> *then no sacrifice can be too great for me to make for Him.*

C. T. STUDD

DAVID JEREMIAH

OCTOBER 4

SHALL I GO?

For You are my rock and my fortress; therefore,
for Your name's sake, lead me and guide me.

PSALM 31:3

Think of all the places you have to go on an average day—literally. You arise in the morning and go to the shower, then to the kitchen, then to the closet to get dressed, then to work, then lunch, then to errands, then home . . . and those are only after you decided where to get married, where to go to school, where to live, where to work, and where to go to church.

Now—think about how many of those "where's" you consulted God about before setting out. Where is the line in your spiritual life between those things that you don't inquire of the Lord about and those you do? Somewhere between what to eat for breakfast and who to marry, you cross that line—and it's probably different for every person. Think of it this way: Is anything too trivial to ask the Lord about? Perhaps the key lies in developing what Paul called "the mind of Christ" (1 Corinthians 2:16)—a combination of asking God about some things and developing wisdom from Him about most other things.

Do you live in an ongoing conversation with God about your next steps? Talk to God this week as if He were right beside you (He is) and cares about every decision you need to make (He does).

Man proposes, God disposes.

TRADITIONAL PROVERB

WHAT'S MOST IMPORTANT?

And now abide faith, hope, love, these three;
but the greatest of these is love.

1 CORINTHIANS 13:13

A good group game asks this question: "If you were given one hour to evacuate your home and allowed one suitcase to hold your belongings, what would you take?" The point is to force people to think about priorities; answers usually include things like family photo albums, keepsake jewelry, a valued gift, important documents—and today most people would probably include their laptop and cell phone!

Everything in life is not equally important, nor is everything in the kingdom of God on the same plane. Of three important virtues—faith, hope, and love—Paul said that love was the "greatest." And Jesus revealed the first and second most important commandments out of the hundreds of commandments in Israel's canon. Today's economic recession has caused many people to think afresh about what is most important in their life. When funds are limited, or the future looks scary, we begin to make choices: God, spouse, family, neighbors, health, savings— we live differently when all things are not possible.

Be aware of changes and choices you are making in these challenging days. Then, hold on to those priorities!

We live by demands when we should live by priorities.

J. A. MOTYER

MEANS AND ENDS

*Better is the poor who walks in his integrity
than one who is perverse in his lips, and is a fool.*

PROVERBS 19:1

Through the ages, ethicists have debated the connection between means and ends: Can immoral actions be justified in order to achieve moral outcomes? Would a prisoner be justified in paying a bribe to get out of jail to try and save the life of his dying child? Does saving the life of the child justify dishonesty?

Fortunately, the Bible offers insight into this difficult question. When David, the new king of Israel, wanted to return the ark of the covenant to Jerusalem, a man was killed by God for handling the ark inappropriately. Earlier in the ark's history, seventy men died when someone removed the lid and looked inside the ark (1 Samuel 6:19). Why the harsh treatment? Specifically, because Israel needed to regain a lost fear (awe) and respect for God's holiness. Generally, because God is as interested in how we do things as in what we do. From God's perspective, the end doesn't justify the means: Wanting to do something good doesn't excuse doing something bad.

If you are planning an action, look as closely at the "how" as the "what." Make sure both bring honor to God.

*Success without honor is an unseasoned dish;
it will satisfy your hunger, but it won't taste good.*

JOE PATERNO

ELISHA

Elisha the son of Shaphat is here,
who poured water on the hands of Elijah.

2 KINGS 3:11

Good to Great, the best-selling leadership and management tome by Jim Collins, talks about Level Five Leaders, men and women in business who effectively combine humility with drive. Level Five Leaders aren't concerned about claiming credit for success. They genuinely care for others; yet they passionately want their companies to succeed, and work hard to make it happen.

Elisha was a Level Five Leader, one of the most powerful and effective men in the Old Testament. He was a miracle worker who stood unflinchingly in an evil nation of Baal worshippers. We first see him described as Elijah's servant (1 Kings 19:21). He was later portrayed as the man who poured water on Elijah's hands—Elijah's attendant. His willingness to perform menial tasks prepared his heart for his later exploits for the Lord.

Don't worry about claiming credit for any success that comes your way. The real question is—are you pouring water on someone's hands? Are you helping another person with their own work today? Are you a servant?

I long to accomplish great and noble tasks, but it is my chief duty to
accomplish humble tasks as though they were great and noble.

HELEN KELLER

RICH IN THIS PRESENT AGE

She considers a field and buys it;
from her profits she plants a vineyard.

PROVERBS 31:16

According to a report just released by the U.S. Department of Agriculture, it now costs as much as $393,230 to raise a child to age eighteen. That's the standard amount for those in the upper income levels. For middle income earners, the figure drops to $204,060. But that doesn't include college.

It takes a lot of money to live, and that's why the Bible tells us to manage our money as wisely as we can. The wise woman in Proverbs 31 was a hard worker, a careful saver, and an astute investor. She provided for today's needs and stored up for tomorrow. The Lord doesn't necessarily want all of us to take a vow of poverty as Francis of Assisi did. Many of the heroes of Scripture were well-off. But the Bible says that those who "are rich in this present age" should not be haughty nor trust in uncertain riches, but in the living God who gives us all things to enjoy. God will provide for us.

It's not our pocketbooks but our perspective that makes us truly rich.

The real measure of our wealth is how
much we should be worth if we lost our money.

J. H. JOWETT

WHO CAN YOU TRUST?

*But it is good for me to draw near to God; I have put my
trust in the Lord GOD, that I may declare all Your works.*

PSALM 73:28

Television reality shows that feature a group of contestants make
trust a central focus. Not surprisingly, the contestants often
betray one another's trust as they joust for advantage and position,
leading to the show's finale. Such a me-first mentality is reflective of
values often found in the world. Becoming transparent and honest
with others is a risk that relationships require.

Fortunately, there is someone whose word is eminently
trustworthy: God Himself. Scripture is filled with proof that
God keeps His word. Indeed, trust is at the very heart of
God's covenant love—first for Israel and then for the Church.
The Hebrew word in the Old Testament usually translated
"lovingkindness" literally means "loyal love"—the kind of love
that never ends. Through the prophet Jeremiah, God said that
as long as the universe—the order of the stars and planets—
remains in place, His promises to Israel would not fail (Jeremiah
31:35-37). There is nothing you can say or reveal to God that
would cause His love for you to fail.

If you have trusted God with your eternal life, shouldn't you
trust Him with the details of your earthly life as well?

Let us learn to trust Him for who He is.

ELISABETH ELLIOT

DREAMS COME TRUE

The preparations of the heart belong to man,
but the answer of the tongue is from the Lord.

PROVERBS 16:1

David Wilkerson tried to speak to the judge presiding over the trial of twelve New York gang members and was kicked out of the courtroom. The next day his picture appeared in the papers, holding his Bible in the air. He thought he had failed miserably with his courthouse blunder. But when he returned to the slums, people recognized him as the preacher who had run afoul of the law. They welcomed him to their neighborhood and many eventually welcomed his message of the gospel of Jesus Christ.

To have a dream, then endure the death of that dream, requires great faith—like another David, the king of Israel. He dreamed of building a temple for the ark of the covenant, but God said "No"—not "No" to the temple, but "No" to David building it. David realized that God's plan was better. Instead of David building God a physical house, God promised to build David a spiritual house. If you've endured the death of a dream, don't give up. Seek God to discover what His purpose and plan are for you.

The secret to "dreams come true" is getting in step with the dream God gives you.

Out of the depths of my prison experience came
the vision for Prison Fellowship's ministry.

CHARLES COLSON

MOBILE COMPASSION

All of you be of one mind, having compassion for one another;
love as brothers, be tenderhearted, be courteous.

1 PETER 3:8

The European Union has approved the use of mobile phones throughout Europe's airspace, but a communiqué from the EU warned that proper cell phone etiquette must be followed. Some passengers "still use the aircraft as a moment of tranquility," and travelers who are resting don't want to spend hours listening to a one-sided conversation.

The creation of cell phones brought a whole new level of communication to our world; and when we realized we couldn't talk openly in all locations, we learned to text message. In trains, restaurants, cars, on the streets, and now in airplanes, we crave fellowship even if it requires pounding little keys with our thumbs. We want to stay in touch with others.

As Christians, we can use this to the advantage of God's kingdom. The same drive that makes us call, e-mail, and text also opens our hearts to warm smiles, loving concern, and acts of compassion. Look around for a lonely person today, and extend the hand of mercy that Christ has modeled for us in His Word. It'll beat texting, thumbs down.

We are the tangible manifestation of the compassionate heart of our
Father. You and I are the expression of God's love on this earth.

FLORENCE LITTAUER

JESUS IN YOUR NEIGHBORHOOD

But whoever has this world's goods, and sees his brother in need, and shuts up his heart from him, how does the love of God abide in him?

1 JOHN 3:17

On its nightly newscast, one of the three major television networks invited viewers to write the network with examples of people helping people during the difficult economic times of 2009—and they received far more examples than they could ever broadcast.

If you knocked on the doors of all the homes in your neighborhood, you would likely find a high percentage of families or individuals who have been hurt by the economic recession. Perhaps unemployment, defaulting on a mortgage, loss of life savings or other funds, unpaid medical bills, retirees having to return to the workforce—the economic downturn has touched almost everyone. What a marvelous opportunity to manifest the love and compassion of God with those who need it most! In His ministry Jesus reached out to everyone, and He wants us to do the same.

Sow the seed of service in your neighborhood. Even if you have been hit hard by the current recession, you can still offer a word of encouragement or a helping hand to those in need. And perhaps share the love of Christ if they ask you "Why?"

If you want your neighbor to know what Christ will do for him, let your neighbor see what Christ has done for you.

HENRY WARD BEECHER

TRUST ONLY IN GOD

The name of the Lord is a strong tower;
the righteous run to it and are safe.

PROVERBS 18:10

The last twenty years have seen Americans lose a lot of money. There were the bankruptcies of companies like Enron and WorldCom in which investors and employees lost out, the bursting of the "dot.com" bubble in 2000, and the housing fiasco in 2008 which led to the economic recession. Trillions of dollars of wealth have evaporated in these and other financial catastrophes.

Tragic as these losses have been to those directly affected, they should come as no surprise to anyone. Everything man builds on earth is constructed with hands tainted by sin—like building a house on a foundation made with cheap cement instead of certified concrete. Any tremor will likely bring it crashing down: "Unless the LORD builds the house, they labor in vain who build it" (Psalm 127:1a). Everything in this world is destined to pass away, either now or in the future. The Bible reminds us that only the truth of God's Word will endure forever.

Our challenge is to invest in this world only what we can afford to lose in this world. That means entrusting our salvation and peace of mind to no one except God.

Heaven will pay for any loss we may suffer to gain it;
but nothing can pay for the loss of heaven.

RICHARD BAXTER

PETER

Simon, Simon! Indeed, Satan has asked for you, that he may sift you as wheat. But I have prayed for you, that your faith should not fail; and when you have returned to Me, strengthen your brethren.

LUKE 22:31-32

Thank God for Peter, the apostle of failure! Though he stumbled, he didn't stay down; and though he sinned, he didn't wallow in his guilt *ad infinitum*, but repented, stood to his feet, and went forward to change the world for Christ.

Proverbs 24:16 must have been Peter's life verse: *"A righteous man may fall seven times and rise again, but the wicked shall fall by calamity."*

Or perhaps Psalm 37:24: *"Though he fall, he shall not be utterly cast down; for the Lord upholds him with His hand."*

Have you stumbled? Failed? Fallen on your face?

Don't just lie there—get up! There were no sinless Bible heroes except Jesus himself; and even the great heroes of the faith had moments of mistakes, missteps, and miserable failure.

But they didn't give up—and neither must you. Get back on your feet, dust yourself off, and go forward for Christ!

Never doubt in the dark what God told you in the light.

V. RAYMOND EDMAN

THINK

Do not speak evil of one another, brethren.

JAMES 4:11

Why is it so easy to point out the faults of others and gossip about them instead of encouraging them? Maybe it makes us feel better about our own shortcomings; perhaps we just enjoy hearing the "juice" about others. Whatever the reason, it is sin; yet many of us continue to do it.

One man found a way to combat this problem in his church. It was a formula he came up with that the members of the church had to apply before speaking to anyone. T.H.I.N.K.: T – is it True? H – is it Helpful? I – is it Inspiring? N – is it Necessary? K – is it Kind? If what they were about to say did not pass the above test, they were to keep their mouths shut. It worked!

Today, we need to pay attention to what we say to others. Are we gossiping and slandering, or are we a source of encouragement? If we cannot honestly say we are the latter, we need to ask God to soften our heart and help us become an example of His encouraging love to those around us. [15]

Kind words do not cost much. They never blister the tongue or lips.
They make other people good-natured. They also produce their own
image on men's souls, and a beautiful image it is.

BLAISE PASCAL

15 ALAN REDPATH, FROM *A Passion for Preaching*

NEITHER CHAOS NOR COLD

Greater love has no one than this,
than to lay down one's life for his friends.

JOHN 15:13

The Reverend John Harper was on his way to America to preach in the famed Moody Church in Chicago. A widower, Harper was accompanied by his six-year-old daughter, Nina, and his niece. Standing at the railing of the great ocean liner, *Titanic*, on the night of April 14, 1912, he said to his daughter and niece, "It will be beautiful in the morning." It was a morning he didn't live to see.

When the *Titanic* began to sink, it is said that Harper added "and the unsaved" to the familiar cry of, "Women and children to the lifeboats." After making sure his daughter and niece were safe in a lifeboat, Harper preached the Gospel to whomever would listen until he was forced to abandon ship—one of 1,498 who went into the freezing North Atlantic. Four years after the tragedy, a young man testified how Harper swam about in the waters before he succumbed, urging people to "believe on the Lord Jesus Christ and be saved." The young man, one of six people rescued from the waters, was one who believed after first refusing Harper's pleas.

Neither chaos nor cold could keep John Harper from laying down his life so that others might live in time and for eternity.

God will be our compensation for every sacrifice we have made.

F. B. MEYER

Planting and Growing

By which have been given to us exceedingly great and precious
promises, that through these you may be partakers of the divine nature,
having escaped the corruption that is in the world through lust.

2 Peter 1:4

In the winter a farmer gathers his seed. He plans how many seeds are needed in order to reap a harvest. He prepares the ground to receive the seed. But nothing happens until the farmer takes the step of burying the seed in the soil. Having seed is not enough. There must be a commitment to plant the seed and nurture its growth until it brings forth fruit.

Jesus was the first to compare the Word of God to a seed (Luke 8:11), followed later by the apostle Peter (1 Peter 1:23). Peter also talked about the "great and precious promises" contained in the Word that allow us to become partakers of the divine nature. But like the farmer and his seed, we only grow spiritually when we plant the Word of God deeply in the soil of the heart (see Matthew 13:1-23). Having the seed of the Word is not enough. We must plant it before we will see ourselves grow.

You probably have more than one seed, more than one copy of the Word of God. But all it takes to see fruit is one that is planted and nurtured.

There is more to Christian growth than knowing what the Bible says;
nobody is ever nourished by memorizing menus.

John Blanchard

David Jeremiah

MARS?

*Many, O Lord my God, are Your wonderful works which
You have done; and Your thoughts toward us cannot be recounted . . .
They are more than can be numbered.*

PSALM 40:5

Astrophysicist Stephen Hawking recently told a conference that human beings must quickly establish a base on the moon and colonize Mars, otherwise global warming or another catastrophe may drive the human race to extinction. "Life on earth is at the ever increasing risk of being wiped out by a disaster such as sudden global warming, nuclear war, a genetically engineered virus, or other dangers we have not thought of yet," he said.

The Bible teaches that earth's days *are* numbered; but the Bible also says that God has not abandoned us, nor has He forgotten His children. Psalm 139 says, *"How precious also are Your thoughts to me, O God! How great is the sum of them."* Jeremiah 29:11 says, *"'For I know the thoughts that I think toward you,' says the Lord, 'thoughts of peace . . . to give you a future and a hope.'"*

We can forget the Lord, but He can never forget us. He loves and knows and cares, and we should think about *that*. When your world is threatened, it's not Mars you need, but the Master.

*God's thoughts of love are very many, very wonderful,
very practical! Muse on them . . . no sweeter subject
ever occupied your mind. God's thoughts of you are many.*

CHARLES SPURGEON

THE FINISH LINE

...let us run with endurance the race that is set before us.

HEBREWS 12:1

It took Edward Gibbon 26 years to write *The History of the Decline and Fall of the Roman Empire*, 36 years for Noah Webster to produce the first edition of the dictionary, and the Roman orator Cicero spent 30 years practicing in front of friends in order to perfect his public speaking. That is persistence personified.

The life we live on earth is merely practice for heaven. So why is it so difficult at times to maintain our spiritual growth and press on toward our goal? We get distracted by the world, we get lazy in our effort, and we live in a culture that demands immediate gratification rather than appreciating long-term goals.

As Christians, we must challenge ourselves to persistently grow in the Lord and mature in our faith as part of this race we are running. We cannot give up or settle for a mediocre walk with God. Let us persist in our efforts, resting in His arms when we need to, and gaining the strength to continue on from the One who is waiting for us at the finish line.

Never, never, never give up!

WINSTON CHURCHILL

SCROLLING THROUGH LIFE

Son of man, eat what you find; eat this scroll,
and go, speak to the house of Israel.

EZEKIEL 3:1

In John Bunyan's classic allegory, *Pilgrim's Progress,* Christian grew weary while clambering up a steep hill on hands and knees. He came to a bench, sat down to rest, and pulled his scroll from his jacket. Falling into a deep sleep, Christian relaxed his hand and the scroll fell to the ground. Only later in his journey did he realize the scroll was missing. Falling on his knees, Christian asked God for forgiveness, and then retraced his steps. Coming to the arbor, he wept for having fallen asleep in the daytime in the midst of the difficulty and for having lost the scroll. But as he wept, his eye spied his book under the bench. So joyful was he that he raced up the hill nimbly, determined never again to fall asleep and lose the precious scroll.

Amid the difficulties of life, we often need rest; but we should never fall asleep spiritually or lose our daily habit of reading from the "scroll" of God's Word. Be diligent at staying on God's pathway. Stay alert and keep your Bible close at hand.

God, as being very tender of me, hath not suffered me to be molested,
but would with one scripture and another strengthen me against all.

JOHN BUNYAN

OCTOBER 21

EARLY WARNINGS

*I myself always strive to have a conscience
without offense toward God and men.*

ACTS 24:16

In Ewa Beach, Hawaii, sits a rather plain-looking white block
building with a small ramp leading to the front door. It is un-
imposing, but what happens there could save thousands of lives.
It's the Pacific Tsunami Warning Center, established in 1949. Its
purpose is to continually monitor the Pacific Basin for seismic
activity and provide early warning flashes for possible tsunamis.

The human heart also has an early warning system, established
in the soul, which continually monitors for the seismic activities
of sin in our lives. It's called the conscience, and the apostle Paul's
desire was to serve Christ with a pure conscience (2 Timothy 1:3).

One man quipped, "Conscience is that still small voice that is
sometimes too loud for comfort."

Are you listening to your conscience? The Bible warns that if
we don't heed this still, small inner voice, it may become seared
and defiled (1 Timothy 4:2, Titus 1:15). When that happens, it's
like disconnecting the sirens and signals from the Pacific Tsunami
Warning Center.

If your conscience is speaking to you about some matter, hear
it and heed it!

There is no pillow so soft as a clear conscience.

FRENCH PROVERB

DAVID JEREMIAH

DORCAS

Dorcas . . . was full of good works and charitable deeds which she did.

ACTS 9:36

If there were a race named "Kindness Klassic" or "Good Deeds Derby," Dorcas would have been the champion. She made garments for widows and sewed the buttons on many a child's coat. When she died, the whole town turned out in grief; and someone sent for Peter. The Bible says, *"Peter . . . knelt down and prayed. And turning to the body he said, 'Tabitha, arise.' And she opened her eyes, and when she saw Peter she sat up"* (Acts 9:40).

In 1982, Berkeley writer Anne Herbert coined a simple phrase: *Random Acts of Kindness.* The idea was: Imagine what would happen if there were an outbreak of kindness in the world, if everybody did one kind thing on a daily basis. Now *Random Acts of Kindness* is an international movement wherein thousands of people seek to adopt a stray animal, smile at a bus driver, compliment a stranger, return shopping carts to the store, treat local police officers to coffee, and give up their places in the grocery line to someone with just one item.

If anyone should be kind, it is the followers of Jesus. Today, be a Dorcas and commit a random act of kindness.

The best portion of a good man's life is his little, nameless, unremembered acts of kindness and of love.

WILLIAM WORDSWORTH

TRUSTING GOD WITH YOUR FAMILY

Unless the Lord builds the house, they labor in vain who build it.

PSALM 127:1A

No couple stands before God on their wedding day and vows to separate within a few years or raise children to choose a wayward path. Every couple vows to do their best with God's help to create a loving and lasting home that will be a refuge and sanctuary, a hospital of the soul to heal the wounds of the world. Family is everything—where life begins, where it is nurtured, and where it breathes its last, surrounded by love and hope of being reunited in eternity.

Sadly, we sometimes have to identify with Job: "For the thing I greatly feared has come upon me, and what I dreaded has happened to me" (Job 3:25). Even the most well-intended families suffer the pain of disappointment, lost love, breakdown, even breakup. But that doesn't mean God's grace isn't sufficient to carry on. Family faith pursues God's ideal, fights for the highest good, loves unconditionally, thinks the best, and always perseveres. And if failure occurs, it gives and receives forgiveness through the blood of Christ and lives to love and believe another day.

Your family is not perfect, but your God is. Let Him give you renewed faith for your family today.

The family circle is the supreme conductor of Christianity.

HENRY DRUMMOND

DAVID JEREMIAH

OCTOBER 24

THE MARK OF THE CHRISTIAN

By this all will know that you are My disciples,
if you have love for one another.

JOHN 13:35

External marks of identification are accepted in our culture. If you work in a company, you may wear an I.D. badge. If you live in a gated community, you may need a windshield sticker to gain access. And, if you want to check your child in or out of a nursery at church or preschool, you will probably need a picture I.D. card.

I.D. marks and badges are so common today that it will likely be no surprise when the coming Antichrist requires every person on earth to receive a mark on his or her forehead or hand signifying their allegiance to him—and thereby, their right to buy and sell in the marketplace. Christians, on the other hand, have an ancient mark instituted by Christ Himself: love for one another. He said the world will know His disciples by the presence (or absence) of love. The Antichrist's disciples will be identified by a bodily mark of some sort, while Christ's disciples will be (and should be today) identified by their love for one another.

The question for every Christian is, "How plain is Christ's mark in your life? How obvious is it that you belong to Him?"

Love is service rather than sentiment.

JOHN R. W. STOTT

RIPPLES

*A posterity shall serve Him. It will be recounted
of the Lord to the next generation.*

PSALM 22:30

Just as tossing a stone into a lake creates ripples to the shoreline, so our simple acts of witness produce results that extend to the return of Christ.

Early one Sunday, a young man dragged himself home from a night of partying. As an instructor at Tampa's Arthur Murray Studio, he was single, popular, and unhindered by morality. He collapsed into bed, setting his radio alarm for mid-afternoon. When the radio came on, he was jolted awake by the preaching of Donald Barnhouse, who was asking: "Suppose you were to die today and stand before God and He asked you, 'What right do you have to enter into my heaven?'—what would you say?"

That's the moment the Holy Spirit touched D. James Kennedy, who became one of America's eminent pastors and teachers. At the time, however, no one knew the results of that broadcast. It was unknown to Dr. Barnhouse, to the producers of the show, or to the supporters who had given their gifts to put it on the air. Only heaven will tabulate the outcome.

You're doing more good than you know. Don't underestimate the handful of stones you're throwing into the pond whenever you say a word for Christ.

Lord lay some soul upon my heart and love that soul through me.

LEON TUCKER

THE WORLD'S PATINA

Pure and undefiled religion before God and the Father is this:
to visit orphans and widows in their trouble,
and to keep oneself unspotted from the world.

JAMES 1:27

Bronze mentioned in the Bible was an alloy of copper and other metals such as tin. Today, copper is widely used in cookware, vases, sinks, pots, and for ornamental purposes. Over time, bronze and copper, exposed to the elements, develop a patina—a greenish sheen, highlighted by dark spots that create an appearance of age. Some people find the patina on copper highly desirable.

The spotting of ornamental copper objects might be desirable, but there is another category of spotting that is not: when Christians become spotted by the world. The apostle Paul says that Christ's goal is to keep His bride, the Church, from becoming spotted or blemished (Ephesians 5:27); and Peter says every believer is to be diligent about being found in Christ, unspotted and blameless (2 Peter 3:14). We become spotted by the world when we become friends with it (James 4:4). Are you developing a worldly patina? Compared to the purity of Christ, the difference will be unattractive.

We avoid spotting by living in Christ—being *in* the world but not *of* the world.

The ship's place is in the sea,
but God pity the ship when the sea gets into it.

UNKNOWN

CASE LAW

Beloved, do not believe every spirit, but test the spirits,
whether they are of God; because many false
prophets have gone out into the world.

1 JOHN 4:1

For police officers, knowing and understanding case law is one of the most important components of their job. Case law refers to the principles and rules of law determined by specific cases brought forth in court, such as Carroll v. United States, 267 U.S. 132 (U.S. 1925), which enables officers to search vehicles without a search warrant if there is probable cause to believe that the vehicle contains contraband. Officers must study and memorize case law constantly in order to know what to look for and how to properly handle each case.

In the same way, Christians must constantly be studying God's Word in order to detect false doctrine. If we have not studied the true doctrine, how can we know what false teaching looks like? We must commit ourselves to learning and understanding as much as we can from the Bible. By doing this, we will build a firm foundation for ourselves that cannot be moved by every new teaching that comes along; and we will in turn live a more sound and victorious Christian life.

Nothing less than a whole Bible can make a whole Christian.

A.W. TOZER

DAVID JEREMIAH

THE LIGHT OF OBEDIENCE

Your word is a lamp to my feet and a light to my path.

PSALM 119:105

Go into any of the big-box hardware/home center stores, and you'll find an entire section devoted to flashlights. Some of them are huge! They advertise millions of candlepower in brightness and light up objects a quarter-mile away. These lights are a far cry from the tiny, hand held oil lamps in biblical times: "one" candlepower in strength, lighting up objects perhaps five feet away!

The psalmist wrote that God's Word was a lamp to his feet and a light to his path. And in the mind of the Israelite, God's Word was something to be obeyed. As I obey God's Word where I stand today, His Word will give direction for the next move I should make. In other words, there is no need to see a quarter-mile down life's path if I am not going to obey and take the one step God has made clear where I stand. If you are seeking direction for your life, obey what God has shown you today. Do that one day at a time and, looking back, you'll realize the entire way has been illuminated.

Obedience is not a matter of seeing the whole path, only the next step. Obedience increases seeing.

The plain fact is that not everyone who professes to seek guidance is honestly desirous of being guided into God's will.

J. OSWALD SANDERS

FLYING FUNDS

Riches certainly make themselves wings;
they fly away like an eagle toward heaven.

PROVERBS 23:5

The Bible warns that money is as transient as a bird on the wing. Proverbs 27:24 says that riches are not forever, and Ecclesiastes 5:14 warns that wealth can easily perish through misfortune. Paul warned us not to trust in wealth, which is so uncertain (1 Timothy 6:17).

If you've suffered financial loss, it might help to remember that sometimes monetary pressures are like winds pushing us onto the shores of God's faithfulness. You can stand on the Solid Rock without a penny in your pocket, without a dollar in your account, without a crumb in your pantry. We can't effectively insure ourselves against financial ruin—there are no truly safe investments—and who knows what the future will hold?

There is one thing we know for certain—there will never be a run on heaven's banks. He tells us to be unshaken and unafraid. He'll provide in His own time and way, and we can trust Him with all our needs. He who spared not His own Son but freely gave Him for us all, how will He not also give us all things we need?

No man can tell whether he is rich or poor by turning to his ledger.
It is the heart that makes a man rich. He is rich or poor
according to what he is, not according to what he has.

HENRY WARD BEECHER

WHEN HE SHALL COME

Now there is in store for me the crown of righteousness, which the Lord... will award to me on that day—and not only to me, but also to all who have longed for His appearing.

2 TIMOTHY 4:8 (NIV)

A morning television show recently presented a film clip of an American soldier who had just returned from Iraq. His return was a bit earlier than expected, so he showed up unannounced at his daughter's school. A film crew was allowed to capture the scene. When he entered the classroom, his daughter looked up and saw him in stunned unbelief, then she burst into tears of joy, covered her mouth with her hands, and ran into his embrace. Lifting her off her feet, he hugged her tightly as she sobbed and classmates cheered.

Maybe that's a small picture of how we'll feel when Jesus comes again.

Perhaps you remember a time in childhood when you looked forward to a beloved family member coming for a visit. The days and hours leading up to their arrival seemed interminable. The eagerness and anticipation were hard to contain.

The Lord wants us to long for His appearing like that.

When He shall come resplendent in His glory, to take His own from out the vale of night, O may I know the joy at His appearing, only at morn, to walk with Him in white!

ALMEDA PEARCE

STRANGERS IN THE WORLD

But now they desire a better, that is, a heavenly country.
Therefore God is not ashamed to be called their God,
for He has prepared a city for them.

HEBREWS 11:16

The American philosopher Henry David Thoreau suggested that we should live so simply that if an enemy overtook our town, we could walk out of the gate empty-handed and without anxiety. It is a reminder to us as Christians that we should travel light, remembering that this world is not our home.

When Pharaoh asked Jacob's age, the old man replied, "The years of my pilgrimage are one hundred and thirty" (Genesis 47:9). Shortly before he died, King David prayed, "We are aliens and pilgrims before You" (1 Chronicles 29:15). In discussing Old Testament heroes, the writer of Hebrews 11:13 called them "strangers and pilgrims on the earth." He said they desired a better country and were looking for a city that God had prepared for them (verse 16); therefore God was not ashamed to be called their God.

The Bible says, "Beloved, I beg you as sojourners and pilgrims, abstain from fleshly lusts which war against the soul."

Remember—this world is not our home; we're just "a passing through."

Christians are not citizens of earth trying to get to heaven
but citizens of heaven making their way through this world.

VANCE HAVNER

November

November 1

Gratitude for Salvation

*But we are bound to give thanks to God always for you,
brethren beloved by the Lord, because God from
the beginning chose you for salvation...*

2 Thessalonians 2:13

As James Chasteen was distributing Gideon Bibles in a nursing home in New York City, he spotted an old man in a wheelchair. The two struck up a conversation, and James asked the man if he was certain of heaven. "I would like to think that I would go to heaven," the man replied with tears, "but I don't think I would. I don't know how, and no one has ever told me how." That day James had the joy of leading this man to Christ; and afterward, he asked him how old he was. The astonishing answer: 100! He would be 101 in another month.[16]

Praise God for a man who found Christ at age 100!

Thank goodness most of us don't wait that long. What a joy to know Christ as our Savior today, to be walking with Him, and to be looking forward to life in His Celestial City. We are bound to give thanks to Him who, from the beginning, chose us for salvation.

*O Father, we would thank Thee for all Thy love has given, our present
joy of sonship, our future joy in Heaven.*

Ada R. Greenaway, in *Hymns Ancient and Modern*, 1904

---

16 *The Gideon Magazine*, June 2009, p. 3.

THE HOUSE HE'S BUILDING

But the salvation of the righteous is from the Lord:
He is their strength in the time of trouble.

PSALM 37:39

Years ago, before Josh McDowell was the well-known speaker and author he is today, he joined the staff of Campus Crusade for Christ. Going to the ministry headquarters at Arrowhead Springs in California, he received his first assignment: washing the floors in the lobby of the former resort hotel. While he thought he was going to be working with the ministry's leaders, he was relegated to watching them walk by as he scrubbed the floors they were walking on. Later, he said it was one of the most important lessons he ever learned: It takes preparation to be used by God.

Moses learned that lesson, spending forty years in the Midian wilderness as a shepherd before leading his countrymen out of Egypt. Jesus spent forty days in the Judean wilderness before being commissioned for ministry at the Jordan River. Difficult periods of preparation are God's way of saying, "Only I know what you need to know to be successful. Trust me." The psalmist said, *"Unless the Lord builds the house, they labor in vain who build it."*

If you're going through a difficult time right now, trust the Lord. The house He is building (you) needs whatever you're learning as you wait on Him.

A season of suffering is a small price to pay for a clear view of God.

MAX LUCADO

NO OTHER NAME

But to which of the angels has He ever said:
"Sit at My right hand, till I make Your enemies Your footstool"?

HEBREWS 1:13

Aprominent religion with temples located around the world honors an angel with a statue in all its temples. The Washington, D. C., temple has a statue of this angel that is more than 18 feet tall, weighing 4,000 pounds. This angel is revered because he supposedly revealed the religion's sacred writings to its founder.

While this religion claims roots in Christianity, it is far from the truth of God's Word and it gets the angel part completely wrong. Nowhere in the Bible are angels elevated or venerated. They are powerful and faithful servants of God, but they are created beings. Only one person in Christian Scriptures is to be elevated and worshipped above all: Jesus Christ. The writer to the Hebrews makes it clear that no angel has ever been accorded the status of God's Son, Jesus Christ. While we are thankful for the work of these created servants of God—and their ministry to us—Christians should never make the mistake of worshipping them (Colossians 2:18).

There is no other name under heaven like Jesus Christ (Acts 4:12).

An angel is a spiritual creature created by God without a body,
for the services of Christendom and of the church.

MARTIN LUTHER

WHO, WHY, AND WHERE

The Spirit Himself bears witness with
our spirit that we are children of God.

ROMANS 8:16

When Princes William and Harry of Wales were born to England's Prince Charles and Lady Diana, the British press lovingly referred to them as "the heir and a spare"—William being "the heir" and Harry being "the spare." In other words, Prince William, being the firstborn son of Prince Charles, stands directly in the line of succession to the British crown. And should he be unable to become king, Prince Harry would step in. When one is born to royalty, one's identity and destiny are fixed simply by being born.

The same is true of Christians. The moment we are born again by God's Spirit, we become children of God and "heirs according to the promise" (Galatians 3:29). Our future and our destiny is set—we know who we are and where we are going. Our purpose in life is to be transformed into the image of Jesus Christ (Romans 8:29), and our destiny is to live for eternity in the presence of Jesus Christ our Lord (Revelation 21:3-4).

If you are a Christian, you should never be confused about who you are, why you are here, and where you are going. That was settled when you were born again.

God made us to be worshippers. That was the
purpose of God in bringing us into the world.

A. W. TOZER

POWER OF THE BOOK

So shall My word be that goes forth from
My mouth; it shall not return to Me void.

ISAIAH 55:11A

The first state constitution written in America was the Fundamental Orders of Connecticut (1639). It was based on the Bible, and it became a model for other state constitutions as well as the Constitution of the United States. Since the American Revolution (1776), America's biblically-based constitution has remained in place. France, by comparison, has had seven constitutions since the French Revolution (1789) that were based on Voltaire's anti-biblical, humanist philosophy.

The influence of the Bible is seen throughout America's government. The founding fathers devised a three-branch system of checks and balances because they acknowledged the depravity of man—man's inability to govern himself. It is hard not to connect America's declining moral state with the removal of the Bible from its original central place in our nation's government and schools. The Bible is alive and powerful; remove it, and its life-changing power is negated (Hebrews 4:12).

Moral and spiritual decline happens to individuals before it happens to nations. Commit to keeping God's Word at the core of your life.

Apply yourself wholly to the text; apply the text wholly to yourself.

JOHN A. BENGEL

REMEMBER YOUR CHROMOSOMES

I will praise You, for I am fearfully and wonderfully made;
marvelous are Your works, and that my soul knows very well.

PSALM 139:14

You inherited 46 chromosomes (23 pairs) from your mother and father, half of each pair from each parent. The half-pairs united at your conception as a single-cell being. From the beginning, human beings have replicated the same shape—two arms, two legs, one head, and so on—while varying in the details—eye and hair color, facial characteristics, height and shape—based on the genetic markers on the chromosomes. Indeed, we are "fearfully and wonderfully made."

The consistency of God's design of human beings (and other animal and plant species) reflects the consistency of His purpose. As Paul said in Romans 1:19-20, the evidence for God's purposeful existence is all around us, not least in those who bear His divine image on the earth (Genesis 1:26-27). Life is not random as evolutionists would have us believe. Rather, the consistency of design in creation reflects the dominance of God's controlling purpose.

On days that appear to be without purpose in your life, remember your chromosomes: steady, purposeful, and unwavering as the purpose of God.

He that is made in the image of God must know him or be desolate.

GEORGE MACDONALD

THINKING ABOUT GOD

I will meditate on Your precepts, and contemplate Your ways.

PSALM 119:15

The *American Heritage Dictionary* says to meditate is to "reflect on; contemplate." How did such a simple idea become so scary to most Christians today? It's because of the influence of Eastern religions that use meditating on a specific word or thought as a way to empty the mind, to move beyond object-oriented thinking to a deeper state of awareness or reality. Ironically, in Scripture, meditation is always focused on something or Someone—a filling of the mind, not an emptying.

In the Old Testament we find Scripture to be the most consistent object of meditation (Joshua 1:8; Psalm 1:2; 119:48). But Old Testament saints also meditated on God (Psalm 63:6) and His majesty (Psalm 145:5), the works of God (Psalm 77:12), and God's name (Malachi 3:16). And in the New Testament we are exhorted to meditate on things that are true, noble, just, pure, lovely, and of good report (Philippians 4:8), as well as on sound doctrine and the spiritual gifts of God (1 Timothy 4:15-16). Psalm 1:1-3 perhaps says it best: the primary characteristic of a godly person is that he or she meditates "day and night" on "the law of the Lord."

The more we contemplate the truth of God, the more our lives will reflect the Author of that truth.

Meditate on the Word in the Word.

JOHN OWEN

NOVEMBER 8

THE GREATEST PARADOX

My brethren, count it all joy when you fall into various trials.

JAMES 1:2

Many things about the kingdom of God seem odd to those who are not its citizens. Kingdom citizens gain by giving, live by dying, and become great by becoming least. But perhaps the greatest oddity in the kingdom of God is when Christians find joy in pain and suffering. There is something unnatural about rejoicing in the midst of trials.

But a clarification must be made. The Bible says we are to give thanks "in everything," not "for everything." The Bible is *transrational*, not *irrational*; it represents thinking at a higher level, not a lower level. "In" the experience of trials and trouble, joy can still be found because we know that every experience has a purpose and place in God's plan for our lives. Who would not find joy in having his faith proved to be genuine? Peter writes that trials and suffering come for that very reason: to prove that the faith we cling to is the real thing (1 Peter 1:6-7). In such revelation and confirmation is found true joy.

If you are experiencing a painful moment in your life right now, you don't have to fake having joy "for" the pain. Your joy is to be in the knowledge that God is in control and your faith in Him is unshakeable.

It is the very joy of this earthly life to think that it will come to an end.

CHARLES H. SPURGEON

GRATITUDE FOR HEALTH

*Beloved, I pray that you may prosper in all things
and be in health, just as your soul prospers.*

3 JOHN 2

Millions of people worldwide suffer from debilitating diseases like Parkinson's disease, arthritis, and multiple sclerosis. And no one can truly understand the frustrations of these illnesses unless they are personally affected by them. Yet many of these individuals are so thankful for the health they *do* have, while others who aren't plagued with a life-altering disease take good health for granted.

In writing to his friend, Gaius, the apostle John said, "I pray that you may prosper in all things and be in health, just as your soul prospers."

Perhaps you've heard people pray, "Lord, we thank You that we are as well as we are." None of us is in perfect physical shape; all of us are subject to illness. In heaven we'll be perfectly whole. But here on earth let's thank God that we are as well as we are, and rejoice that in Christ we can enjoy abundant living in body, mind, and soul.

Make each prayer a prayer of thanks and every day Thanksgiving.

HELEN STEINER RICE

BE A FRUIT INSPECTOR

*For every tree is known by its own fruit. For men do not gather figs
from thorns, nor do they gather grapes from a bramble bush.*

LUKE 6:44

Grafting merges the fruiting portion of one plant or tree with
the rooting portion of another. The trunk of an apple tree of
one variety, for instance, called the rootstock, will have grafted to
it the flowering or fruiting portion of a different apple tree, called
the scion. When the tree matures, it bears fruit that the rootstock
tree would never have borne.

That may work in the world of horticulture, but it does not
work in the spiritual world: The fruit cannot be different from the
root. Or, as Jesus put it, *"Every tree is known by its own fruit."* Jesus
spoke these words when warning against false prophets: Test
the prophet's fruit and you will know the prophet's root. But the
principle applies across the board—even to Christians. Galatians
5:22-23 describes the fruit of the Spirit—the character traits of a
true follower of Jesus. Anyone bearing fruit unlike the character
of Jesus calls his own spiritual rootstock into question.

Fruit inspection is always in order—not others' fruit, but our
own. Make sure there is no discrepancy between fruit and root in
your life.

*It is no use to anybody for a tree to bud and blossom
if the blossom does not develop into fruit.*

MARTIN LUTHER

THANKING BY GIVING

*You will be made rich in every way so that you can
be generous on every occasion, and through us your
generosity will result in thanksgiving to God.*

2 CORINTHIANS 9:11 (NIV)

This is the month when Americans pause to give thanks for
their blessings. While we normally think of Christmas as the
holiday for giving, perhaps Thanksgiving is a time to give as well.
At the first "Thanksgiving" feast held by the Plymouth colony in
1621, the members expressed their thanks by inviting the native
Wampanoag people who helped them survive their first winter.

Giving to others is a good way to express thanks to God. Paul
told the Macedonian Christians as much when he wrote that
God's blessing to them would allow them to be generous to
others, which would result in "thanksgiving to God." In Romans
15:28, Paul called the Macedonians' financial gifts "fruit,"
meaning it was a result of their relationship to Jesus Christ (John
15:1-8). When they gave to others, it was because of what God,
through Christ, had given to them. This Thanksgiving might
be a good opportunity to join the Plymouth and Macedonian
Christians by sharing with others.

Look around—who do you see with a need you could meet? Or
who could you bless with an unexpected gift?

No duty is more urgent than that of returning thanks.

AMBROSE

SNARED OR SAFE?

*The fear of man brings a snare, but whoever
trusts in the LORD shall be safe.*

PROVERBS 29:25

Recently a man in New York turned down a promotion because his new office would be on the tenth floor. The problem? He suffers from a fear of elevators—evidently a combination of acrophobia (fear of heights) and claustrophobia (fear of enclosed spaces).

When a fear takes hold of us, it doesn't like to let go. For some, it's the inability to relax at night because of squeaks in the timbers or noises near the windows. For others, it is panic attacks or anxiety disorders. And then there are people who experience apprehension whenever a loved one is traveling, or a sense of dread when fetching the bills from the mailbox. Many of us are afraid of other people, those intimidating souls who frighten, bully, harass, or torment us.

Proverbs 29:25 gives us two options: We can fear others, which becomes a snare. Or we can trust God, which leads to safety. The devil is the source of fear, and his goal is to confuse and confound. The Savior of our souls replaces fear with faith, and whoever trusts in Him is safe.

*I have learned over the years that when one's
mind is made up, this diminishes fear.*

ROSA PARKS

No Room for Bullies

For an overseer, as God's manager,
must be blameless... not a bully....

TITUS 1:7 (HCSB)

There's a long list of bullies in the Bible: The brothers who bedeviled Joseph, the Pharaoh who bullied Moses, those foreign invaders who threatened Judah, Haman who hated Mordecai, Jezebel who threw Elijah into fits, the Pharisees who tried to intimidate Jesus, and Alexander the coppersmith who did harm to Paul. Bullies can show up anywhere, even at home or church. At some point, we have to take a stand in the name of Christ and resist bullying.

Bullies don't always come in human form. The devil sends doubts, fears, and worries to browbeat us. James said that if we resist the devil, he will flee from us—as bullies usually do. Let's think of ourselves as children whose older brother stands at our side. Because of Him we are more than conquerors.

The Bible says, "Don't be bluffed into silence by the threats of bullies. There's nothing they can do to your soul.... Save your fear for God, who holds your entire life—body and soul—in His hands (Matthew 10:28, the *Message*).

The fear of the Lord tends to take away all other fears...
This is the secret of Christian courage and boldness.

SINCLAIR B. FERGUSON

FOLLOW THE OXEN

Now then, we are ambassadors for Christ.

2 CORINTHIANS 5:20

Cape Town was a bustling outpost when Barnabas Shaw arrived in South Africa in 1815, intending to preach the Gospel and plant a church. Unfortunately, the authorities controlling the city were hostile to missionary efforts, and Barnabas was banned from engaging in evangelistic work. Not knowing what else to do, he bought a yoke of oxen and a cart, packed his belongings, and headed into the interior, letting the oxen lead the way. On the twenty-seventh day of the trip, he camped for the night near a party of Hottentots who were also traveling through the region. The Hottentots explained that they were traveling to Cape Town, hoping to find a missionary to teach them the "Great Word."

Had either group started a half-day earlier or later, they would not have met. Had either traveled at a different speed, they would have missed one another. God ordained the encounter, and His providence led Barnabas Shaw to his appointed field.

God has uniquely put you where you are to be His witness. Someone is "camping" near you, needing the Lord Jesus. You're His ambassador, so look around you and find your mission field.

Oh, it is the only thing worth doing, to save souls.

R. A. TORREY

SPIRITUAL SQUATTERS

Nor give place to the devil.

EPHESIANS 4:27

A "squatter" is a person who moves in and takes over an unoccupied or abandoned piece of property without permission and without paying for the privilege. In 2004, in his book *Shadow Cities: A Billion Squatters, A New Urban World*, author Robert Neuwirth estimated that one in every six people in the world is a squatter.

From a biblical perspective, demons that move in and take over the life of a human being can be called spiritual squatters. They move in without permission, or at least with very little resistance, and gradually cause spiritual, emotional, and even physical derangement. To use biblical terms, these people have become fully demonized. A Christian is the opposite: fully Spiritualized—totally indwelt and controlled by the Holy Spirit of God. A Christian cannot be demon possessed, but can be harassed or influenced by demons. That is why the apostle Paul wrote to the Ephesian Christians to give no place to the devil (Ephesians 4:27).

Submitting to God and resisting the devil (James 4:7) is the way to keep spiritual squatters off your property. Make sure you have given no place to the devil and his agents.

*Angels have a much more important place
in the Bible than the devil and his demons.*

BILLY GRAHAM

NOVEMBER 16

BEST PRACTICES

You shall love the LORD your God with all your heart,
with all your soul, and with all your strength.

DEUTERONOMY 6:5

The term "best practices" is used in organizational settings to refer to any activity, process, method, or behavior that is judged to be the most effective. Best practices are those methods that are most efficient, effective, and result in fewer complications and failures. Best practices are not "good ideas" or suggestions. They are proven strategies for anyone who wants the best possible outcome in a given endeavor.

Jesus Christ put into words what might be considered spiritual best practices: First, love God with everything in you—heart, soul, and mind; second, love your neighbor as yourself (Matthew 22:37-39). He called loving God "the first and great commandment," making it "job one" in the Christian life. No one who wants to be a fruitful Christian can ignore the priority of loving God. Loving other people is good; but since God is the source of our love for others, our love will be found wanting if we have not loved God first.

Priorities are given for a reason: They are proven best practices that we ignore at our spiritual peril.

Beloved, let the fact of what our Lord suffered for you grip you,
and you will never again be the same.

OLIVER B. GREENE

PRESSING ON

I press toward the goal. . . . I press on.

PHILIPPIANS 3:12, 14

If you're planning to travel during the Thanksgiving break, you're probably mapping the route, arranging lodging, and eager to be with family and friends around a roasted turkey. Everyone's travel plans are different, but each trip has three parts: the starting point, the journey itself, and the destination.

In the Christian life, our starting point is Mount Calvary. The German hymnist Paul Gerhardt penned these poignant words: "Upon the cross extended, see, world, thy Lord suspended." Jesus shed His blood on the cross to set us on the road to heaven.

Our destination is New Jerusalem, the Celestial City described so brilliantly in Revelation 21-22. Just as we study travel brochures of our destinations, we should frequently study the subject of heaven in the Bible.

The Christian's journey is a series of steps in Christ-likeness. Are you more like Jesus today than yesterday? Are you pressing on? Does your life now demonstrate the love, joy, and peace of Jesus more than it did a year ago? Today find a way to be a little more like the Savior as you press, step by step, toward the goal.

I will look upward and travel onward and not be afraid.

MISSIONARY ELLIS GOVAN,
DURING THE JAPANESE INVASION OF CHINA

HOPE FOR THE FUTURE

Cast your burden on the Lord, and He shall sustain you;
He shall never permit the righteous to be moved.

PSALM 55:22

Many people are fascinated with the future. Successful television series like *Star Trek* and *Flash Gordon* were created around Imaginary places in time. The possibilities were endless for storylines and unusual happenings. Those who enjoy science-fiction are entertained by the future and what it holds, and then there are those who want nothing more than to know what the future holds and to control it by carefully planning every detail of their lives. That, of course, is impossible. Planning and working toward a successful life is good, but we cannot ultimately control what we do not know or understand, but we know Someone who does. We can speculate and postulate about what we think will happen, but isn't it far easier to trust in the One who created all things to guide and direct our lives?

God is our strength and shield. He'll either shield us from trouble, or strengthen us in it. The One who holds the future also holds us tightly in His hands. So we can look forward with thankfulness.

Never be in a hurry; do everything quietly and in a calm spirit.
Do not lose your inner peace for anything whatsoever,
even if your whole world seems upset.

FRANCIS DE SALES

HEAVY BACKPACKS

Praise be to the Lord, to God our Savior, who daily bears our burdens.

PSALM 68:19 NIV

Pediatricians are concerned that many children are carrying too much weight in their school backpacks. Lugging a heavy burden around all day can trigger chronic back, neck, and shoulder pain. The rule of thumb is: A child's backpack shouldn't be heavier than 10-20 percent of his or her body weight.

Many of us carry around burdens that are too heavy. Here are some of the Bible's best "burden" verses:

The burden is too heavy for me—Moses in Numbers 11:14 (NIV)

We were burdened beyond measure, above strength, so that we despaired even of life—Paul in 2 Corinthians 1:8.

I am the Lord your God who brings you out from under the burdens—Exodus 6:7.

Cast your burden on the Lord, and He shall sustain you—Psalm 55:22.

When I was burdened with worries, You comforted me and made me feel secure—Psalm 94:19 (CEV).

For My yoke is easy and My burden is light—Matthew 11:30.

Is your backpack too heavy? Cast your cares on Him by faith, and say with the psalmist: Blessed be the Lord who daily bears our burdens!

> *If you want rest, O weary souls, ye can find it nowhere until ye come and lay your burdens down at His dear pierced feet.*
>
> CHARLES SPURGEON

THE LITTLE POT OF OIL

Nothing . . . but a jar of oil.

2 KINGS 4:2

In her book, *A Little Pot of Oil,* Jill Briscoe describes a time early in her ministry when she confided in an older friend that she had run out of strength and was resentful and exhausted. Jill's attention was directed to the little pot of oil within her. "You have all you need within you, Jill," said the woman, "in the person of the Holy Spirit. You have heavenly help a heartbeat away. It works as you begin to appropriate what you have. Go home, shut the door, and spend time with the Lord. Then begin to pour out whatever you have into the empty vessels of your neighbors."

That wasn't exactly what Jill wanted to hear; but she went home, shut the door, and asked God to show her where to begin pouring. "Give me an idea, Lord," she prayed. Then she arose, called a babysitter, and set off for the town center where she began pouring her life into high-risk teens, opening a period of ministry that transformed the lives of many young people.

If you're at the place God wants you to be, don't quit. Instead, shut the door, pray, and ask God to give you a fresh idea for His work. Then begin pouring out of your little pot of oil. And as you pour out, God will pour in!

*We have to step out and pour out, trusting that the
Holy Spirit will fill us and give us what we need to continue.*

JILL BRISCOE

MINISTERING SPIRITS

Then an angel appeared to Him from heaven, strengthening Him.

LUKE 22:43

The phrase "there for me" has entered the cultural conversation in recent years, appearing everywhere: song titles, tributes, testimonies, eulogies, and the like. Rarely is the phrase illustrated by specific examples, but readers and listeners generally get the idea: one person steps in to bring aid, comfort, advice, or resources to another person in need.

While it may sound trite to apply it to them, we could say that the angels were always there for Jesus. At least twice in His life that we know of, in moments of weakness and stress, one or more angels appeared to support Jesus: following His forty days of fasting and temptation in the wilderness, "angels came and ministered to Him" (Matthew 4:11); and during the hours of His agony in the Garden of Gethsemane an angel appeared in the Garden to strengthen Him (Luke 22:43). While it is hard for us to imagine Jesus needing ministry or strengthening, in His humanity He suffered the same tests as we do, yet without sin (Hebrews 4:15; 5:8).

Fortunately, angels are there for us as well, "sent forth to minister for those who will inherit salvation" (Hebrews 1:14).

Beside each believer stands an angel as protector and shepherd leading him to life.

BASIL THE GREAT

DAVID JEREMIAH

GRATITUDE ATTITUDE

While I live I will praise the Lord;
I will sing praises to my God while I have my being.

PSALM 146:2

Assume you are a Christian who lives in a politically and spiritually repressive country. You learn one day that all who refuse to renounce their faith in God will be killed. What would you do? Would your activities on that day be any different than the day before? Would your activities include prayers of thanks to God?

If you were the Old Testament prophet, Daniel, nothing would change. After learning that the King of Babylon had signed a decree stipulating that anyone caught praying to another God would be thrown in the lion's den, Daniel went home and did what he normally did three times each day: He prayed and gave thanks to God—thanks that he was now a wanted man? Not likely. Daniel's gratitude was based on knowing that God is sovereign over all things; that God knew his life would be threatened long before Daniel knew it; that he could entrust his future to God without fear of the outcome.

If gratitude and thanks to God are part of your daily pattern of life, then no unforeseen circumstance can create fear.

It is only with gratitude that life becomes rich.

DIETRICH BONHOEFFER

RAISE WITH PRAISE

I will bless the LORD at all times;
His praise shall continually be in my mouth.

PSALM 34:1

The Massachusetts Medical Society released a document entitled *Raise Your Child With Praise* in July of 2006 that included a printable tip card on how to use praise alongside discipline to raise children in a happy home. They tell parents, "Your child needs your love and attention. Sometimes your child learns that the only – or the best – way to get your attention is to misbehave!"

Children need discipline to be sure. The Bible even says "Do not withhold correction from a child" (Proverbs 23:13). But a child's tender spirit can be crushed with the constant presence of criticism and correction, and God's Word tells us not to exasperate our children (Ephesians 6:4 NIV). There must be a balance of godly discipline and deserving praise.

As Christian parents, we need to fill our homes with praise, both toward God and toward our children. In doing this, we will create a positive environment that motivates our children toward obedience and teaches them to live a life filled with praise and thanksgiving rather than discontent or criticism.

Spare the rod and spoil the child – that is true. But,
beside the rod, keep an apple to give him when he has done well.

MARTIN LUTHER

LEMONADE

Indeed it was for my own peace that I had great bitterness.

ISAIAH 38:17

The financial panic of 1907 started with a run on the Knickerbocker Trust Company of New York, exhausting the bank's reserves in a day and a half. In a matter of weeks, the panic had spread across the country and banks everywhere closed. One family was especially hard hit. Their investments and business enterprises foundered, and their dreams for the future evaporated. But they were resourceful, for they had two assets they could still use. The first was the mother's cooking skills, and the second was an old adobe building near the train station.

And so the Hilton family opened their first hotel.

There's an old saying that if life hands you a lemon, make lemonade. Problems bring possibilities to us that would not have otherwise occurred, and it's important to prayerfully consider how we can turn liabilities into assets.

In Isaiah 38, King Hezekiah suffered a debilitating illness; but by the end of the story, much good had come from it, including an extension of his life and a song of praise. If you're suffering through bitterness and pain now, remember that God has promised to work all things together for good to those who love Him. Look ahead in hope, and make some lemonade.

Every problem has a purpose.

RICK WARREN

THANKS IN, NOT FOR

*In everything give thanks; for this
is the will of God in Christ Jesus for you.*

1 THESSALONIANS 5:18

What could have motivated Horatio Spafford to pen the words to the mighty hymn "It Is Well with My Soul"? Before writing the hymn he had lost his only son in 1871, been financially ruined by the great Chicago fire of the same year, and then lost his four daughters at sea in 1873. His motivation was likely the truth of 1 Thessalonians 5:18: "In everything give thanks."

Many claim the verse is unrealistic: How could anyone give thanks for events like Spafford endured? But the verse says to give thanks *in* all things, not *for* all things. God expects no one to be thankful for tragedies that befall us in this life. But He does expect us to trust Him in the midst of such circumstances. *In* those difficult times, we can thank God that He will cause all things to work together for good in our life (Romans 8:28). While we grieve *for* those events and the losses incurred, we can give thanks even while *in* their midst.

Giving thanks when things are good requires enthusiasm, but giving thanks in hard times requires faith. If you are in the midst of difficulties, begin each day with a prayer of thanks.

Prayer without thanksgiving is like a bird without wings.

WILLIAM HENDRIKSEN

JOINING THE FRATERNITY

We . . . comfort those who are in any trouble,
with the comfort with which we ourselves are comforted by God.

2 CORINTHIANS 1:4

One day when Earl McQuay was a professor at Columbia International University, he received an emergency call. The news was devastating. His son, Tim, had been in a terrible wreck.

After Tim's death, Dr. McQuay wrote of the experience in a poignant little book, *Beyond Eagles: A Father's Grief and Hope.* He said: "Only someone who has experienced such a loss, we have found, is able to understand the agony of grief. Once in a while, we meet someone who has experienced a similar heartbreak, and we sense a certain kinship with them. It appears that we have become members of what someone has called 'the fraternity of the bereaved.'"

We each have our own set of hardships in life; and whenever you face any sorrow, you become a member of a fraternity. Parents of prodigals, for example. Or cancer sufferers. Or those who struggle with addictions. Or those who have buried a child.

There is a purpose in it all, and your hurt isn't wasted; it can provide balm for someone else's healing.

God does not waste suffering . . .
If He plows, it is because He purposes a crop.

ISOBEL KUHN

GREAT IS HIS FAITHFULNESS

If we confess our sins, He is faithful and just to forgive us our sins and to cleanse us from all unrighteousness.

1 JOHN 1:9

Everyone has done it—gone to bed with the weight of the world on our shoulders over a sin committed during the day. It's certainly destined to be a long night if we didn't settle accounts with God and others quickly (Ephesians 4:26). But even if we confessed our sin to God (1 John 1:9) and received His forgiveness, there is the discouragement factor. No one likes to disappoint a good friend, especially *that* Good Friend. How could we have been so (arrogant, foolish, disobedient)? How can we face the Lord Jesus in the morning after failing to be loyal to Him today? Feeling like Peter on the night of his three betrayals of Christ (Matthew 26), we toss and turn through a fitful night of barely-sleep.

With the morning's light it dawns on us—"The LORD is righteous in her midst, He will do no unrighteousness. Every morning He brings His justice to light; He never fails..." (Zephaniah 3:5). All night, God has been true to His promise not to leave us or forsake us and to greet us with unfailing mercy with every new morn.

Never forget: Though we may fail Him, He cannot deny Himself (2 Timothy 2:13). His mercies never fail. Great is His faithfulness!

Let God's promises shine on your problems.

CORRIE TEN BOOM

NOVEMBER 28

I HAVE EVERYTHING!

*So we, Your people and sheep of Your pasture,
will give You thanks forever.*

PSALM 79:13

Erma Bombeck once wrote about the subject of thankfulness, saying that when she forgot to be thankful among cancer survivors, she would hear the voice of a particular eight-year-old named Christina, who had cancer of the nervous system. When Christina was asked what she wanted for her birthday, she thought for a moment and then responded by saying "I don't know. I have two sticker books and a Cabbage Patch doll. I have everything!"

Sometimes a momentary thought about someone other than ourselves is all it takes to remind us to be thankful for what we have and who we are. In the same way, when we turn our attention away from ourselves and upward, toward the Giver of all life, the many blessings He has poured out on us come rushing back and overwhelm us with thanksgiving.

If we find ourselves complaining about our situation or longing for a better life, we need to take a few moments to worship God and allow His goodness to wash over us until we are consumed with gratitude.

The optimist says, the cup is half full. The pessimist says, the cup is half empty. The child of God says, my cup runneth over.

ANONYMOUS

FIVE SIMPLE RULES

My little children, let us not love in word or in tongue,
but in deed and in truth.

1 JOHN 3:18

The best way to have friends is to be one, and we can all do that. Fortunately, the rules for being a friend are simple enough for anyone to master.

First, work on your relationship with the Lord every day. The love we need for others comes from Him; and if we walk in the light as He is in the light, we'll have fellowship with one another. And with His love comes His joy, peace, and patience.

Second, avoid the use of the word "I." When you're with others, ask about *their* day, *their* health, and *their* burdens.

Third, don't be easily offended. A prudent person overlooks an insult (Proverbs 12:16, NIV). Good friends have thick skins.

Fourth, be cheerful. No one wants to be around a grumpy, irritable, or depressed spirit. Be friendly!

Fifth, drop everything to help your friend in a time of crisis or emergency. After all, you never know when you'll be on the receiving end.

Cultivate your friendships, and they will come back to bless you.

A friend knows when you have a need and
comes to strengthen you in the hand of God.

DAVID JEREMIAH

NOVEMBER 30

GO TO HIM FIRST

*Trust in the Lord with all your heart, and lean
not to your own understanding; in all your ways
acknowledge Him, and He shall direct your paths.*

PROVERBS 3:5-6

Christian musician Wayne Watson has a song entitled "Friend
of a Wounded Heart" that says when we're looking for a
friend, we can always turn to the Lord. "You'll find Him there,"
says Watson, "arms open wide, love in His eyes."

It's wonderful to have a few good friends in whom we can
confide, and who will pray for us and with us. But it's easy to run
to our friends when we should be running to our Friend.

Our friends may like us, but He loves us with an everlasting
love. Our friends may listen, but His ears are always open to our
cries. Our friends may try to advise us, but in Him dwells all the
treasures of wisdom and knowledge. Our friends may encourage
us, but He strengthens us with all power in our inner being. Our
friends may give us a good word, but He gives us His precious
promises. Our friends may brighten our lives, but He gives us
abundant life.

There's not a friend like the lowly Jesus. So learn to go to
Him first.

*Though by sin oppressed, go to Him for rest;
our God is able to deliver thee.*

WILLIAM OGDEN

December

GOD'S TWO THERMOMETERS

But whoever keeps His Word, truly the love of God is
perfected in him. By this we know that we are in Him.

1 JOHN 2:5

How do I love thee? Let me count the ways...."
Have you ever tried out Elizabeth Barrett Browning's
famous line on a dating partner or spouse?

From a biblical perspective, there are only two correct answers.
If you're speaking to another person, love means meeting his
or her needs. We love others by being more concerned for their
needs than for our own (Philippians 2:3), so we seek ways to
serve and to provide for them. But God, being God, has no needs
we can fill; so if we're saying, "How do I love Thee?" to Him, the
answer is different. Loving God means obeying Him. Jesus said,
"If you love Me, keep My commandments" (John 14:15). He said,
"Whoever has My commands and obeys them, he is the one who
loves Me" (John 14:21 NIV). He said, "If anyone loves Me, he will
obey My teaching" (John 14:23 NIV).

These are the Great Physician's two thermometers for testing
the health of our love. Do we care for the needs of others and are
we obedient to God?

Spiritual growth consists most in the
growth of the root, which is out of sight.

MATTHEW HENRY

DAVID JEREMIAH

GOD'S MESSENGERS

Bless the Lord, you His angels, who excel in strength,
who do His word, heeding the voice of His word.

PSALM 103:20

When someone in authority gives a directive, that command finds its way to the appropriate person who makes it happen. Commands don't execute themselves—it takes a person to carry out the authority's desires.

Isaiah 55:10-11 pictures God as an authority who sends forth His word. And it is always carried out: "It shall not return to Me void, but it shall accomplish what I please, and it shall prosper in the thing for which I sent it." But how does that happen? Who carries out God's words and translates them into action? Angels do—like the angel found in Daniel 10. This angel was dispatched from heaven to deliver to Daniel the answer to his prayers. The angel was delayed for three weeks by an evil angel, the power behind "the prince of the kingdom of Persia," and only the angel Michael, "one of the chief princes," was able to defeat the evil angel and see the messenger on his way to Daniel.

When you pray, realize that angels are at work to execute God's answers. And they may be opposed by "principalities and powers in the heavenly places" (Ephesians 3:10).

Angels mean messengers and ministers. Their function is to
execute the plan of divine providence even in earthly things.

THOMAS AQUINAS

JACOB

Then Jacob was left alone.

GENESIS 32:24

It must have been a "slow-news" day, for the headline of the Fort Wayne *Journal Gazette* was: "Naming Your Car Assuages Loneliness." The article was based on comments by a Tufts University professor who noticed a growing trend in car-naming. "Naming is the beginning of a conversation and a relationship," said the expert. "Many people spend a lot of time alone, and one place we spend a lot of time alone is in cars."

One man, who named his vehicle "Mimi," said he talks to his car all the time. "I'm sorry you're so dirty," he might say. "I have to wash you."

As we head into the holidays, perhaps you're already worried about spending Christmas alone. Well, you don't have to talk to your car. When Jacob found himself alone, he wasn't alone at all. The Angel of the Lord was there, and the two wrestled until Jacob received the blessing.

We can be alone without being lonely, even at Christmas. Devote this month to earnest prayer, acknowledge His presence, and "wrestle" with the Lord until the blessing comes.

I have a great deal of company in my house;
especially in the morning, when nobody calls.

HENRY DAVID THOREAU

YOU ARE NEVER ALONE

*Are they not all ministering spirits sent forth
to minister for those who will inherit salvation?*

HEBREWS 1:14

In the beginning, God established the principle of community when He said, "It is not good that man should be alone" (Genesis 2:18). That referred first to marriage, of course, but the theme of relationships and community is carried forth throughout the New Testament (1 Corinthians 12). But there is another form of community that is just as real but to which we pay little attention—to our detriment. And that is the community of the angels of heaven.

One of the purposes of the angels is to minister to the needs of God's people—"those who will inherit salvation" (Hebrews 1:14). The template for their activity is established in the life of Christ: Angels attended His birth (Hebrews 1:6), His life on earth (1 Timothy 3:16), His temptation in the wilderness (Matthew 4:11), His agony in the Garden of Gethsemane (Luke 22:43), and His resurrection (Matthew 28:2). At every crisis point of Christ's life, angels were with Him.

Regardless of the number of people around you, you are never alone in times of trouble. If you are a child of God, angels are sent forth from heaven to minister to you.

Jacob saw angels ascending and descending, but none standing still.

ANONYMOUS

The Best Place to Be

*Not that I speak in regard to need, for I have
learned in whatever state I am, to be content.*

Philippians 4:11

A quick survey of Internet dating sites—as well as brick-and-mortar "speed dating" businesses in major cities—would lead one to think being single is a disease that needs to be cured. First it was websites devoted to matching up singles—and they took the Internet by storm, quickly becoming the most popular new category of websites. But now dating websites are specializing into sub-sites that help singles find each other more quickly on the basis of religion, age, location, and most recently, lifestyle preferences such as cooking and fine foods.

But that's a sign of the times, not a sign of what's right. In God's eyes, singleness is a season of life like any other—no better and no worse. By activating their singleness for the Lord, singles are able to experience the joy of service. They are able to live with peace and thanksgiving, not in a state of anxiety. If you are single, be thankful for the time and ability you have to walk uninterrupted with Christ (1 Corinthians 7:33-34).

It has been well said that the best place in the world to be is the place to which God has led you today.

*Next to faith this is the highest art—to be content
with the calling in which God has placed you.*

Martin Luther

David Jeremiah

A DESIRE TO KNOW

*To them it was revealed that, not to themselves, but to us they
were ministering the things which now have been reported to you
through those who have preached the gospel to you by the Holy Spirit
sent from heaven—things which angels desire to look into.*

1 PETER 1:12

The most famous example of role reversal is probably Mark
Twain's *The Prince and the Pauper* (1881). Two young English
boys, identical in appearance, one a prince and the other a
pauper, become friends and decide to switch clothes and roles in
order to see what the other's life is like.

While that story is fictional, there is a literal case of role
reversal with profound circumstances: when Jesus Christ left
the glory of heaven and descended to earth to take on the form
of a lowly man. This must have been a shocking thing for the
angels of heaven to witness since they had known Christ only
in His glory. This must be only one of many things about God's
redemptive plan that Peter says "angels desire to look into" (1
Peter 1:12). Because angels are created beings like us, they share
the same inquiry into the ways of God as we do.

We can learn from the angels: If they desire to "look into" the
depths of the mysteries of God, how much more should we who
are the objects of His saving work?

With God there are mysteries, but no mistakes.

MICHAEL GRIFFITHS

DECEMBER 7

PEACE ON EARTH

Glory to God in the highest, and on earth peace, goodwill toward men!

LUKE 2:14

One of the most startling revelations of NASA's first ventures to the moon came in the form of photographs of earth. The most famous showed the earth like a fragile blue ball hanging in the black night of space. It was simultaneously a reminder of how isolated our outpost is in the vastness of the universe, yet how special it is: blue oceans contrasted with white covering clouds say "life" like no other heavenly body.

The uniqueness of earth is confirmed many ways in Scripture, but nowhere more clearly than in the Christmas story. God so valued His creation that He sent His only Son to redeem it. This blue orb hanging in the silence of space was invaded by hosts of angels who proclaimed "peace, goodwill toward men!" on the night of Jesus' birth. Every resident of this globe—past, present, and future—was the recipient of that blessing. Even if global peace is yet to cover the earth, it can fill the hearts of earth dwellers.

As you hang beautiful round ornaments on your Christmas tree this year, think of the earth hanging in space—and those who dwell on it whom Jesus came to save.

Cast out our sin and enter in, be born in us today.

PHILLIPS BROOKS

THE URGENCY OF THE NIGHT

And [the shepherds] came with haste and found
Mary and Joseph, and the Babe lying in a manger.

LUKE 2:16

For many years in small communities all across America, there was one word that caused every resident to drop what he or she was doing and come running: "Fire!" Many communities still have volunteer fire departments today, manned by local residents who are willing to serve their neighbors at a moment's notice.

On the night when the angels from heaven announced the birth of Jesus to the shepherds of Bethlehem, the shepherds responded with the same urgency. The news they heard would allow for no other response than to go immediately and see what had come to pass. This Christmas, we should be like those shepherds, like those volunteers who are singular in their focus to save their community from fire. We should let nothing stand in our way of focusing on the entrance of Jesus Christ into this world.

Be willing to set aside anything that obstructs your view of Jesus this Christmas season. To miss seeing Him is to miss the whole of Christmas.

"To you in David's town this day is born, of David's line,
The Savior, who is Christ the Lord, and this shall be the sign."

NAHUM TATE,
"WHILE SHEPHERDS WATCHED THEIR FLOCKS"

BEWARE OF MASQUERADES

*And no wonder! For Satan himself transforms
himself into an angel of light.*

2 CORINTHIANS 11:14

Masquerade balls gained prominence in Europe as early as the fourteenth century and have been popular ever since, spreading to America and South America via celebrations such as Mardi Gras and Carnivale. But ancient Greek actors also wore masks to create a facial impression consistent with their character.

Masquerades are fine when it comes to fun but can be dangerous in the spiritual world. Paul warned the Corinthian church against Satan masquerading himself as an "angel of light"—pretending to be one of God's good angels. In the same way, he could empower "false apostles" to transform themselves into "apostles of Christ." Indeed, Paul suggests that his "thorn in the flesh" was a "messenger of Satan." "Messenger" in Greek is *angelos*, or "angel" (2 Corinthians 12:7). Was his thorn a false apostle who was empowered by Satan, acting as an "angel of light"? It takes discernment to see an imposter.

There are good angels and evil angels in the world. It pays the Christian to be on guard against the evil (1 Peter 5:8) while giving thanks for the ministry of the good (Hebrews 1:14).

Satan does far more harm as an angel of light than as a roaring lion.

VANCE HAVNER

DAVID JEREMIAH

NAOMI

Do not call me Naomi; call me Mara,
for the Almighty has dealt very bitterly with me.

RUTH 1:20

Naomi was a widow whose sons had died. She was alone in the world, living on a shoestring, stranded in a foreign nation, and lonely.

Maybe you can identify with her if you're single, widowed, divorced, overseas, or grieving the loss of a child. You feel like crying out, "Call me Mara, for the Almighty has dealt bitterly with me."

But finish reading Naomi's story in the book of Ruth. She had a God who knew how to meet her needs; and in His good timing, He gave her a friend named Ruth, a caregiver named Boaz, a village full of friends, and—best of all—a grandson named Obed. By the end of the story, her friends were praising the Lord for restoring Naomi's life and nourishing her old age.

If the Lord is your Shepherd, you shall not lack anything you need—including friends. Our God supplies our needs out of the riches of His grace. Reject self-pity, and trust Him to restore your spirits and to nourish you through all the seasons of life.

Self-pity is our worst enemy and if we yield to it,
we can never do anything wise in this world.

HELEN KELLER

THE CLARITY OF THE NIGHT

When they saw the star, they rejoiced with exceedingly great joy.

MATTHEW 2:10

Many residents of metropolitan areas rarely see the glory of the stars against a clear, midnight sky. "Light pollution" from streetlights, neon signs, and commercial districts washes out the brightness of the stars against their backdrop.

But there was no light pollution outside ancient Bethlehem. The shepherds would have been awash in the glory of the heavens when an even greater glory appeared to them: an angel accompanied by an angelic choir. As clear as the night sky was the angel's message: "Born to you this day in the city of David [is] a Savior, who is Christ the Lord." There is much cultural "pollution" at Christmas that can wash away the clarity of the Christmas message if we allow it. Our voice must remain as clear as the angel's: The One born at Christmas is the Savior—Christ the Lord.

Be clear this Christmas about the reason for the season. Don't allow the bright lights to wash out your vision of the Savior.

It came upon the midnight clear, That glorious song of old,
From angels bending near the earth to touch their harps of gold.

EDMUND H. SEARS,

"IT CAME UPON THE MIDNIGHT CLEAR"

DAVID JEREMIAH

GOD WILL APPEAR

*Nebuchadnezzar spoke, saying, "Blessed be the God of Shadrach,
Meshach, and Abed-Nego, who sent His angel and
delivered His servants who trusted in Him."*

DANIEL 3:28

How would you have felt if you had been Peter? King Herod began a persecution of the church in Jerusalem, highlighting it with the murder of the apostle James, the brother of John. When he saw that this pleased the Jewish leaders, he seized Peter also and put him in jail. If you had been Peter, wouldn't you have thought that Herod planned to murder you as well?

The church prayed diligently that night for Peter who was chained to two Roman soldiers, and there were guards at the doors of the jail. He was bound in chains through the night with the prospect of meeting a sword in the morning. But suddenly the church's prayers were answered as an angel appeared to Peter and set him free. When Peter realized that God had appeared, he said, *"Now I know for certain that the Lord . . . has delivered me"* (Acts 12:11). You may not find yourself chained and condemned to die for Jesus. But whatever your predicament, if you will wait, God will come to you with peace, protection, or a promise.

It is not a question of whether God will appear when you are in trouble, but how.

When Jesus is present, all is well, and nothing seems difficult.

THOMAS À KEMPIS

AGE AND ATTITUDE

So teach us to number our days, that we may gain a heart of wisdom.

PSALM 90:12

In his book, *Coming Home*, James Dobson notes that Immanuel Kant wrote one of his most famous philosophical works at age seventy-four; Verdi was still composing when he was eighty-five. When Michelangelo completed *The Pietà*, his greatest work of art, he was eighty-seven; and Ronald Reagan was the most powerful man in the world as president of the United States at age seventy-five. Instead of sixty-five being the presumed age for retirement, it ought to be seen as the age when a lifetime of learning is focused on new achievement.

Consider the following: Moses and Aaron were over the age of eighty when they lead the children of Israel out of Egypt, through the wilderness, and to the Promised Land. The fact is, the older we get, the more accumulated wisdom and perspective we should have to bring to bear on new goals. Regardless of your age, consider replacing "retirement" with "transition" in your vocabulary. See life as a continual process of moving from one accomplishment to the next with God as your guide.

Yes, age is a small part of growing old, but attitude is the largest.

Instead of counting the days, make the days count.

UNKNOWN

DAVID JEREMIAH

NO OTHER NAME

Nor is there salvation in any other, for there is no other name under heaven given among men by which we must be saved.

ACTS 4:12

Christian leaders who appear on secular television talk shows are often asked whether they believe Jesus is the only way to heaven. If the answer is *Yes, Jesus is the only way*, the interviewer often paints the Christian as intolerant, arrogant, narrow-minded, out-dated, and fanatical.

But if the interviewer were talking to a physician who had made a medical breakthrough for a terrible disease, would he say, "Doctor, is this really the only cure for this disease"?

If he were talking to a mathematician about the multiplication table, would he say, "Professor, how can you be so arrogant as to believe that three times three always equals nine"?

By its very nature, truth is narrow, precise, and factual. Jesus said, *"I am the way, the truth, and the life. No one comes to the Father except through Me"* (John 14:6). In this day of pluralism and political correctness, it's important to know that Christ is still the only one who can save from sin. Do you think God would have given His own Son had there been some other way?

Trust in Christ alone, and trust Him today.

> *God help us if we preach anything else but Jesus and Him alone for salvation.*

PAIGE PATTERSON

JOY TO THE WORLD

Then the angel said to them, "Do not be afraid, for behold, I bring you good tidings of great joy which will be to all people."

LUKE 2:10

Understandably, the initial reaction of most people in the Bible who encountered an angel was fear (Numbers 22:31; Matthew 28:5; Luke 1:13, 30; 2:10). Once the shock subsided, those who saw an angel usually received a message of comfort or assurance. In the case of the shepherds on the night of Christ's birth, the angel's message was one of "good tidings of great joy"—the message that "Christ the Lord" was born in Bethlehem (Luke 2:10-11).

The great hymn "Joy to the World" remains one of the most beloved hymns in the world. Angel ornaments are often placed at the very pinnacle of a Christmas tree to picture the angels who appeared in the sky above Bethlehem, announcing the joy that had come into the world that night. The joy that filled Bethlehem is the same joy that should fill our hearts this Christmas: "Joy to the world, the Lord has come!"

If you hang an angel ornament on your tree this year, be reminded of the joy they came to announce—and be a messenger, spreading that joy to others.

The King of Kings salvation brings, let loving hearts enthrone Him.

WILLIAM DIX

DAVID JEREMIAH

SENIOR STRENGTH

And now, here I am this day, eighty-five years old. As yet I am as
strong this day as on the day that Moses sent me.

JOSHUA 14:10B-11A

Caleb was a faithful man at age forty and had lost none of his vim and vigor forty-five years later. When he, Joshua, and ten other Israelite men went up to spy out the Promised Land for Moses, only Caleb and Joshua returned with a report based on faith: "Yes, there are obstacles, but God will give us victory." As a result of Caleb's faithfulness, Moses promised him an inheritance in the land. Caleb had to wait forty-five years to receive it.

After the unfaithful generation of Israelites died off in the wilderness, Israel entered the land to drive out the inhabitants. Now eighty-five years of age, Caleb was still raring to go: "*It may be that the Lord will be with me, and I shall be able to drive [the Anakim] out as the Lord said*" (Joshua 14:12). Caleb felt as strong at eighty-five as he had at forty, and not just physically. His vision for fulfilling the promises of God had lost none of its clarity. How many people do you know like that? How about the one you see in the mirror each morning? If you need a fresh vision for "senior strength," ask God for it today.

As we age, our physical strength may diminish, but our spiritual strength should be on the rise.

God never goes back on the man who stakes his all on Him.

WILLIAM BARCLAY

Friend in Deed

*And the Scripture was fulfilled which says,
"Abraham believed God, and it was accounted to him
for righteousness." And he was called the friend of God.*

James 2:23

Everyone has a circle of friends that gets more intimate as the circle gets smaller. Jesus had 120 in His largest circle after His ascension (Acts 1:15). Then there were 72 that were trained disciples (Luke 10:1), and then 12 who were with Him for three years (Matthew 26:20). Within that group were His three closest friends, Peter, James, and John (Mark 9:2), among whom John seems to have been the closest (John 13:23; 20:2).

In John 15:14, Jesus drew the lines of friendship a different way: Anyone who keeps His commandments can be considered His friend. By "friend" Jesus meant someone with whom He would communicate and co-labor, someone He could trust to carry out His will when He returned to heaven. The question for today's believer is, Are we the kind of disciple that Jesus would see as a friend? Are we committed to obeying His commands? Can He count on us to fulfill His mission in His absence?

It's one thing to be the friend of man, another to be the friend of God.

*The golden rule for understanding
in spiritual matters is not intellect, but obedience.*

Oswald Chambers

David Jeremiah

THE SILENCE OF THE NIGHT

*Now there were in the same country shepherds living
out in the fields, keeping watch over their flock by night.*

LUKE 2:8

The Christmas season is a noisy season. There are carolers
singing in the streets and the squeals of children as they
hurry to unwrap their presents. And the wonderful Christmas
music broadcast over the airwaves and played in our homes. But
there is also the sound of traffic at the mall, impatient shoppers
in the stores, and commercials on television imploring us to help
the economy by spending more.

On that first Christmas night in the fields outside Bethlehem,
the silence was almost deafening. The occasional soft bleating of
a sheep . . . the muted murmuring of the shepherds . . . perhaps a
distant voice in the village. The first Christmas night was a silent
night, allowing the shepherds to give full attention to the message
of the angel—the announcement of the birth of the Savior.

Be sure to set aside some quiet time this Christmas to reflect
on the Savior who was born Christ, the Lord—and thank Him for
bringing heavenly peace to your life.

*Silent night, holy night, all is calm, all is bright
Round yon virgin mother and child. Holy infant so tender and mild,
Sleep in heavenly peace, sleep in heavenly peace.*

JOSEPH MOHR, "SILENT NIGHT, HOLY NIGHT"

BECAUSE HE CAME

*And suddenly there was with the angel a multitude
of the heavenly host praising God and saying: "Glory to God
in the highest, and on earth peace, good will toward men!"*

LUKE 2:13-14

Bill Gaither wrote a beautiful gospel song, "Because He Lives," the chorus of which explains why Christ's resurrection is so important: "Because He lives, I can face tomorrow, because He lives, all fear is gone; because I know He holds the future, and life is worth the living, just because He lives!" (©1971 William J. Gaither)

But we might also go back about thirty years to Christ's birth and write another song titled "Because He Came." Think how His coming into the world changed everything. Because He came, we can know God, we can have our sins forgiven, we can know purpose in life, we can be sure of our eternal salvation, we can understand the plan and purpose for all creation, and we can live in perfect peace. The entrance of no other man or woman into this world has provided benefits such as those. But to experience the benefits of Christ's advent, we must know Him! Don't let this Christmas season pass by without discovering why He came for you.

Because Christ came, we can know that He will come again.

*The fact is that the greatest mystery of all—
the incarnation—comes at the very beginning [of faith]
and is the central reason why we believe in God.*

OS GUINNESS

WATCH YOUR EYES

*For all that is in the world—the lust of the flesh, the lust of the eyes,
and the pride of life—is not of the Father but is of the world.*

1 JOHN 2:16

Eyetrack III was a study conducted by researchers to determine
what peoples' eyes do when they land on an Internet web
page. If a viewer's eyes always followed a consistent, predictable
path, then web pages could be designed to maximize that
natural tendency. (Result: upper left quadrant got the most first
looks, then center-top and center-middle, then far right edge
and bottom.)

If it's true that the eye is the window of the soul, then it's no
wonder marketers do everything they can to capture the eyes and
hold them in place. And it's no wonder that the Bible cautions us
against the "lust of the eyes." Things that are wrong can be dressed
up to appear as if they are right. When the devil tempted Jesus by
showing Him all the kingdoms of the world, Jesus rebuked him
with the admonition from Deuteronomy to "worship the LORD
your God" and serve "Him only" (Matthew 4:10).

Whatever our eyes want becomes an object of worship. Guard
your eyes today against desiring anything but God.

Guarding our hearts begins with guarding our eyes and ears.

JERRY BRIDGES

SOURCE: HTTP://WWW.POYNTEREXTRA.ORG/EYETRACK2004/MAIN.HTM

WAITING EXPECTANTLY

"But you, Bethlehem Ephrathah, though you are little among the thousands of Judah, yet out of you shall come forth to Me the One to be Ruler in Israel, whose goings forth are from of old, from everlasting."

MICAH 5:2

When you order something online, you must choose a shipping option based on how anxious you are for your package to arrive: Regular ground shipping (5-7 days; cheapest), expedited ground (faster), USPS Priority Mail, next-day business, next-day afternoon, or overnight (most expensive). If it's a digital product (book, music, software), you can often receive it instantly by downloading it to your computer. Once you've paid for something it's hard to live without it; the temptation is great to pay a high price to have it delivered ASAP.

Think how Israel must have felt knowing her Messiah had been promised and was coming, but not knowing when He would appear. The promise (in veiled fashion) began thousands of years ago in the Garden of Eden (Genesis 3:15) and was gradually made more specific—except for the time.

We know Jesus is coming again. Like Israel of old, we don't need to know when, only that we are ready when He appears.

Anyone can devise a plan by which good people go to heaven.
Only God can devise a plan whereby sinners,
which are His enemies, can go to heaven.

LEWIS SPERRY CHAFER

TUCKED IN

Be strong and of good courage, and do it; do not fear nor be dismayed, for the Lord God—my God—will be with you.

1 CHRONICLES 28:20

When Corrie ten Boom was a little girl, her father used to tuck her into bed at night. He talked and prayed with her, then laid his big hand on her little face. Later, when Corrie was imprisoned in a brutal concentration camp, she would ask God to tuck her in and lay His hand on her face. "That would bring me peace, and I would be able to sleep," Corrie wrote in her book, *Each New Day.*

One of our Lord's names is Emmanuel, meaning "God with us." Our dads or moms may no longer be around to tuck us into bed, but our Emmanuel never leaves us. Sometimes it helps to envision His presence beside us in the car, sitting by us in the pew at church, or leaning over us in bed as if to tuck us in. It's not a matter of visualizing an imaginary person but of recognizing a Friend's presence.

Jesus said, "Lo, I am with you always." So be strong and of good courage, and do not fear or be dismayed, for the Lord God will be with you.

Jesus, thank You that because of Your constant presence,
I am never alone. Hold my hand tightly, Lord. Although
afflictions may torment me, they can never defeat me.

CORRIE TEN BOOM

AS GOOD AS DONE

. . . Eye has not seen, nor ear heard, nor have entered into the heart of man, the things which God has prepared for those who love Him.

1 CORINTHIANS 2:9

If you stretched a 2,700-mile-long piece of string from the East coast to the West coast, that would represent eternity. Then if you went to Kansas and put a pencil dot on the mid-point of the string, that would represent time as we know it on earth. Then if you went up in the Space Shuttle and looked down on the string with the little dot in the middle, you'd see time relative to eternity—the way God sees everything at once.

Our little pencil dot is small compared to the "everlasting to everlasting" that God sees, yet it's still significant to Him. But because He sees our dot all at once, He sees past, present, and future at the same time. So when God moved the prophets in the Old Testament to tell of the coming Messiah to be born in Bethlehem, the prophets had to wait for it to happen. But God saw the prophecy and its fulfillment all at once. Prophecy is important because it represents a completed event in God's sight. Jesus was born in time, but God saw it in eternity.

Don't ever doubt God's promises and prophecies. Once spoken, they're as good as done.

Bethlehem and Golgotha, the Manger and the Cross, the birth and the death, must always be seen together.

J. SIDLOW BAXTER

THE HOLINESS OF THE NIGHT

Then the shepherds returned, glorifying and praising God for all the things that they had heard and seen, as it was told them.

LUKE 2:20

For many people, the true spirit of Christmas is finally experienced in the last few hours of Christmas Eve. Many churches have a Christmas Eve service in the latter hours of the night. Indeed, many non-Christians attend these services to catch an annual glimpse of the meaning of Christmas.

Beautiful music, soft candle light, the fellowship of like-minded souls, and a chance to hear the Christmas story read reverently—all this and more makes a Christmas Eve service a holy night for the Christian church. But it's not just the surroundings, meaningful as they are. Holiness is a matter of the heart above all else. And just as the shepherds left the holy stable where they found Jesus in Bethlehem and went back to their workaday world glorifying and praising God, so should we do the same. The holiness of Christmas Eve and Christmas Day should be a prelude to living a holy life the rest of the year.

Make sure you sanctify Christ in your heart this season that He might live gloriously through you in the New Year.

O holy night the stars are brightly shining,
It is the night of the dear Savior's birth.

JOHN S. DWIGHT, "O HOLY NIGHT"

THE GIFT OF HIMSELF

*For there is born to you this day in the city
of David a Savior, who is Christ the Lord.*

LUKE 2:11

Long ago, there ruled a wise and good king in Persia who loved his people and often dressed in the clothes of a working man or a beggar so he could visit the poor and learn about their hardships. One time he visited a very poor man who lived in a cellar. He ate the coarse food the poor man ate and spoke cheerful, kind words to him. He later visited that poor man again and told him, "I am your king!" The king thought the man would surely ask for some gift or favor, but he didn't. Instead he said, "You left your palace and your glory to visit me in this dark, dreary place. You ate my coarse food. You brought gladness to my heart! To others you have given your rich gifts. To me you have given yourself!"[17]

God gave us the gift of Himself when He sent His Son to this dark, dreary place. Have we accepted Him graciously and thankfully as the poor man did, or do we take this gift for granted? This Christmas season, let's remember to thank Him for His most precious gift to us: Himself.

*Out of the ivory palaces, into a world of woe, only
His great, eternal love made my Savior go.*

HENRY BARRACLOUGH

17 HTTP://WWW.CROSSWALK.COM/PASTORS/ILLUSTRATIONS/

ALONE BUT NOT FORGOTTEN: JOB

I loathe my life . . . Let me alone, for my days are but a breath.

JOB 7:16

It's the season to be jolly, but depression strikes millions of people during the holidays, especially those living alone, recently bereaved, or facing money problems. Sociologists tell us that suicide rates increase ten percent during the holidays, and crisis centers are unusually busy.

The secret to joy, however, is learning to be controlled by the Holy Spirit instead of by our temperaments. Dr. Martyn Lloyd-Jones wrote, "Our feelings are always seeking to control us; and unless we realize this, they will undoubtedly do so."

Sometimes we have to preach to ourselves, like the writer of Psalm 42 who said, *"Why are you cast down, O my soul?"* We have to pick ourselves up and give ourselves a sermon. We have to remind ourselves to hope in God. We have to quote His Word, recall His promises, submit to His authority, and be filled with His Spirit.

Job didn't linger in depression. He worked through his circumstances, saw the Lord, and revived in spirit. You can do the same!

The Christian is never meant to be carried away
by his feelings, whatever they are—never!

MARTYN LLOYD-JONES

MEEKNESS, NOT WEAKNESS

He must increase, but I must decrease.

JOHN 3:30

The famous nineteenth-century London preacher, Charles Spurgeon, wrote a book with an unusual title: *Humility and How to Get It*. That title would be more suited to modern marketing methods than the staid style of Victorian England due to its catchy nature: Surely no humble person would declare himself a teacher of humility!

We have a false idea of humility today. It is not self-abasement or groveling; not a Caspar Milquetoast personality—timid. Take Moses, for example. No one could accuse him of being timid or weak. Yet the Bible says he was "very humble, more than all men who *were* on the face of the earth" (Numbers 12:3). Rather than weakness, humility is meekness: a right understanding of one's place in the grand design of God's economy. Jesus was humble when He came to earth and submitted Himself to earthly limitations and the Father's will (Philippians 2:3-8). We are humble when we recognize Jesus as Lord and bow our knee to Him. There is strength in humility, but not grasping for advantage; desire but not desperation for advancement.

Ask God today for a fresh perspective on Christ and what He has done for you. And then enjoy a humble day.

The surest mark of true conversion is humility.

J. C. RYLE

THE BACKDROP FOR LIFE

In everything give thanks; for this is the
will of God in Christ Jesus for you.

1 THESSALONIANS 5:18

When young lovers are courting, they can think of little except one another: "What is she doing right now?" "How will he like the cookies I made?" "What did she think about what I said?" "How can I convince him I love him?" In other words, everything in their lives is viewed against the backdrop of their relationship, their love for one another.

That's how Jesus lived in His relationship with the Father. He did nothing on His own initiative, but did only what He saw the Father doing in order to please Him (John 4:34; 5:19; 6:38; 8:28, 42; 12:49). Everything that happened in Christ's life was viewed against the backdrop of the Father. And the same should be true of us in our relationship with God. If we trust Him completely, we will "rejoice always" and "pray without ceasing" (1 Thessalonians 5:16-17). And we will also give thanks in everything (verse 18). Why? Because everything happens against the backdrop of God's sovereign will and His love for us. It's easy to forget that truth, easy to let grumpiness replace gratitude.

Today, try to view everything that happens as being part of God's will for your life. And "in everything give thanks."

The essence of Christian ethics is gratitude.

R. C. SPROUL

DAY-TIGHT COMPARTMENTS

*Do not worry about tomorrow, for tomorrow will worry
about its own things. Sufficient for the day is its own trouble.*

MATTHEW 6:34

The most widely-read book of the twentieth century on the
subject of anxiety was Dale Carnegie's *How to Stop Worrying
and Start Living,* in which the famous self-help expert suggested
thirty ways to overcome worry. Carnegie's first rule was: "Live in
day-tight compartments." While we should plan for the future,
we shouldn't worry about what tomorrow may hold.

Carnegie said, "You and I are standing at this very second
at the meeting place of two eternities: the vast past that has
endured forever, and the future that is plunging on to the last
syllable of recorded time. We can't possibly live in either of those
eternities . . . but, by trying to do so, we can wreck both our bod-
ies and our minds. So let's be content to live the only time we can
possibly live: from now until bedtime."

Jesus taught us to pray, *"Give us this day our daily bread,"* and
the psalmist said, *"This is the day that the Lord has made; we will
rejoice and be glad in it"* (Psalm 118:24).

Just take life one day at a time, trusting God's grace from sun
up to sun down.

> *Our main business is not to see what lies dimly
> at a distance, but to do what lies clearly at hand.*
>
> THOMAS CARLYLE

DECEMBER 30

SUFFICIENT FOR THE FUTURE

And He said to me, "My grace is sufficient for you,
for My strength is made perfect in weakness."

2 CORINTHIANS 12:9A

It's hard for us to imagine the apostle Paul in a state of weakness. But a perusal of 2 Corinthians 6 and 11 shows us that he suffered terribly as an apostle for the sake of Christ. But the most unique experience with weakness that Paul had was one we can learn the most from because it was unnamed. It is the sustaining principle, not the specific problem, which is important.

Paul was made weak by some affliction, and it no doubt concerned him because of its likely impact on his future ministry. How could he serve if he was sidelined by a serious problem? But God said, "Trust me, Paul. I know *the* future and *your* future. I will give you grace to do all you need to do." And He did. Paul became thankful for His weakness because it highlighted God's strength. Just as God knew Paul's future, so He knows yours. If you are worried about your future, perhaps this coming year, trust God. The same grace He gave Paul, He will give to you.

Your future is not bigger than God, nor are your limitations larger than His grace. Your faith in Him means your future is with Him.

Trust the past to God's mercy, the present to God's love,
and the future to God's providence.

AUGUSTINE

JESUS

Then the devil left Him, and behold,
angels came and ministered to Him.

MATTHEW 4:11

Anita Deyneka of the Slavic Gospel Association told of a man named Yuri who was sentenced to a Siberian prison for his faith. Facing intense loneliness, Yuri asked God to let him be with a group of believers with whom he could pray and observe the Lord's Supper. One night, Yuri was awakened by a voice saying, "Come with me." He opened his eyes to see a stranger before him.

The stranger led him outside the prison gates onto the road leading to the nearby village, and then the man disappeared. Yuri hurried toward the village where he discovered a bright cottage, crowded with Christians having a prayer meeting. Entering, Yuri worshipped with them and shared the Lord's Supper. Then he sensed a voice telling him to return to prison, which he did without incident.

Though we cannot often see them, the Bible teaches that angels are "ministering spirits" sent to serve those who inherit salvation (Hebrews 1:14, NIV). After His temptation, Jesus was alone in the wilderness—but He wasn't alone. The angels were with Him.

The angels of the Lord surround you, too, for you are in His care.

Angels descending, bring from above, echoes of mercy, whispers of love.

FANNY J. CROSBY

DAVID JEREMIAH